Acclaim for Penelope Jean Hayes'
THE MAGIC OF VIRAL ENERGY

"Life is often a mysterious journey and author Penelope Jean Hayes has offered her personal recollection of the many interesting revelations she encountered along her pathway towards wisdom and enlightenment. You will find this a welcome guidebook for your own passage through the bewilderment we all meet up with in finding what truly makes you happy."

—**Dr. Fred Alan Wolf**, winner of the National Book Award in Science, bestselling author of *Taking the Quantum Leap,* and cast of the films *What the Bleep Do We Know!?* and *The Secret*

"*The Magic of Viral Energy* could not be timelier, in my opinion. We live in an age when everything we do affects not only our own health, but also the bio-diversity and health of the planet on which we depend. We all proceed through life taking so much for granted, tuning-out our inner-selves, oblivious to the ways in which our inner beings impact firstly on our own health and then on our surrounding environment. *The Magic of Viral Energy* helps us recognise and understand ourselves. We gain so much as individuals when we understand what it is we have to give, and, in turn, the enormous return we get when we do so. Viral energy is food for our soul—that's why it's magical."

—**Peter Egan**, British actor best known from *Downton Abbey, Unforgotten,* and *Ever Decreasing Circles*; animal rights activist; Ambassador for Animals Asia Foundation

T0160289

"We know that there is a home team advantage in sporting events. We know that we get good vibes or bad when walking into a meeting or even at a party. However, until now, no author has focused on the magic of viral energy as a technique for improving the quality of everyday life. It's not the next *The Secret*, rather, *The Magic of Viral Energy* is what's next."

—**Bill Gladstone**, bestselling author of *The Twelve*, co-author with Jack Canfield of *The Golden Motorcycle Gang*, and famed literary agent to mega-bestselling authors Dr. Barbara De Angelis, Neale Donald Walsch, and Eckhart Tolle

"Penelope Jean Hayes shows us the way. With humor, happiness, and whole-hearted smarts, Penelope clarifies the path to true fulfillment. Her work—and this *move*ment—is for everyone who craves helpful and kind guidance to 'get out of your head' and plug into your greatest potential. Brava!"

—**Jeffrey Marsh**, author of *How to Be You*; inspirational speaker; Ambassador for GLSEN; called "A Master of Video" by *O Magazine*, the Oprah Winfrey magazine

"From one strong motivational public speaker to another, I find Penelope's inspirational message to be contagious! Her viral energy message is powerful, timely for our society today, and necessary. She offers something new in personal growth and she has a voice of wisdom and confidence that *move*s people."

—**Mandy Gill**, Health and Fitness Cover Model, Reebok Super-Athlete, and International Speaker

The Magic of Viral Energy

PENELOPE JEAN HAYES

The MAGIC OF VIRAL ENERGY

An Ancient Key to Happiness, Empowerment, and Purpose

NEW YORK

LONDON • NASHVILLE • MELBOURNE • VANCOUVER

The MAGIC OF VIRAL ENERGY

An Ancient Key to Happiness, Empowerment, and Purpose

Published in New York, New York, by Morgan James Publishing. Morgan James is a trademark of Morgan James, LLC. www.MorganJamesPublishing.com

ISBN 9781642796087 paperback
ISBN 9781642796094 eBook
Library of Congress Control Number: 2019941628

Cover Design and Interior Illustration by:
Andrew Green
www.AndrewGreenArt.co.uk

Interior Design by:
Chris Treccani
www.3dogcreative.net

Morgan James is a proud partner of Habitat for Humanity Peninsula and Greater Williamsburg. Partners in building since 2006.

Get involved today! Visit
MorganJamesPublishing.com/giving-back

For you—
so you know for certain that the dream inside you
is both on purpose and your birthright

ACKNOWLEDGMENTS

I am blessed to have a number of close family and friends who help to shape my experiences (some of which are incognito-mentioned within these pages), fill my heart, and make the sweetest memories. I do wish to single-out "Walks with Lions," an individual who, when I was a teenager, shared with me his near-life story; its mere knowingness set me on a path of endlessly seeking answers to life's biggest spiritual questions. (I hope that someday, someone shares their true unbridled story with you. And, I hope the many short stories within these pages can spark that odyssey for you, too.) Although he might not have intended its full impact, that one conversation changed everything for me, and it turned my head and my journey's trajectory.

This acknowledgment, however, is not for my every beloved but it is where I am bestowed the great honor to publicly thank those individuals who have been intimately and specifically involved with—and instrumental in—the creation process of this book. So, here goes.

While the "viral energy" philosophy was conceived within me some years before we met, my husband Burton, by his very presence in my life, has made this book's birth possible. Burt has never wavered in his encouragement of my purpose and has endlessly supported the deal that I made with Life about what I would create in this walk in the world, even when I had moments of not believing in my own success at it. Some women hope for a soul-mate while others look for a life-partner and teammate. I prayed for and held out for all-of-the-above, and with Burt, I got all of that, *and a bag of chips*! Burt is the person who is most definitely "my person." (Oh, how for so many years I had longed for a "my person.") He is the one person who is always "home" to me, no matter where I am or where we live or how life challenges me in what has been, at times, a spine-fortifying journey. He has gifted me with finally knowing the long-elusive-to-me feeling of stability. He embodies the precise definitions of doing-life-together, fierce loyalty, and unwavering and unconditional love. While I'm not saying that my husband is perfect, he *is* every dream that I ever dreamt when I was vision-boarding the loneliness away and learning to ask big. *Did I ever get lucky with Burt!* And, I know it.

My agent, Bill Gladstone, needs no introduction in literary circles and so I will not list here his many mega-bestselling clients, nor his bestselling book titles as an author in his own right. I will proudly say that Bill was an early supporter of *The Magic of Viral Energy* and from the start, he wholly believed in me and my message. I will never forget the Sunday in late 2017 when Bill agreed to represent me; I will forever remember my gratitude, disbelief, and awe to be validated and taken-under-wing by "Bill Gladstone," a name that is most often said in full, as are those others on this earth who have, in various ways, earned such an introduction by their reputation alone. I continue to be honored to work with him as my literary agent.

Ainsley Schoppel, my editor. If you are fortunate, there are those people who come into your life with whom you are meant to do important soul-work together. Ainsley is such a person for me and her contributions as Editor of *The Magic of Viral Energy* have been invaluable. Rather than taking up space here to sing her praises solely for her editing skill and craft, please trust that she is among the very best of book editors today. Incidentally, Ainsley is Co-Editor-in-Chief for the international aspirational magazine, *Face the Current*, and I believe that my work has benefited tremendously to be scoured over by an editor who specializes in auditing writings of new-consciousness wisdom. Throughout the editing process of this book, Ainsley and I have had exceptional synergy. She is more than my editor; she cared enough about *you*—the reader—to challenge me when my thoughts on paper weren't quite clear and to raise in advance the questions that she felt you would have, making sure that I answered them fully within these pages.

For a new author, being offered a book deal by a bona fide publisher, especially a *New York City publishing house*, is like getting a dinner invitation from Big Foot; it's a tall order and the very rare alignment of how-well-you-write, what-you-have-to-say, and the-size-of-your-platform. My yeti, Morgan James Publishing, was in my crosshairs due to their author-centric business model. Authoring can be a solo vocation and when seeking a publisher, I really wanted a team. With Morgan James, I got one! My very heartfelt appreciation goes out to David Hancock, Founder and CEO of MJP, who gave my book a wonderful home and ensured that I had a partner and a trusted friend.

When I began the search for an artist to create the five illustrations within this book, I had a picture in my mind of what I was looking for: I needed a professional who could translate my metaphysical philosophies and cosmology concepts into form and figure while giving them depth and story. The moment that I set eyes on British illustrator Andrew Green's work, I knew that he was the one. The process of working with Andrew was pure joy for me, and so naturally I asked Andrew to also draw the cover. Springboarding off my vision for *The Magic of Viral Energy*, Andrew Green produced a cover that hit all of the right notes for Best Book Covers Ever Created! From its colors to creative imagery, the *MOVE* cover is a brilliant, light, and magical piece of art. When I mentioned to Andrew how fortunate I felt to have him as my illustrator, he said, "I think it was ENERGY that joined us up!" And, I cannot agree more.

My sincere thank you to all those individuals who lent their true, personal, and sometimes humorous and/or self-deprecating stories so that I might share them.

I would be remiss if I let pass the opportunity to mention the other love of my life and to put her name in ink—the one who has been with me through every move, break-up, and challenge over the last twenty-three years; my beloved cat Sabrina. She has been my companion through the joy and the pain since 1996 (not a typo), and I thank her—deeply and sincerely—for spending her life with me and for getting me through the nights when my soul poured in sorrow and the mornings when I held a cold toilet bowl.

I must give my final shout-out to the little engines of positive viral energy who nap together daily in a basket on my desk whilst I write: our kittens, Max and Andy. They make me smile and they add light to my light.

CONTENTS

FOREWORD

I first sniffed out a review copy of *The Magic of Viral Energy* when I found it nearly buried in a rather large stack of manuscripts and books—daily deliveries to the network by authors and publishing houses, all hopeful that their message will be considered by the Executive Producer of *SuperSoul Sunday*, and of course noticed by Oprah herself. This particular title stuck out from the rest (perhaps serendipitously) so I snatched it away to one of my favorite lounge spots in the office that I frequent when I visit with Mamma O. I flopped down on my special pillow, pawed open the cover, and began to read.

I immediately noticed that this book offered something different in the new-consciousness movement: the concept that energy has a contagious nature as it moves within social interactions and the environment around us all. As a very astute canine, I regularly witness this phenomenon in the light energy emitted when Mamma O, Stedman, and the rest of our pack go on nature walks, and conversely, in the heavy energy that I feel when we get bogged down in stressful, stagnant, or sometimes septic spaces—and yes, even when I'm around humans who carry these low energies.

We (our entire team here at the network, of which I very much feel a part) are in the business and soul-work of thought-provoking and inspiring content that needs to be shared with the world. Our viewership is forward-thinking seekers who are dedicated to their own self-development and that of others. And yet, though they have read all of the great works of today's best spiritual teachers, and they know all about the law of attraction and visualization, many still struggle to reach their highest goals and dreams. Whilst I've been reading *The Magic of Viral Energy*, I'm starting to think that what people need is the rest of the formula that explains how energy works, and it's actually more than just attractive—it's osmotic and viral, too!

I have observed that people today are desperate for purpose and are still searching for the key to happiness. More than ever before, the current generation is at risk because the human species has created and entered into an era of artificiality and it has taken its toll. Except, there's good news: I'm happy to tell you that there are tangible how-tos, wisdom for enlightenment, and true joy available to all those who understand and utilize *The Magic of Viral Energy*. This book gives simple but powerful solutions to everyday problems.

In the first half of the book, the concept of "viral energy" is explained through the use of dozens of true short stories; some brought tears of laughter to my puppy eyes and others made my heart ache in empathy. Author Penelope Jean Hayes gives the reader many tools for protecting their light and positive energy, as well as several examples of what to say to those who might try to undermine their dreams or sap their internal power. Penelope also provides a simple ten-question test to help identify a true-love partnership versus a relationship that might be intended only as a growth opportunity, and she even talks about the cure for the common cold, or as she's coined it, "viral-energy-sickness." In the second half of the book, Penelope raises new and audacious philosophies including the replacement of the Big Bang theory, and she answers some age-old questions such as why we only experience time as a forward-moving construct. In the final chapter, Penelope pulls together exactly how and why the cosmology of the universe is important to you and your everyday life—and trust me, you'll want to hear this! *The Magic of Viral Energy* is full of inspiring and fresh new ideas that will change the way people think of external power, force, and true empowerment.

I have a feeling—*you could call it a dog's sense*—that one day in the soon-time, Mamma O will be sitting under the oaks with author Penelope

Jean Hayes, discussing *The Magic of Viral Energy*. I hope that I, too, will be there at Mamma's feet, soaking in the light energy as this ancient wisdom is ushered into the now-generation and shared with all those who, in the depths of their souls, need this message today.

—Oprah's Dog

(I believe I'm the favorite, but we'll keep that between us.)

INTRODUCTION

I was fifteen-years-old and a runaway, slinking from one shady acquaintance's apartment to the next. Somehow, I ended up at a house rented by a stripper named Sally (her stage name was Samantha). She was in her mid-thirties and I recall that she had bright red hair extensions that were frayed and so grown out that I could see the exposed bits of glue. Sally didn't like me; she barely regarded me at all but begrudgingly put up with me that night because I was brought over by one of her "colleagues," also a stripper. Although I was many years younger than legal, I had become acquainted with a new group of friends by frequenting a dance club on the weekends. (*Well, pseudo-friends for a brief time that, in hindsight, I would dub "The Freeing of a Caged Tiger." This was a term that my dad had used for me—half endearingly—due to my unmanageable demand to be unruled. I was fearless and curious. Although, I was more of a dove than a tiger and the hum of the city attracted me like a wide-eyed dove to a live wire.*)

At the back-end of Sally's house, the building narrowed to a dirty caboose-like kitchen where Sally and her boyfriend were heating a pair of butter knives on the coiled element of the stovetop and then pressing tiny balls of what they called "oil" between the hot blades. I watched them suck in the smoke from the burnt oil and they motioned an offer for me to try it. I said, "No, thanks," and they burst into laughter. Annoyed, Sally told me to go to sleep in the basement; it was after three o'clock in the morning and I was tired anyway. I flipped on the stairwell light and as I crept down the grey-painted wood stairs I heard her say, "Dumb effin' rich kid. What's she doing here?" (*I was thinking the same.*)

The smell in the basement was worse than the acrid cloud of the burning drugs; it was rank with mildew. I left the light on—a bare bulb centered in a ceiling of floorboard underbellies. The wall-less space was empty apart from a washer and dryer, a furnace unit, and a sloppy line of plumbing pipes. In one corner there was a purple curtain fringed with long tassels and beaded with metallic ends that divided off a seven-foot wedge from the rest of the room. On the concrete floor behind the curtain was an old comforter spread open, devoid of a pillow and blanket but still conspicuous in its use as a bed. I knelt down on it and, barely believing that this moment was real, removed my jacket, rolled it up, and laid my head on it. *It's just like camping*, I told myself.

The basement was cold, but I was colder. Pride was the reason I was there and I knew it, yet *there* I was, sequestered and penniless. I wondered what my mum had made for dinner that night and if she still kept fresh sheets on my bed. I wondered if my dog Sparky missed me as much as I missed him. Thinking of Sparky reminded me that I still hadn't forgiven my parents for euthanizing Charlie, my beloved cat, earlier that year. He was my best friend from the age of four and was taken from me when he was just eleven. It wasn't his fault that he repeatedly peed in the corners of our dining room floor; he was confused by our last move and quite frankly, so was I. To their credit, my parents did try with Charlie. They replaced the carpet and padding and painted the subfloor underneath, all in an effort to block the smell and hopefully the behavior. After that, I guess they believed that euthanasia was the only logical solution. (*I didn't know much, but I knew that love isn't logical.*)

As I lay there on the cold floor, I recalled that day when I went with my dad to bring Charlie to the vet. I had to be brave for Charlie and so I used my time in the car to fight for a stay of execution. Like a skilled lawyer, I stated my best case to my dad, but that got me nowhere. I pleaded and sobbed, but it was a heavy and fast train that could not be stopped. With his carrier on my lap, I locked eyes with Charlie, pushed my fingers through the bars and felt the plush mane of fur that framed that familiar face. I chanted, "*I love you. I love you. I love you. I love you,*" as the car pulled into the gravel parking lot of the veterinarian's clinic, the familiar odor betraying our destination before we'd even parked. Stones popped and crunched under the wheels of our Park Avenue and we inched to a stop in the same ominous motion as a hearse.

Charlie would normally cry in the car, protesting a trip to the vet. That day, he only stared me down with his beautiful, big green eyes, wide and blameless, tender and consoling as if to say, "Well, I guess this is it, Kid. We had a good run."

"*Noooo,*" I whimpered as if I could will away this whole horrible idea. Ending Charlie's life was unimaginable to me, especially at that moment as I felt the warmth of his body straight through the plastic box between us. He was not a hit-and-run victim in need of humane mercy, he was a family member with a distinct personality and he was a being of vital meaning in my world.

With a firm voice, Dad said, "You stay here."

As he got out of the driver's seat, I resumed my chant and vow to Charlie, "*I love you. I love you. I love you.*" The passenger door opened and in one slow-motion sweep, Dad gently lifted the crate and Charlie off my lap and then disappeared inside.

I was gasping in grief. No word, no cry, no sound was worthy to mark the intensity of my pain. My world was collapsing upon itself and in an irreversible moment, on the authority of my own father, my only lifelong friend was gone forever.

In mid-memory, the furnace kicked in with a loud bang. My heart responded with a single wild beat high in my head, and a vacuum of air pressure from the furnace began moving the dangling tassels on the curtain. Although the curtain was hideous, it still looked like it didn't belong in that dank basement. A tear rolled down my cheek and into my mouth. I tasted its salt and wiped it away.

"You don't belong here," a woman tending bar had told me just a few hours prior. I had ordered a free water because I didn't have money for a real drink, yet I was satisfied with that because I was at the bar for the music, dancing, and a feeling of being alive that I hadn't felt before. In so many ways, the bartender was right that I didn't belong there, but I believed that I didn't belong anywhere. As a child, I was a shy girl and my family moved around so much that a thick skin slowly grew around my soft innards. I hid behind the ruse of aloofness to cover up my terror of being conspicuous and friendless. It wasn't long before I was full of indignation, hormones, and confusion, all of which led to commonplace parental clashes that would end with me locking myself in my room. One day, a squall of shouting and crying ended with me blurting out, "I'm leaving!" Before I knew what had happened, I was stuffing a supply of my clothes into a large black garbage bag with snot choking my breath and the armor of indignation and ego blocking my logic. I was already deeply regretting my exit even before my well-groomed heels crossed the threshold out of my home.

As a vexed fifteen-year-old, I was a primitive impression of the girl that my mum once called, "the laughing gizzard," known then for my joy but now for not belonging. This shift was grossly obvious to me from my perspective of lying on a stranger's floor and gazing, not at stars, but at gaudy basement curtain tassels. Yes, they were atrocious, but somehow, as I lay in my makeshift bed, I appreciated their smack of color in contrast to the walls around and inside me. I watched the tassels swing like children in a playground and I soon fell asleep.

How I got "there" was unlikely given the safe and comfortable life in which I was raised. Yet, getting "there" was surprisingly easy and much more effortless than how I later got out of a life that could have killed me, if not merely murdered my soul. That was supernatural. Through all of the pitiful aloneness and vulnerability (in the corporeal sense of that word), there was a knowing inside me. I *knew* that I couldn't take this dark and lost existence too far. Occasionally I would come back home like a stray cat; I suppose I was a runaway and a runback, an in-and-outer. And yet, I knew that this was not the life I was meant to live and that I needed to find a way out of my self-inflicted despair. Yes, even while sleeping on the stripper's basement floor, I knew that I had a purpose to live out, although fully waking up to that purpose didn't become realized for nearly twenty more years.

It was in 2002, at twenty-nine, that I consciously began seeking true happiness and the meaning of my life. Even though I was searching, I was still painfully unfulfilled into my early thirties. I realized that I was shoehorned into a career that I was well-suited for but didn't suit me. Then finally in 2007, I took a leap into the abyss of the unknown, and teetering between gumption and irresponsibility, I took my car, clothes, and my cat, and left Canada for Nashville, Tennessee. I often say that I found happiness on my journey to purpose, yet it was more than that; I found a hidden code to life. I discovered the "**M**agic **O**f **V**iral **E**nergy" and by understanding and utilizing it, my spirit has *moved* from emptiness and loss to true and lasting joy. I'm now sharing with you the magic and everything I've discovered in this journey to supernatural happiness.

In reading these pages, you can embark on your own journey to purpose, true love, and joy. As you begin, it's important to understand that "viral energy" is not the law of attraction, which is like-energy-vibrations attracting like-energy-vibrations in the same way radio waves from a transmitter are picked up by a receiver tuned in to the same frequency. While the law of attraction is always a factor, there is another energetic power at play and it's rather different; it's viral energy. Virality is inherent to energy in social interactions and the environment around you. Viral energy is working right now to co-create your circumstances, experiences, relationships, health, wealth, and happiness. In order for any of us to reach our true destiny, we have to start thinking differently.

My message is for seekers—those intrepids who want to squeeze the lemons of life and discover their full potential. It's for people of all ages and genders who are socially aware, lovers of quantum theory and spirituality, science buffs with inquiring minds, animal lovers, environmentalists, compassion advocates, and seekers of answers to universal questions. It's also for those who enjoy a good short story and want to be deeply inspired by something new.

There is a knowing inside you; it's an ancient truth as old as time and I hope that it jolts you wide-awake.

PART ONE:
WHAT'S VIRAL ENERGY?

CHAPTER ONE:

ENERGY IS CATCHY

Osmotic-Energy-Balancing
(The Fourth Dimension)

More than a decade ago, I experienced an encounter with a giant owl that opened me up to energy recalibration and synchronization. The profound effect of this experience is the phenomenon that I instinctively dubbed "osmotic-energy-balancing."

After moving to Nashville in 2007, I frequently visited the surrounding parklands to hike, think, and write. Like many, I feel greater creativity and wisdom when surrounded by nature. In that area of Tennessee just outside Nashville's city center, the fragrance of late fall is musty and earthen with a trace of soft tannins like cellared red wine. With the exception of the unseasonable warmth and bright sunshine, this October day was no different.

After a long trek, I arrived at my spot in the woods; the spot on top of a ridge that made a perfect hiking destination. (It was the very spot that I had once carved a heart in oak containing my now husband's name joined with mine. It was a symbolic remembrance that I continued to visit even when we were broken up for a few months, perhaps to keep vigil over the trees and love itself.) Prepared to stay for hours, I had water, a bag of almonds, a pen and paper, and a cushion for comfort. There was nowhere else to be and I was content to stay all afternoon, if for nothing else than to breathe in stillness.

The forest was dense; a different world from the nearby city. There were no sounds of traffic, only the rhythm of a twig-crackle followed by silence, trailed by a birdcall, punctuated by more silence. I pondered life, wrote about it, and sat in gratitude. My practice was a meditative form of spiritual medicine. The foliage canopy of the expanse before me opened up to a vantage point exposing rolling hills of orange and green backcountry that transitioned to a spectrum of monochromatic yellows and reds. I sat and admired the trees gracefully bending in the wind. I listened to the leaves dancing and ruffling in the breeze like a hundred million tiny chimes. Together, the music and choreography of the spectacle were as ironic as an animated Disney classic, replete with the flitting of busy birds and the stumbling of lanky fawns. Chipmunks nosed their way under groundcover, making a ruckus louder than I would have expected from the pip-squeaks that would eventually emerge. The scene was a symphony of the senses and each layer of it was in harmony with the next. The forest was alive with movement and sound, yet also calm and peaceful. Soon, I was not writing or thinking; the impulse to attribute or label my experience with words had dissolved. I was just perceiving and *being*. I might have already been immersed for two or three hours when a shift began.

I slowly started to see the colors around me grow more vibrant. It was beyond three-dimensional; I was seeing the forest in another dimension as it popped up before me with incredible depth.

The wilds were exposing the fourth dimension.

It was not a hallucination or the result of a substance-enhanced trip, and it wasn't a vision or even a dream. Rather, it was a clear-headed perception of the environment around me in its raw and unmasked state. Everything became lighter, shimmering as though I could see the actual energy-field of the forest. It was ethereal and vaporous, where each element of the environment was a fraction of something unbound, like the in-between essence of a bubble and a burst.

Just then, a large body moved in my right vision. With a span as wide as a car is long, it kited on the air, slowly, silently, and seemingly with authority. The Overseer had arrived, and he was a giant owl. Without a single flap, he pulled in his wings and mutely landed on a branch in front of me. Not six feet away, he was directly across from my position on the cliff. For long, peaceful minutes, I remained locked on him as he went about his wide-eyed business of surveying the area with a confidence that was both steadfast and resolute. Time slowed, yet I was not measuring it or concerning myself with doing anything; I was only observing and being observed. The owl was aware of my presence but was neither concerned with nor bothered by me, and it did not fear or avoid me. Nature had accepted me and I was one with the forest. This reminded me of the experience by primatologist Dr. Jane Goodall in her first immersion in the jungle of Tanzania's Gombe Stream National Park in 1960, and how she did nothing but sit in close proximity to the wild chimpanzees without imposing herself upon them. In time, Jane's energy assimilated to the natural world and the great apes accepted her. There on the cliff, exchanging energy acceptance with the owl, I understood the state of balance of which Jane spoke, because I was in it.

You, too, can practice osmotic-energy-balancing. It's an exercise, a personal custom, and a spiritual routine, just like you might practice meditation or yoga. To really wrap your mind around osmotic-energy-balancing, think of your energy field as a balloon filled with hot water. (It's hot because you're coming from the city with all of its associated hopped-up thoughts and emotions adding to the mash of viral energy you've assumed over time.) Now, your hot water balloon is dropped in a very large pool of cool water. Unless somehow insulated to be impermeable (which is indeed possible), the temperature inside the water balloon will equilibrate with the temperature of the pool. This cannot happen the other way around, because the pool is the field with the more significant concentration of energy—it's more potent and has greater power and effect than the water-filled balloon.

In this same way, you take on the energy of the great outdoors, while the great outdoors does not take on your energy. Only temporarily, and to a very small and nearly immeasurable extent, does your energy rub off on nature. Again, I'll use the hot-water-filled balloon analogy: The effect of your energy on the "body" of a forest is similar to the effect that the temperature inside the balloon has on the water in the pool. The water in the pool immediately around the hot-water-filled balloon will ever so slightly warm via the osmosis of heat. Then, just as efficiently and without effort, that water will equilibrate back to the temperature of its more significant larger body, the greater pool temperature.

In any scenario, it is the energy source with the higher concentration of energy that will more profoundly vibrate. Here's another example: If you're feeling light and joyful, and then you spend three hours on the floor at the New York Stock Exchange surrounded by shouting people and hot energy, your light energy will most likely sync with the force of the heavy energy in which you are submerged. In the same way, if you are sad or stressed out from a difficult day and then later spend the evening at a comedy show, the powerful light energy of the latter will likely wash away your stress. Indeed, your own energy field can become tuned to the higher-concentration energy vibration.

When I encountered the giant owl that day in the forest, my energy field synchronized to vibrate in harmony with my surroundings. It was through my own experience of this visceral intimacy with Creation that I gained awareness of its built-in process of osmotic-energy-balancing; one of nature's magical portals to Universal Intelligence. In that state, I was incapable of causing discord to the energy around me; I was one with it. The great owl recognized me as part of its environment and for those moments, my energy was balanced with nature and I glimpsed an interior world.

It was truly like seeing something that we're not supposed to see, or that most of us do not see. Perhaps this is how the owl sees, and the chipmunk, and the trees. It was like a curtain or veil had been pulled away to reveal the backstage of a play where all the moving parts are visible, but in this case, the moving parts were energy currents. The colors were so illuminatingly vivid that my surrounding popped out at me, more than three-dimensional. There is another dimension behind the scenes and it connects everything to each other and then to you and me: it's a fourth-dimension that swirls, moves, and dances as it interacts. It was exhilarating and electrifying to be with it for those moments. Perhaps it's what we will all see in time.

You're an Emotion Mime

For better or worse, all energy is contagious. Good vibes, chronic sadness, and lasting joy are all contagious through the energy around you and the people with whom you spend time. Do you ever think about the quality of energy that you're emitting and the ways in which others are subconsciously responding to you? How might this be affecting your companionability, your happiness, and the happiness of your loved ones, your success at your job, your earning potential, your relationships, and your health?

Physicists report that swinging pendulums in close proximity to one another, such as those found inside clocks, will synchronize. While the pendulums initially swing at different moments, they soon begin to swing to the exact same rhythm and pace—they move together. This happens because of pulses or waves of sound energy that become entangled in close proximity. The pendulums transmit vibrational information through their permeable energy fields and they naturally come to an agreement as to how they will swing. And, get this: It's more than just clocks and pendulums (and tassels on purple curtains). For instance, heart cells sync up to create your heartbeat. Studies show that closely in sync romantic couples will have heartbeats and breathing rates that are in concert with one another. The topic of the synchronicity of women's menstrual cycles has been well documented and well known amongst female roommates or family members within a household. (*I think you're getting the idea now.*)

What if all of life functioned on a pulse—a movement of energy—and synchronized within a system of shared energy? It does. What if the quality of your life is the product of the intentions and energy patterns of those people with whom you spend the most time, the energy of your own deep inner intentions, your outer environment including the energy of your city, the tone of what you watch on TV, and everything else to which you are exposed in your surroundings and interactions? Well, it is.

You probably know that people who are likable get many of the best opportunities in life. Jobs are more often given to the likable candidate over the slightly more qualified, yet less likable applicants. Others are repelled or attracted to you on your overall likability and how you make them feel when they're around you. So, how can you make others smile and feel good around you? It's simple—smile and others will smile at you; feel good and others will feel good around you. You see, you're an emotion mime, and so is everyone else.

Have you ever noticed face mirroring, or mimicking? When you're watching TV, do you sometimes catch yourself having the very same expression as the character that you're watching? My husband Burt does this and it's so funny to watch. His expression-mimicking is more pronounced than in anyone that I know. He's the very definition of an open book and as such, he's extremely readable. For instance, he might be watching an episode of Discovery Channel's *Naked and Afraid*, listening to someone give an in-the-moment report of the tough environmental conditions and how hard it is to make fire when the humidity is so high. Burt will deeply nod in agreement. I smile because I know that he doesn't realize he's mimicking.

Energy is transferable and emotions are a form of energy. The advertising world knows this and they use it on you every day. Emotion-mimicking is being monetized all around you from billboards to commercials. When you see someone smiling a big, beautiful, open smile, it makes you smile, too. By simply observing someone else's emotion (happy, sad, or any feeling in between), you can take on that exact emotion. Masters of social media know this as well. Users don't often even read a post or article, but they might "like" it for a photo that makes them feel something good. Across social media platforms, the best click-bait photos used to advertise products or accompany news articles are tight face shots of genuinely joy-filled people, happy couples, or playful pets. Just like sex, happiness sells.

Emotions are also mirrored through senses other than sight. People talk louder and faster when they are upset, out of control, feel wronged, or know that they are in the wrong. If someone is yelling at you, use this trick: lower your volume, slow your voice, and deepen your tone. They will soon lower their voice to match yours and will calm down.

Take the knowledge of emotion-mimicking through viral energy and flip the script in your favor. Be cognizant of the emotions that you take on from the media around you and the people in your life—protect your happiness! And remember, you have the same effect on others who observe you. Whether you are deliberate about it or not, you are an emotion mime and having awareness of this phenomenon can prove very useful. You can improve your influence and likability just by transferring positive emotions to those around you.

Deflector Shields Up! You Have a Permeable Energy Field

Matt is one of the most positive and pleasant people that you could ever meet. He's not a person who lets others get under his skin very often; negativity tends not to permeate his being. Let's just say he's one of those rare enlightened individuals, but that doesn't mean he's not a little "sticky."

One evening, Matt attended a homeowners' association meeting in the community where he lives with his wife, Jennifer. Jennifer didn't join; she stayed home, lit a candle, and worked on one of her favorite projects. The meeting was charged with disgruntled neighbors airing grievances and mixing bickering with gossip. Matt came home over an hour later, unscathed and unaffected in his typical water-off-a-duck's-back manner.

Within minutes of Matt walking through the door, his wife's tranquil environment was disrupted by a thick, negative energy that filled the space like a silent intruder. Matt's mood had been good, cheerful even. Jennifer's mood had also been good until it suddenly disintegrated into frustration and agitation.

Could it be that the negative energy from the HOA meeting, while not absorbed by Matt, clung to him and went viral in his environment? Could it be that while Matt was immune to the viral energy, Jennifer was not? Absolutely!

We are ready for a cultural awakening to the phenomenon and magic of viral energy. Energy transfer *is* possible because energy itself is permeable, allowing for flow and exchange.

You have a permeable energy field that allows energy to pass through, but sometimes it can stick and linger. Basically, you are holey, so be deliberate about what energy you allow in and be mindful to shake off any negative or frantic viral energy that you may have picked up. Being tuned in to clingy negative energy allows you the opportunity to discard it before continuing on with your day. *That is, if you want your day to go well!* Even if you don't let the negative energy of others or your environment bring you down, it is possible that while you're not affected (and infected), you can be a carrier of heavy viral energy.

Both light and heavy energy are at large in the world around us. The degree to which energy is heavy or light is dependent on the purity ratio or composition of light energy. (We will get into this more later.) These qualities of energy make up the presence of everyone and everything including creatures of the land, sea, and air, plus mountains and forests, and chaos, pain, joy, and our everyday intentions. Every unit of Life, including you and me, is *being* in a vibration of creation-energy and that should matter to you very much because energy created outside of your own being can permeate your space and personal power as if you had sponsored and created the energy yourself. These energies sort of float around waiting to latch on—ask Jennifer! But, why does energy behave this way? Because, energy is forever moving and seeking balance—to be made whole again, to equilibrate, to reunite with its equal level. Energy is the stuff of life; it is Life itself, it's the Alpha and Omega, the beginning and the end, the what is and the what always was and what shall be. Yeah, I know—it sounds metaphysical, biblical, and a little Sci-Fi, but it's a real and natural phenomenon. And frankly, it's high time that we see the world with **move** clarity.

What the Heck are You Marinating In?

The following is an interesting case of viral energy. It is a known fact among dentists that their profession is linked to abnormally high suicide rates. According to a Wayne State University study conducted by Steven Stack in 1995 and published in 2010, being a dentist increases one's risk of suicide by a whopping 564 percent. Numerous studies have addressed this shocking statistic and have attempted to determine why this is the case. Could it be due to occupational stress? Hmm, let's see. Air Traffic Controllers have high rates of depression and suicide, which can be linked to the stress associated with the massive responsibility of having passenger safety in their hands. However, life and limb are not often at stake in the dentist's chair. Perhaps it's the burden of financially supporting their families? Well, farmers also have above-average suicide rates, which are frequently linked to the precarious nature of a business dependent on weather conditions and ever-changing trends in consumer appetites and food marketing. But, in comparison, dentists have fairly stable client bases and market insecurity is a non-factor. So, what is it that causes dentists to be at risk of depression and suicide? There is one answer that makes sense: viral energy.

Dentists are in an occupation where nobody wants to see them. Most dental patients would rather be anywhere else than in the dentist's chair because going to the dentist is associated with discomfort, pain, and fear. "I hate the dentist," is a phrase that you've probably uttered; most of us have. So, guess what happens with all of the negative energy produced from fearful words and nervous energy? It goes viral and it's palpable to the dentist. They know that they are, in a sense, hated and feared. Just like a dental water jet, dentists are blasted and soaked with heavy energy every day.

Energy affects you and you affect energy.

You've said it before: "I could cut the tension in the room with a knife," and "His energy is contagious," or "Her laughter is infectious." You know that you get good or bad vibes when you walk into a room. The nature of energy is that it's catchy; it's contagious and can be picked up when you're tuned in, open, or lingering in it. Chronic exposure to light energy results in the good stuff in your life, while chronic exposure to heavy energy results in what you perceive as bad.

Try this visual; it will help you further understand how viral energy works: Think of viral energy as a marinade and think of yourself as a piece of meat. (*Don't get too excited, it's a metaphor!*) You're soaking in a marinade comprised of ingredients that are hot, flavorful, savory, and salty.

To deconstruct our metaphor, the marinade includes the energy of the people with whom you spend time, the work that you do, and what you are exposed to all around you. Whatever's in there, that's what you're soaking in. Remember, you have a permeable energy field, so you can take on all that you're marinating in. Perhaps you have a loving partner, a loyal dog, a stressful work environment, some positive friends, others that are quite negative, clutter in your closets, a barrage of violence through your entertainment choices, a peaceful garden in which to repose, an ornery neighbor, a morning traffic jam, and a good audiobook to get you through it all. It's a spicy sauce.

I wanted an expert's opinion on the subject of viral energy in social interactions and our environments, and the ways in which it can affect you and me, so I asked Dr. Stephen Hinshaw, Ph.D., about this phenomenon. He's Chair of the Department of Psychology, University of California, Berkeley, and Editor of the *Psychological Bulletin*. He said, "It's really an interesting concept, these infectious agents that you're calling them. Maybe you're a person who doesn't have enough 'Teflon' (emotional armor), so things stick to you. Turn off media and social media at a certain point. I think social media can make it hard to have Teflon these days because sometimes you can be constantly reminded of what is negative. I think there's something to what you're suggesting; it's like you get this virus, you get this infectious agent."

Viral energy appears in negative and positive forms (more accurately worded as heavy and light, and also well-described as dense and light), with a full spectrum existing in between. As an example, what do you think is the viral energy of a traffic jam? Well, it's not good. It's full of tension, stress, people running late, held up agendas, angry people, idling motors, beeping horns—those are the energies in a traffic jam. What's the energy vibration of an argument or a situation where a person or group is being verbally berated? If you are playing a team sport, you are more likely to lose the game if your coach or teammate is yelling at you in a frantic or demeaning way, saying things like, "You idiot! Get the darn ball!" That kind of heavy energy can cause you to lose focus, put up a mental energy block, and derail your gameplay. In a complete juxtaposition, consider the energy of a walk in the woods. It's a much lighter feeling, right? Chirping birds, fresh air, harmony and balance, soft earth underfoot, and adventure—it's a very positive viral energy mixture.

If you were about to sing the national anthem at the Super Bowl, I bet you would want to get your energy right in the hours and minutes leading up to this once-in-a-lifetime moment. You might be a person who wants all of your best friends and family around you that morning before the big game, pumping you up with encouragement and love. Conversely, you might want to be still and focused, practicing meditation and swimming in the gentle vibration of your go-to classical music to get you centered. Either way, on that day, chances are you would avoid dealing with a person with whom you have a tumultuous relationship history or seeing the frantic friend who gets you nervous and agitated. Surely you wouldn't expose yourself to negative energy by reading hateful posts on social media, and you would also be likely to arrive early so as not to get stuck in a traffic jam and stress about running late. In your own way, you would strike a balance between filtering out the energetic noise and bringing in the good stuff that fills you up.

But, you see, your life and whatever you're trying to accomplish in earnest is *that* important every single day. Because of this, it is mission-critical that you monitor your viral energy on a daily basis. You need to try, at the very least, because we both know that you let in a lot of heavy viral energy when you don't have to. You can and should be mindful of what the heck it is that you're marinating in!

Look, you're a superstar. You are the protagonist of your own life. Who else could possibly lead or be in charge of your life? No one. You already know that your career is worth your effort and you believe that the people in your life are worth your effort. I'm here to tell you that *you* are so worth your effort, so please mind what you're marinating in. To attain what you're trying to achieve—your personal mission or simply happiness itself—each and every day should be treated like the Super Bowl of your dreams.

CHAPTER TWO:

LIGHT ENERGY CREATES

Are You in a New Torque State of Mind?

N ow that you've been introduced to the magic of viral energy, you might be wondering: how can I positively boost my thoughts, experiences, successes, and my life as a whole, in order to gain an *advantage*?

Well, there's a guy who knows a lot about that. As a matter of fact, he's one of today's top global experts on the "psychological advantage." British survival expert John Hudson is a co-host and competitor for Discovery Channel's reality survival game, *Dude You're Screwed*, and he's also the Chief Instructor at the UK Royal Air Force Military Survival School where he trains the next generation of military survival instructors.

To get a psychological advantage in a survival situation, Hudson often begins by making himself a strange brew of wilderness tea concocted from twigs and berries or whatever he can find. Tea makes him feel at home even when lost—he's English after all. In one show episode, Hudson had this to say (*I liked it, so I wrote it down*) about the benefits of a psychological advantage when in a survival situation, on a mission, or lost in the wilderness: "It definitely goes back to psychology. One of the first things that you should try to do in a survival situation is something familiar, and if that's got a net benefit to you, like having a warm drink, then that gets your mind on the right track. So, making a cup of tea is a really good thing to try to do. It's like a fire; you get the warmth and the morale. I just feel like I'm much more in charge of the place."

You know as well as I that sometimes life itself can feel like a survival situation. However, you don't have to wait until you're screwed before you draw on your psychological or energetic advantages. No matter what the task at hand, why not have a toolbox of your own advantages? Viral energy is conducted through the vibrational tone of consciousness—your state of mind—and through thoughts and words, all of which create ("good" or "bad") experiences and outcomes.

You also know that you can advantage or depress your state of mind, and I believe both happiness and depression can be understood from a quantum physics perspective. After all, thanks to the discovery of quantum mechanics at the end of the eighteen-hundreds, the science is responsible for opening up the entire fields of electronics and computers and is credited with the invention of cell phones and most everything technological that we know. It's energy and particle science at the smallest level, and because our mind is a powerful computer, I figure it's a pretty important topic to wrap our minds around.

I spoke with the quantum physicist of quantum physicists, Dr. Fred Alan Wolf, otherwise known as Dr. Quantum. He's a genius professor, bestselling author, and world-famous cast member from the films *What the Bleep Do We Know!?* and *The Secret*. If you've seen these movies, then you're sure to remember Dr. Wolf—he sort of looks like Albert Einstein.

Here's what he said: "Okay. Let's say that right now you're sitting and you're saying, 'Oh, I'm so depressed. I feel so bad. I feel terrible.' Just do one simple thing. It's very simple. Ask yourself this question: 'Who is feeling depressed?' But don't answer the question. Just posing the question without answering it changes the chemistry inside the body, and just by asking, you can begin to lift yourself from that depression. You've got to keep doing it for a while because it isn't like automatic pilot. It's not like throwing a switch. You've got to keep doing it, and after a while you begin to realize that the person who is saying 'I am depressed' is not you. The mind is a process, and it's related to what is happening at the level of what we call the quantum field of reality. At this unobservable invisible level of reality, we are dealing with a field of possibilities, not a gathering of physical objects. Think of a magnetic field produced by a bar magnet. The field is invisible. But sprinkle iron filings on a sheet of paper and then place the bar magnet beneath the sheet and you see the effect of the field on the filings. Changing the field of possibilities changes the pattern of behavior. Your brain is like the iron filings. It's a bunch of 'stuff.' Your mind is like the quantum field and is not made of 'stuff.' In fact, it's not made of anything. From the point of view of quantum physics, your mind doesn't even exist in the material 'spacetime' world. It comes before it."

(KABOOM!! My mind comes before space and time!?)

"The Magnetic Field" provided by Dr. Fred Alan Wolf

Now, to be clear, Dr. Wolf—*winner of the National Book Award in Science*—is not suggesting that getting out of depression is easy; he is suggesting that when we reprogram our habitual self talk and—even deeper—our beliefs about our Self, the energy quality created by our mind (the part of us that can *choose* this or that) will change our state of being and our state of mind. How that change occurs is very plainly the result of how we know energy to behave and to produce outcomes. The essential sentence is, as Dr. Wolf said, "Changing the field of possibilities changes the pattern of behavior." Of course, in this example, the "pattern of behavior" is an actual change in the chemistry of the brain (an organ no different than any in the body, with the body being the part of us that experiences the output of our choices).

He continues, "That which is *aware* is not in spacetime, hence it is a *spiritual entity* perhaps related to the quantum field of the mind itself and inherent in the whole universe. As far as I could speculate, and *mind* you, I am only speculating here, the simple technique I explained should work to change your mindset and therefore the observer in you causing you to change your perspective on whatever you observe, be it feelings, intuitions, senses, or thoughts. The ancient key lies in the usage of the word 'I' in English, 'Ya' in Russian, 'Ich' in German, 'Anee' in Hebrew, and 'Je' in French. Although a simple word, it represents many different people living inside of our brains and nervous systems and muscles and skin and bones."

I love this insight from Dr. Quantum. So, thoughts create the torque—the moment of force—to manifest into form.

Your thoughts can either disrupt or advantage the quality of what you're manifesting in your life, your experiences, and happiness. Heavy energy will depress your state of mind. Light energy will advantage your state of mind and provide the torque.

As I pursue my goals and dreams, I actively try to get my mind "on the right track" as John Hudson says. I deploy my go-to psychological advantages while writing, painting, visualizing, or dealing with a difficult time or situation. *What can I do to get a net benefit that will supercharge my creativity or opportunity*, I wonder? Here's what gives me a mental boost: Classical, French, or jazz music; lighting a candle; and a quick reset meditation. When attending an important meeting or event, I also like to wear a favorite dress or shoes to feel the most comfortable in my own skin.

Advantages are not fix-alls; they are small ways to make a big difference in your morale and momentum because *you* still have to do the work. Change your mind and change your direction. Torque your mind and torque your success. Open your mind and open your world. Advantage your mind and advantage your life.

The Hidden Treasure that Every Successful Person Knows About

Laura, forty-two, is a vocalist with a life-long dream to be rich and famous. Every time she is asked what her highest goals are, she says that she wants to win a Grammy as a recording artist, an Academy Award as an actress, and be known and recognized all around the world. The problem is that Laura has been circling the fringe of the music industry for a solid twenty-five years and can't figure out how to break through to the fame and fortune that she desires. And in terms of being an actress, well, she hasn't done any acting since high school.

I see it all the time. Laura has a clear case of confused-passion-picker. There is a disconnect between what she thinks she wants and what will make her happy. I told her, "'I want to be rich' will not make you happy because your being rich does not create anything. 'I want to be famous' will not make you happy because the degree to which you are a recognizable public figure does not create anything."

At the heart of it, what Laura truly wanted was to feel that she mattered. In working with celebrities in my former role as a publicist, I have found that most of the people who want to be famous are the ones with the most profound insecurities. These people hold beliefs that they don't really matter and so they subconsciously figure that becoming famous would be the antidote to any doubt that they matter and are indeed important. They might also think that money and fame are the tickets that will finally get others to admire or respect them.

Of course, there are those who are already quite rich and famous. Some got that way through an unintended bi-product of following their deep inner purpose. Others, while successful according to the world's standards, chased and caught the wrong dream and are still left wanting and unfulfilled—they picked the wrong passion and are some of the most unhappy and searching people in the world.

When you say that you want to be successful in your life, career, as a parent, or in the love department, what you really want is to be happy. But did you know that true success and happiness are synonymous with each other? You can't have one without the other. It would be a good bet to say that if you were journeying toward your true purpose in life, you'd probably be pretty darn happy.

So, do you want the secret to success? And, while we're at it, would you like to know the entry-key to happiness? Sure, no problem. Here it is: *inspiration magnetizes the resources required to fulfill the dream.*

Inspiration is the magnetic ingredient to fulfill your dream. Inspired passions, inspired goals, and inspired intentions supercharge the dream, goal, or intention. The key is the word *inspired*. Albert Einstein famously said, "I have no special talents. I'm only passionately curious." Vincent Van Gogh said, "I would rather die of passion than of boredom." Bob Marley said, "I have no education. I have inspiration. If I was educated, I would be a damn fool." And it's not just artists and philosophers that *get* this; titans of business get it, too. Kevin O'Leary, TV's infamous "Shark" has many times said, "I have to be excited to invest." His panel-mate Barbara Corcoran adds to that, "You can't fake passion."

Laura didn't understand the formula for success. She never stopped to ask herself how or what she wanted to contribute to humanity or to life itself. When thinking about your passion, think of it this way: what need for others am I fulfilling? (Not, "What do I need? What do I want?") After all, to market yourself in any business you must create something that people want to buy, do, or have. Even the word "purpose" can only make sense when it is a solution to a need.

You could wander for many years asking yourself the question, "How do I get what I want in life?" But you will get nowhere and have nothing with that question. Instead, ask yourself, "What's my unique contribution?" or "What can I create and who can I serve?" and "What inspires me?" or "What gives me goose bumps?" Then, replace the question with the key. Replace the word "what" with the answer. For instance, "Making people smile and laugh inspires me. Collaboration with other musicians gives me goosebumps."

When I spoke with Dr. Fred Alan Wolf, I had one last question for him that was different from the quantum physics questions he usually fields. I said, "I'd like to share that for me, happiness was found on the journey to purpose. May I ask you, what is happiness to you?" He told me this, "We all are born and we die. I believe that aside from the law of attraction, each of us has a purpose on the planet, and that the event of your birth is not an accident, and that your death is not the end of the road. Finding your purpose in life may take years or decades, but you will eventually find it and act according to that purpose or frustrate yourself by doing what you really don't wish to do. The really big secret is not the law of attraction; it is the action that people who realize their purpose take in their lives. In every case where I have met successful people, I tend to find that the happiest people are those who do what they enjoy doing. The richest people are those who do what benefits others. To be rich and happy, do what you enjoy doing for the benefit of others and you can't fail to be rich and happy. It is absolutely guaranteed, provided you take the right action."

From my own experience, and through the shared wisdom of some very enlightened individuals, I have learned that inspiration is always an experience shared from a high source of light energy. The hidden treasure that successful people know is this: let true passion and inspiration point the way and success and happiness will follow.

Illuminati

Alan was a light for everyone around him; a conduit for conveying wisdom. He had no jealousy to cloud his light and his capacity for absorbing light was ever expanding and non-resistant. He was a being of contagious light, kind of like the Santa Claus of viral energy, working the magic all the time. Although, Alan wasn't bearded and jolly, nor was he even handsome or rich; Alan was a very thin twenty-something-year-old janitor at a high school with a lisp and a lazy eye. In an act of reverse bullying, the students of the school embraced Alan and would give him a cheerful, "Good morning, Alan," when they passed him in the halls. They would even bring him an extra snack from home on occasion. The teachers and students got together every year to help celebrate Alan's birthday with heartfelt displays of balloons and cards—they felt good about their inclusion of Alan into the body and family of the school.

When Alan suddenly died in a drowning accident at twenty-eight years old, everyone grieved for him. But they then realized that they were grieving for themselves. In the absence of his wide and bright light energy, the students and teachers came to understand that *they* had not been doing something for Alan; *he* had been doing something for them. It was Alan who first acknowledged each person that he passed and gave them a shiny, "Good morning," or "Good afternoon," or "What a beautiful day it is today!" It was Alan who first smiled at each person he passed in the halls. The students and teachers eventually smiled back, progressing from a muttered, "Morning..." to enthusiastic variations of, "Good morning, Alan!" It was Alan who was the force that moved people to kindness and mobilized their charity and goodness. It was Alan who brought the power of one to so many. It was Alan who brought out the best in others and elevated them with his light.

Do you know an illuminati? I bet you do. You likely know a few of these enlightened ones. They're all around you, hidden in plain sight. If you don't, keep a look out for them. They are the person who inspires you when you don't have the words, the ideas, or the fuel to get through today—a mentor who stands out among all mentors because they embody both wisdom and light. They have more than sage words; they are the one with the infectious presence and contagious joy. Illuminati are often philosophers, teachers, inventors, writers, moviemakers, playwrights, artists, and great contributors to our spiritual evolution. Here are a few famous ones that you would know by name: Mother Theresa, Maya Angelou, Princess Diana, and Mahatma Gandhi. They can also be a stranger in the supermarket, or the seemingly ordinary person seated next to you in a waiting room.

Audit the quality of light energy radiating from the people around you. Are they inspiring, well-intentioned, and do they add to your joy? You can supercharge your light quality as a result of whom you spend time around. I go out of my way to seek illuminati in my life. Somewhere along the way I realized that being positive within myself wasn't enough; I needed to be around people with a presence of light so that I could soak in the glow.

An illuminati can be anyone at any time that adds light to your light. Lightness from others is light energy from a source *outside* of you, correct? So then think about this: while it isn't your light, you feel it and experience the light and it becomes your light. Because you know that you didn't sponsor the light and it didn't come from you to start with, what you're feeling is the impact of viral energy. It works exactly like osmosis: the spontaneous net movement of solvent molecules through a semi-permeable membrane into a region of higher solute concentration in the direction that tends to equalize the solute concentrations on the two sides. (*Bingo!*) Enlightenment is much more likely when your inner and outer environments are congruent with each other. It's actually not as fancy as it sounds; it's plainly the magic of viral energy. So, you might want to spend more time with an illuminati. Bathe in their light—it's catchy. Just remember these three words and you can't go wrong: I choose Light.

Are You Ready for Your Biggest Paradigm Shift, Ever? (Seven Consciousness-Energy Strata)

Okay, so it's clever to know that you can take on the energy with which you surround yourself. But, then what? What difference does that make in the long-term? Actually, a great deal. For your happiness and fulfillment in life, the heavy or light energy to which you assimilate makes all the difference in the world. And, why? Because, in part, the effects of viral energy set your energetic-presence and your presence is being in the field to which you have access.

Let me explain by introducing you to the "Seven Consciousness-Energy Strata." Consciousness-energy is a measure of awakening and, once you begin to work with the mechanics of energy, it will be a game-changer in your life.

So, what are the Seven Consciousness-Energy Strata? These are seven levels of awakening. To visualize this, think of it like a layer cake with seven different flavor levels. Or, visualize layered rock—like you might have seen in an archaeological dig on TV—as it displays years of Earth's stories with one stratum on top of the next. However, with the Seven Consciousness-Energy Strata, the layers are of contagious vibrational energy—the stuff that creates.

Each of the energy layers is empowered to create. Some create heavy and others create light, and they evolve from heavy to light.

In ascending order, the layers are: Hell, Ignorance, Indifference, Wanting, Awareness, Creation, Heaven.

As you might expect, the lowest, thick, and sluggish energies are in the very bottom layers. There is less of the good stuff down there. This is where guilt and illusion reside. These energies create narrow (mindedness), less (opportunities), and low (emotions and actions), and are obstructions to the light that is always available to you.

The upper layers of energy are the highly inspired, light, and unobstructed energy. Up there is everything good that you want, and more of it. This is the limitless space where love, enlightenment, and creation reside. This energy creates light.

In between the two opposing ends lie other strata of energy. The strata are further divided into two awareness realms by a separation line (literally and spiritually) between "Wanting" and "Awareness." Through my own meditations, I have come to believe that when each soul crosses over this delineation threshold (by way of their own spiritual awakening to the mechanics of creation-energy and the interconnectedness of all of Life), it is one of the grandest moments in humanity's spiritual evolution and is collectively celebrated by all of Heaven. (*Now, this is a big deal. Cue the choir of angels!*) This awakening signifies freedom, recognition of the true meaning of life, and authentic happiness, and yet so many of us are stuck living in a state of wanting. We *want* to find our soul's mate and/or companionship. We *want* financial security. We *want* to be out of emotional and physical pain. If this sounds at all like you, I bet you would love to know how to finally transcend wanting. (*Read on.*)

The stratum of energy that you are "in" is also how your energy is tuned. The way in which your energy is tuned becomes your being's pulse and presence. Here is where the word *presence* becomes so very important to everything that you want and dream of in earnest. Your presence is both a noun and a verb and it is a state-of-being moving in spacetime in a horizontal pulse of consciousness-energy.

Your presence encompasses everything that you get and what you give off. Unless you are in stratum flow with it (whatever the "it" is that you are wanting), no amount of commiserating about what you want will get you "it." No one else can help you get "it" or do it for you. No one and no thing around you is responsible to lift your presence; your presence is not a victim and it's not passive.

This is most likely not the understanding of "presence" you might have had before, am I right? But hang with me because this is so important and key to your happiness and success. Before we go any further, let's pinpoint the kind of presence that we're talking about.

International bestselling author Eckhart Tolle talks about presence as a guide to "the now"—the ever-present moment of now. Tolle teaches the benefits of being consciously aware of the present moment, including ways in which to practice presence. (*But this is not the presence we're after here.*)

Here's a different take on presence: In the entertainment industry, we use the word presence to describe an actor or performer that just has "it." Perhaps it's their *je ne sais quoi*—that special something that they bring to the stage or when they walk into a room, and we just can't put our finger on what it is about them that's so special. Is it their personality, their mystery, their talent?

In another context, social media sensations are said to have an online presence or platform. In this case, presence is a voice, an audience, and the ability to influence.

The English language is really very limiting and like many words doing triple duty, "presence" is used for several unique meanings. The magic of viral energy has its own definition and meaning of presence, and understanding it is imperative to properly utilizing the magic to your benefit and the benefit of others.

Your being's presence is an energetic attainment in the consciousness-energy strata.

Your presence is something—an energy—that you earn as a product of everything that you are, do, experience, intend, and with which you surround yourself.

This energetic attainment should not be confused with your physical energy level, which is a result of your caloric intake and physical exertion. Furthermore, your presence has nothing to do with your influence in the world, popularity, or status. It also doesn't have anything to do with how much sleep you did or didn't get, it's not affected by caffeine or alcohol, and it's not even about your personality, humor, appearance, or confidence. Presence has nothing to do with being outgoing, aloof, or talented, and it does not change with today's good or bad news, or today's good or bad mood. Viral energy presence is not about being physically "there" in a location, or about "showing up" for someone physically or emotionally. Viral energy presence is not the location of your body, your mind, or even your spirit. It's also not about a singular moment or about trying "to be in the moment." Presence isn't concerned with being consciously aware of the eternal moment of now, and it's not something that you can practice. It's what you are being.

In terms of viral energy, your presence is the energy **quality** of your being. Your energetic-presence is where you are being in the consciousness-energy strata—it's how you vibrate, what you give off, and it fuels everything that you create.

I know a man—we can call him Disgruntled Nick (think: Jason Bateman's character in the 2011 comedy-classic *Horrible Bosses*)—who did everything right by his employer and had high-achiever work ethic, yet was not being recognized for his contributions. And worse, his boss repeatedly told him *not* to change the status quo. Over a few years of trying to make a positive difference and consistently being road-blocked, Disgruntled Nick went from disheartened and frustrated to all-out angry and miserable. (I mean, *really* miserable!) Unlike Bateman's character, Disgruntled Nick was not passive; he fought back at injustice. He also started looking for another job. He applied for dozens of well-suited opportunities and attended numerous interviews, putting on his best "happy face" even though he was deeply miserable and entangled in drama and fights with the same old people at his current job. Lo and behold, no one wanted to hire him. Even though Disgruntled Nick had a stellar work history and had earned several impressive awards during his career, no job offers were extended and he couldn't figure out why. Disgruntled Nick had considered all of his assets, and yet, he never considered his energetic-presence as a factor in the way people were responding to him.

Before I finally "got it"—that is, the magic of viral energy—I too used to feel like I was creating the same relationships all the time, or constantly repeating the same failures and disappointments. I kept cycling through the same old breakups, the same old heartbreaks, and repetitive letdowns. Even when it seemed that this would be the time that things would work out, things would suddenly fall apart and it wouldn't make sense. These dreams of mine that were practically guaranteed, locked down, already promised, and all but contracted, would disintegrate before my eyes. Poof! Gone. At times, I bet you've felt like that, too. For instance, you'll face the same old job problems and dissatisfaction even when you change jobs. There may be new people, but the issues remain the same. Maybe you've thought, "Why am I going through this again? Why do I have to go through this same old crap, again?" What is the answer, do you think? Why *are* you going through this same disappointment and loss again? *This* dream was looking like a ringer, right? Well, what happened?

I'm going to tell you what happened (or what's still happening) by way of a little shopping trip that you're going to take—right now.

You open your eyes and find yourself in an unfamiliar building. The sun is streaming through perfectly clear windows, lighting up all corners and passageways throughout the space. Everything about this place feels good and natural, but somehow you don't remember where you are, so you look around for signs. You come to a corridor that appears to be a landing area or foyer and there you find an elevator. Next to the lift, there are "Up" and "Down" call buttons, so you push the down arrow to call the elevator car. The door opens and you step inside. Once inside, you notice an informational panel displaying buttons for seven levels. Now you can see that you are on the sixth floor of a seven-story building, yet the ground floor is actually level three, and the floors are not simply labeled one through seven. They are labeled:

H – 7th Stratum and Penthouse Access
C – 6th Stratum
A – 5th Stratum
W – 4th Stratum
In – 3rd Stratum or Ground
I – 2nd Stratum or Parking
H – 1st Stratum or Lower Level

You press "W." The elevator begins to move with a sudden drop that you feel in your stomach and a moment later the door opens to floor "W." As you look around, you now see that this is a department store. There are sections for home appliances, home repair tools, kitchen dishware and accessories, and exercise equipment, but you don't want any of that. As you walk around you know that this stuff is not what you want; you want yellow tulips. Hmmm. You return to the home repair section and look for flowers thinking that they might carry gardening supplies. When you can't find any flowers there, you look around again in the kitchen accessories—

maybe tulips can be found *there*, you hope. After much scouring and finger-crossing, you can't find yellow tulips. You're now starting to give up on yellow tulips and so you decide that you could be somewhat happy with any color of tulips.

Just then, you see a large, shiny, backlit poster of a very satisfied looking woman wearing a wide-brimmed hat (the kind that you only wear on vacation) and boasting an armful of multicolored tulips. The poster reads: "Wake Up Your Senses." Ah-ha! So, they *do* stock tulips here, you tell yourself. You continue to search but continue to have no luck.

As you put more and more effort into finding tulips, you're giving up on ever getting any flowers of any color or variety. You know exactly what you want in your mind—it is your dream and deep desire after all—but you've looked and looked (and even panicked and feared and hoped and prayed) and now you're starting to get frustrated and disheartened. Your vision of flowers is waning. *Maybe I'm not meant to have the fresh flowers that I want*, you start to think. You reason with yourself that you will strive only for plastic flowers—*that's not asking too much*, you think. And so you keep wanting in a cycle of futile effort.

During all of your dreaming and searching and wanting and praying and wishing and reasoning and compromising, you never notice the sign that reads: FRESH FLOWERS—ONE LEVEL UP.

The fact is, flowers were never going to be available on level "W" because they are on level "A." To reference my own past—when I was experiencing nonsensical loss and defeat, I didn't have access to my dreams because of the "level" of my presence. I didn't know it, but I was running on a treadmill within the stratum of "Wanting" when all along my dreams were not there. My dreams were big and bold and beautiful and they vibrated and shared energy with the "Creation" stratum. No matter how much I chased and wanted my dreams, I didn't share energy with them—not in the presence that I was being at that time; not on that level. I didn't flow with them. I didn't pulse with them. (*Not then at least.*)

I wish I knew then what I know now, and that is that we each have the ability to change that to which we have access. You should be very empowered to know that no matter your repeating issues, or what you've been told (or have told yourself), you can absolutely change your presence—that vibration that sets your presence—and therefore change your stratum flow.

You do all of this through the management of viral energy.

(Maybe your sign reads: TRUE LOVE—TWO FLOORS UP. Or: DREAM JOB—LEVEL C.)

Consistent exposure to light or heavy energy does indeed impact and raise or lower your presence. By way of the process of your spiritual evolution coupled with the osmosis of light or heavy energy, your presence ascends or descends, evolves or devolves, all within the consciousness-energy strata.

Once again, think of it like a marinade. Your energy field is permeable, and you soak in the energy that exists all around you. After some soaking, you take on the flavor, temperature, and quality of the viral energy sauce. Even still, *you choose* what you accept into your presence. *You* have the power to let in light and filter out the heavy energies.

So, what stratum are *you* being?

It won't be too hard to figure out; you'll identify it right away. What do you recognize in yourself? What do you often experience?

HEAVEN (Truth)

SPIRITUAL PENTHOUSE
UNCONDITIONAL LOVE
HEAVEN ON EARTH
ENLIGHTENMENT

GOING UP?

CREATION (Truth)

Right-Action	Wonderment	Becoming	Happiness
Creativity	Abundance	Ease	Acceptance
Wholeness	Wisdom	Light	Guardianship
Well-being	Bliss	Fulfillment	
Authenticity	Joy	Purposeful choices	

AWARENESS (Truth)

Forgiveness	Patience	Enthusiasm
Balance	Seeking	Introspection
Expectation	Purpose-Pursuit	Empathy
Optimism	Open-Mindedness	Awakening
Compassion	Intention-Awareness	

WANTING (The Cusp)

Beginning-of-Spiritual-Curiosity   Conditional relationships
Infatuation   Overwhelment   Loneliness   Unfulfillment
Achievement-driven   Need   Regret   Concern
Gratification based choices   Confusion   Vanity   Impatience
Boredom   Depression   Desire   Worry   Hopefulness

INDIFFERENCE (The Great Con)

Inner struggle   Septic energy   Detachment   Jealousy
Pessimism   Inflexible beliefs   Disloyalty   Identity crisis
Relationship instability   Criticism   Energetic blockages
Hurt-regret pattern   Judgment   Apathy   Arrogance
Self-loathing

IGNORANCE (The Great Con)

Energetic toxicity   Smallness   Being stuck   Selfishness
Disappointment   Anger   Unconsciousness   Envy
Rejection   Greed   Powerlessness   Obsession
Lack   Relationship Drama   Stagnation   Hatred

HELL (The Great Con)

Guilt	Material Underworld	Fear
Lust	Violence	Illusion
Lostness	Separation	

Let's look at the Seven Consciousness-Energy Strata.

At the bottom is the stratum of "**Hell.**" This level creates the polluted energies of guilt, violence, separation, lostness, fear, illusion, and the material underworld. One layer above is the stratum of "**Ignorance**" and it creates in stagnation with energy-toxicity, being stuck, obsession, smallness, envy, selfishness, consistent drama, repeated failures, and powerlessness. Ascending next is the "**Indifference**" stratum that is characterized by discord, inner-struggle, judgment, hurt-regret pattern, criticism, disloyalty, jealousy, and self-loathing. Above that is the "**Wanting**" stratum and it includes worry, confusion, unfilfillment, conditional-relationships, impatience, boredom, achievement-driven behavior, dissatisfaction, and the beginnings of spiritual curiosity.

As we get lighter still, we reach the stratum of "**Awareness.**" (Notice the big jump in enlightenment from "Wanting" to "Awareness.") "Awareness" offers forgiveness, seeking, purpose-pursuit, introspection, empathy, balance, and open-mindedness. As you enlighten further, you have access to the stratum of "**Creation**" and there you live with abundance, fulfillment, creativity, guardianship of life, authenticity, wonderment, and joy.

The soul's ultimate consciousness-energy attainment is the stratum of "**Heaven,**" but this is not the same Heaven that we refer to when speaking about the afterlife. The consciousness-energy of "Heaven" is full enlightenment, and if attained in the physical form, it is Heaven on Earth. All souls—including you—will eventually reach Heaven, though not because this incarnation of your soul has passed from the physical lifetime, but because Heaven is the vibration to which all of Life is magnetized, remembers with, and returns to. For most souls, that journey to remembering takes many, many lifetimes. Yet, "most souls" is not all souls. For instance, Jesus Christ attained oneness with Heaven in a single physical lifetime. Indeed, He was divine. The Light energy vibration of fully united consciousness flows in the upper chamber of "Heaven"— souls "there" are no longer identified as beings, but rather as *being*.

(You got it—this is deep spiritual philosophy, but you're hearing it because you're looking for more and because you're ready for more.)

Now, back to you and your vibrational stratum. I'm going to suggest that you are most likely on the cusp of two sequential strata, as you are either evolving (expanding), devolving (minimizing), or stagnating (turning off).

As you study the qualities and experiences as defined in each stratum, they might sound like emotions. While they overlap with emotion, the qualities and energies of presence are not emotions; they are purities of light and heavy (or dense) energy. Therefore, the consciousness-energy strata are different from the emotion spectrum (which is a range of emotions from hatred to joy and every feeling in between). Emotions can be situational and transient and luckily for you and me, emotion does not make up your presence. Unlike your presence, emotion can instantly change. For instance, you were happy but then you heard some bad news and now you're sad. Some days I'm in a crabby mood or something unpleasant has happened to me, but luckily, I don't have to worry about it knocking down my presence; it takes more than that. Emotions can be a byproduct of chronic exposure to the contagious creation energy with which you most often surround yourself. Remember, light energy creates light (from your Higher-Self) and heavy energy creates low. For this reason, emotions are found inside your consciousness-energy stratum—they are being created and contribute to creation.

But, get this—your presence is not the only creator in the energy field. Think about it: what and who is in the stratum with you?

Perhaps you recognize traits or experiences of some of the key people in your life within these strata. What's their energy stratum? What have other people been bringing your way? If you have been experiencing a tremendous amount of *energetic-toxicity* from several people in your life (that's an experience of the "Ignorance" Stratum), or a years-long *hurt-regret-pattern* with a family member (the "Indifference" Stratum), even though it is not *your* behavior or intention, you're in the flow with those folks; your consciousness-energy stratum includes that experience. On this level, you're getting tools and exercise equipment, but you're not getting the flowers you want.

Let's expand on that. You might have a family member who feeds off the negative energy of a *hurt-regret-pattern* with you. This is when they hurt you, then they regret it, then you feel empathy for them, then they hurt you again, and regret it again, confounding the relationship into absurdity. But why do they have access to hurt you? Oh, that's an easy one—you're in the same stratum with them, Silly.

However, now (*finally*) you can choose to step out of the flow. Move your energy lighter. Get out of the flow of the stuff that you no longer choose. Your parent, child, or sibling will still be just that and you will continue to have a relationship with them. They might indeed continue their *hurt-regret-pattern* with someone else; it just won't be with you—once you awaken to the magic of viral energy.

Your energetic-presence is the fuel and power for all that you create and to which you have access. The energy that you are being—in the process of your spiritual evolution—is your presence. If you want to be in flow with a higher consciousness-energy stratum, *be* it.

Let's do a quick audit of your presence. Where are you at with your dreams and goals? Write it down. From one to ten, where are you in relation to your dreams? One is "I haven't yet taken the first step," or "I don't know what I want," or "I'm a mess," or "I just lost my dream—it slipped through my fingers." And, ten is "I'm there. I'm living my dream." Maybe, you are somewhere in the middle yet you feel you know how to get from here to there. Or, do you feel like you're not even in the same neighborhood as your dreams, or that perhaps you're on a different path to your dreams? (*A different stratum layer, channel, or flow.*) If you find that you're not in the same place, space, or energy as your dreams and goals, then what can you do to get in the flow or oneness with them?

Look at the stratum of your goal. Check out the chart of the Seven Strata while thinking of your big goal or inspired dream. Where does it likely reside? What stratum is it? Now consider this: What type of experiences, people, influences, daily practices, mindsets, and soulsets are there in *that* stratum? And, in what stratum are *you* currently operating? Look at your surroundings, influences, experiences, attitudes, thoughts, and practices. Are all things around you, and all that you are currently creating, congruent with the creation-energy that would be found in the stratum where your dreams flow, move, and create?

You only create within your stratum. You only have access to the "stuff" in your stratum flow. All that is in your stratum flow (those energies) are the ingredients for all that you can create. Inside your stratum flow are the makings of a deconstructed recipe. You can create anything with those ingredients—(*caveat*) anything using *just* those ingredients!

So, you might want to be conscious of your presence and get in the flow of what you would love to do, be, and have. The level at which your energy resonates is everything about your being; it's what you take in, give out, and what you then experience. Ponder this: Where is all the good stuff that you want? Where is your true love, paid fun, unobstructed health, inspired dreams, happiness, and pure creation energy? Oh yeah, you got it Baby—it's up there! So, enlighten to it. You have the power. Make your *move*.

CHAPTER THREE:

HEAVY ENERGY CREATES

*Little-Known Toxins in Your Environment
(And How to Avoid Them)*

In June of 2017, actor Daniel Day-Lewis, the only person to win three best actor Oscars, made the shocking announcement that he was retiring from acting. Shortly after his announcement, he said that the decision was directly related to shooting the dark film, *Phantom Thread*, saying that filming it made him so sad he decided to quit acting. In this quote, Day-Lewis references the movie's Director, Paul Thomas Anderson: "Before making the film, I didn't know I was going to stop acting. I do know that Paul and I laughed a lot *before* we made the movie. And then we stopped laughing because we were both overwhelmed by a sense of sadness. That happened during the telling of the story, and I don't really know why," Day-Lewis told W magazine.

While Daniel Day-Lewis doesn't know why sadness overcame him, I believe I do.

Likely due to his method acting (a total immersion technique), heavy viral energy was the culprit that actually ended the career of Daniel Day-Lewis. In time, I do hope that he can detox from that deep immersion into sadness and return to the joy of his vocation—that is, if he so chooses. It takes a concentrated and potent heavy viral energy to end a career or manifest in depression, yet it's the same stuff that is responsible for many bad days for many people.

Here's how it works in your day-to-day life: The news is on in the background. Four commentators are ranting and arguing, and you're getting edgy. Your social media page is laced with opinions, debates, and political talk—the talk these days feels more like hate-slinging. Your desk is a mess with piles of papers, tax filings to do, letters from lawyers, or bills to pay, and it's overwhelming and exhausting just looking at it. Maybe you work in an office environment where there's a lot of complaining and gossip. Heavy viral energy is all around you. The atmosphere can feel heavy with tension, anxiety, and grief, because it is. You might have picked it up while watching the women fight with each other on *The Real Housewives*, or maybe it came from the chaotic noise of blasting horns while stuck in traffic. Perhaps it's the result of the frantic tone of a friend who's having relationship trouble and called to regurgitate the whole thing on you.

Let me give you this true example: Ashley is a friend of mine who called to tell me about an issue with her new boyfriend and to solicit my opinion on the matter. In this scenario, she sincerely didn't know if her boyfriend was being insensitive and inattentive, or if she was just expecting too much from him. Here's what she said happened: The day before, she had sent the exact same text message to three people—her new boyfriend, her childhood best friend, and me. The text message read: "I'M HAVING THE WORST DAY, EVER! I feel so helpless and angry! I lost my necklace, the one that my mom gave me! I can't think of anything else or even move on with my day until I find it. I will never forgive myself if I don't find it! I will never recover if I don't find it! And I'm not sure if the matching earrings are lost, too; I'll have to check when I get home. But if I lost the necklace, the same thing could have possibly happened with the earrings, too. I am absolutely beside myself!"

(*Yep, that's a real text message.*)

Sooo…I responded when I got Ashley's message, telling her that she would probably find it and that she should try not to worry about it too much for today. Her new boyfriend responded as well, with a very brief message saying something like, "I'm sorry to hear that." Her best friend did not respond at all, yet it was the boyfriend's response that bothered Ashley the most, making her question their compatibility and call me for my opinion on the matter. She felt he was not giving her the sympathy and tenderness that she wanted from a boyfriend, and perhaps (and I quote), "A future life partner, for goodness sake."

I told her, "Well, because you asked, I will say that I feel that this one is you, not him." I explained to her that when I had gotten her message, as much as I felt badly for her, I was in the middle of a work project and was having quite a productive day. However, when I read her message, it felt as if she was vomiting all of her fears and negativity all over me. I also let her know that she frequently did this and that I didn't like it at all. I explained that if she had come on softer and communicated in a less frantic way, I would then have felt much more moved to give her a soothing response and more of what she needed. I added that her boyfriend may well have felt the same vomiting of heavy viral energy from her into his workday. I let her know that her message was high-strung and even aggressive.

The next day she found the necklace and also discovered the earrings had always been safely stowed at home.

Maybe you think this doesn't sound like you because you're contained and pleasant with people even though you often experience inner turmoil. Well, that's super-duper that you don't dump on others, but that doesn't determine your viral energy stratum. You can't see your viral energy—no one can. And, you can't fake your stratum either; you're either in flow with the good stuff, or you're not. Your words are very powerful energy formations, and so are your inner thoughts and feelings.

This should matter to you because the way in which others respond to you is essential to your happiness. If others are consistently getting a frantic, low, or miserable vibe from you, chances are you're not going to get a positive response back from them. You see, you succeed, fail, create, destroy, live, die, fight, and love *energetically*. It has everything to do with the viral energy stratum in which your presence resides, and therefore what you're putting out into the world.

Lucky for Ashley, your viral energy stratum is not determined by your current mood or the good or bad thing that happened today. *Your viral energy stratum is a product of chronic exposure to light or heavy energy from within yourself or the people and energy around you.* Both good and bad stuff build up over time. Think of it like dieting and exercise—if you haven't exercised in months but you do so today, you won't see the results today. Although, assuming you maintain the exercise regime, you will see results over time. If you eat poorly today, you won't see the effect in your body and health today. If your poor eating habits become chronic, you will see a change in your body over time. Concentration and duration is also how it works with the energetic influences within your surroundings. Viral energy affects your presence and your presence affects others around you. Your life is the way it is because you are in the same viral energy stratum as everything you are experiencing.

I have another friend, Melanie, who has always had a challenging relationship with her sister, Wendy. They recently had a misunderstanding and, according to Mel, her sister started a big drama. But this time, Melanie had chosen to squash the tension and therefore thought that the subject was done. Until, that is, she got a text message from Wendy asking if she had time to talk about it, *today*. However, Melanie didn't have the time and more importantly, she couldn't risk bringing in any negativity because it was a big day for her—she was expecting good news on an opportunity that she had been diligently cultivating. Of course, that's just the day that her contentious sister wants to talk about recent drama. (*Murphy's Law, right? Or maybe, Melanie's Law.*) So, Melanie told her sister, "No, I don't have time today, but any other day I can make the time."

This was a really big step for Melanie. She usually drops everything when one of her family members needs something or wants to talk. But on this day, she deployed her energy filters at the right time. Later that day, Melanie got the phone call that she had been waiting for with the positive news that she had hoped was coming—and it did.

Saying "no" to heavy viral energy is saying "yes" to light viral energy. As you experience your everyday life, you experience the science of energy—it's as if you are stewing in a petri dish of viral vibes. Yet, no matter how you infer the intentions of others and the "noise" around you, and no matter how you experience viral energy—both the heavy and the light—simply being mindful of these toxins allows you to make choices that limit your exposure and protects your good energy and your presence.

To sum it up, I borrowed this adage from the medical field, and it perfectly applies to viral energy toxicity: *Dilution* is *the solution* to *pollution*.

Loony Bin Life

When I was in my mid-twenties, I woke up one morning to recall that I had checked myself into an asylum the night before. I opened my eyes to the harsh glow of fluorescent lights. I've always disliked fluorescent lights and the way they taint everything with artificial blue-green. Yet on this day, I wasn't sure which I disliked more—florescent lights or dropped ceilings. The hovering rectangles of achromatic tiles speckled with dirty grey dots reminded me of elementary school. I was freezing too, wearing nothing but a faded, open-backed gown the color of a dusty teardrop, with a single white sheet tucked up around my neck.

From previous hospitalizations due to bouts with pneumonia, an inguinal hernia, and a broken ankle, I had decided that I hated everything about hospitals including the chatter from the nurses' station that was inevitably just outside my door, the threat of people invading my personal space without invitation, the way some nurses spoke to me like I was a child, and the way others regarded me more like a potted plant.

"Good morning...'ur Penny?" A robust forty-something woman burst into my room while studying a clipboard. "I'm Sheila. I'm the Charge Nurse. I see that your parents brought you in last night." She hadn't yet looked at me.

"Actually, my parents drove me here, but I brought myself in. I can leave anytime I want to."

"Hmmm," she muttered, as if to say, "Are you sure about that?" She went on to instruct me on the breakfast protocol.

"I'm not really hungry. I'd like to take a shower." I noticed it was a double occupancy room, yet I hadn't a roommate. The door was open to a tiny room where I could clearly see only a toilet and micro-sized sink.

"There is one shower on this floor. You will be told when you can shower. But that's not now." I decided that she must be a mother.

I was on a ten-year bender of what started as fear and loss and was now clinical depression. Sure, I tried all of the antidepressants, but they never got at the root of my sadness; they usually made things even worse, adding a layer of cognitive film to my woes. What I know now is that all energy is viral and viral energy creates. It works the same for the good, the bad, and the ugly of energetic varietals. At this point in my life, I had been resonating in dark emotion and low energy for far too long.

My energy was heavy from the inertia of disappointments and the story that I carried around about who was to blame for my miserable circumstances. No wonder I couldn't see my way clear of negativity—I was thoroughly soaked in it. It's really quite simple: *light energy creates light and heavy energy creates heavy.*

In looking back, I sought to understand why I was so lost for so long. I wanted to know what some leading doctors of psychology thought about my many experiences of viral energy and so I asked Dr. Gerald J. Haeffel, Department of Psychology, University of Notre Dame, a researcher of potential contagious properties of emotion. He told me this: "It's really interesting. We're social creatures and we do give off energy and vibes. A lot of times when you talk about something being contagious, you catch it and you know it right away—you start feeling worse, you start feeling sick. Yet with contagious energy as you say, you didn't go from being an extremely positive person and then go right to being negative or depressed, or vice versa. But an event or influence can have a small effect and start to work on you in a positive or negative way. You probably don't realize that you are starting to think differently, so it really is like you're catching a silent factor that you might not be aware of."

I would agree with that: the depression that I was experiencing was not my true nature, but rather the climacteric of years of disappointment, insecurity, and on-my-ownness. So there I was, discussing shower protocol with a nurse named Sheila. You might not have experienced a solid three-week interlude in a psychiatric hospital as I have, but I think you will appreciate this next story all the same.

We showered every other day and this, I thought, was the most humiliating and degrading part of what I affectionately called Loony Bin Life. (*I figure that I'm allowed to pick fun here, because I was there; I was a Loony.*)

The shower room was at the very end of the ward in a little-traveled cubby entombed entirely in polished stone. It was hang-proof with no shower curtain and no towel hook, however it did have a small shelf the size of an airplane seat-back tray. No shower curtain meant that the water sprayed everywhere before leaving through a drain in the middle of the sloped floor. Slippers, a threadbare hospital gown, and a towel were the only items that we were allowed to bring in the shower room. We had to change in and out of our regular clothes in our own room, then travel up and down the hallway in this open-backed number, which I promise you wasn't the sexiest thing that I had ever worn. This of course also made it known to all other prisoners—I mean patients—exactly who was on shower day. The towels were inventoried and individually doled out—a fresh one left on the stainless-steel shelf, set out by staff as needed for scheduled showers—to avoid the making of ropes, halters, or nooses.

It was the end of my first week there and time for my second shower. When I finished and turned off the tepid water, I reached for the towel and found only an empty shelf. *Uh oh.*

I stood naked for several minutes, thinking, dripping from my hair down, and shivering. *Maybe someone would realize that I'd been gone a long time and would come looking for me,* I hoped; but no such luck. *What to do?* I could have wrapped my soggy self in the hospital gown, but it was paper-thin and I envisioned wet spots circling my private parts, water trickling down my legs, and nipples poking at the fabric like antennae. (*No, thank you.*) Instead, I poked my head and shoulders out in the hallway while sheltering the rest of my body inside and looked around.

"Hello?" I waited.

"Hello? Hello?" I called again.

"HELL-LOW!" (*And it truly was a heck of a low, even for me.*)

Still, no one heard me. This end of the ward was also where linens and paper products like toilet paper were stored in locked metal cages on wheels. I could see the towels—right there, only about eight steps away. *Could I sprint to the cage and tug one through the grill? Yes, I think so.*

I vaulted the lip of the shower doorsill and darted out of the room— naked—taking flight towards my target where I started to shimmy and pinch a towel through the crossbars of the cage. Unfortunately, because the towel was folded, it didn't slip through as planned. A puddle had already formed underneath me and I was freezing cold but committed (literally), so I twisted and wiggled the towel until it was halfway through, looking like a long pour of soft-serve vanilla ice cream.

"Ah-hem." I jumped at the sound of a bogus throat clearing.

A man stood behind my left shoulder. I didn't turn around, but from a half-cocked side view I glimpsed his facial profile and saw that he was wearing a hospital gown. *Great, one of the crazies.*

The man calmly reached past me, took hold of the towel that I had been wrestling, and with a firm tug and in one smooth move he yanked the remainder of the towel free and draped it over his own shoulder. Before my jaw fell and just as expeditiously, he Houdini'ed a second towel through the bars and placed it over my shoulder, then tipped the ball cap on his head like a gentleman from the 1940s would do with a fedora, turned, and coolly walked to the shower room. Without peeping in my direction, he chucked my abandoned things outside on the hallway floor and closed the door behind him.

How to Get Their Straw Out of Your Milkshake (Calling Out Energy Suckers)

I wonder, do you know what your most basic needs are? Do you, *really*? You might have heard this one before: you can live without food for weeks, without water for days, and without oxygen for minutes, but you cannot live without energy; not even for a fraction of a second.

You operate from your personal power: your presence. And when you don't feel seen or heard—when your presence is weak—you sometimes turn to anger, frustration, jealousy and all kinds of low thoughts, emotions, and actions.

Have you ever felt drained after visiting with a negative or frantic person? Of course you have. What about being left exhausted from a phone call with someone who is down and miserable? Yep, and often. That's your light energy being drained by the denser energy around you. However, what it feels like is your energy being drained away. Your friend, co-worker, or relative might not mean to, but they're being an energy sucker.

You see, when they stick their metaphorical straw in your "energy milkshake," they unconsciously want to feed off of your light energy— they "suck" what was yours in order to fuel themselves. Sure, they feel a little bit better after unloading their low and uploading your high, but what does that leave for you? What kind of day are you now going to have when you're operating from a depleted tank, poisoned with frustration and agitation? (And yet, you *can* be there for others without allowing their energy to drain yours.)

"Watch your viral energy" has become a euphemism between my husband Burt and me when we want to remind each other to be aware of time spent with a negative friend or family member, or even when monitoring our exposure to violence on television. While writing this book, Burt periodically reminded me to censor the deluge of messages and phone calls that I received from certain friends who far too often wanted to share every detail of their precarious relationships, daily problems at work, some sad thing that happened to their neighbor's cousin, the things that angered them in the news, the thing they wanted to buy or do but can't afford, or how they have too much to get done in too short of time. I mean, I pride myself in being a listening ear, but sometimes too much is too much! Burt would say, "I can tell when you have talked to so-and-so. Now, remember what you always say—*watch your viral energy.*"

So, this happened recently: Another close friend, let's call her Britney, warned me that she had a number of issues building up—love life, decisions regarding marketing expenses for her business, the confusion of a guy friend who likes her (so, more love life), and what to wear for her upcoming birthday dinner. She had apparently been saving up a litany of topics and she needed my help to figure out everything. One of the issues involved her boyfriend whom she would be seeing again the next night, therefore putting a clock on her reception of my feedback and advice. She texted to give me the overview of what was coming and then sent nine voice memos totaling one hour and twenty-six minutes that I could listen and reply to when I had "time in the next twenty-four hours." (*Yes, this happened.*) But this next part is where the mistake was made and I did it to myself.

The following morning was Saturday and the day of Britney's scheduled date with the boyfriend that she had teetering on a fence. Burt and I had planned to decorate our Christmas tree early that day—it was Thanksgiving weekend—and while he was hauling all of the decorations in from the garage, I thought it would be a good time to get it over with and listen to all (yes, all) of Britney's voice memos of concerns, complaints, guesswork, conjecture, anger, and fears. *Um, big mistake.*

I had opened the floodgates of heavy viral energy right into my day. I couldn't shake it. I was beyond irritated by Britney's messages and what I felt was a load of narcissism, making me mad at myself for taking it all on at once, or ever. Heavy viral energy had robbed both me and Burt of the peaceful morning that we had planned and to which we had looked forward. And needless to say, the Christmas tree didn't get decorated that day. (*Poor Burt! Thankfully he understands the power and magic of viral energy.*)

I have come to know how important it is to watch and protect my viral energy. I know that the quality of my energy—that is, my *presence*— is the quality of my creation fuel for everything that I write, say, produce, and am. If my presence is polluted, so is my work, mood, happiness, physical health, and output in every way.

It took me nearly half the day to get back to a good place energetically. I did a meditation specifically to purge anger; it's all about breathing out with force and purging negativity from the heart chakra. I then actively filled our home with pleasant music and built up the atmosphere with a lovely pumpkin-coconut scented candle. Oh, and I also did some shoulder blade squeezes to release tension. Yeah, it was no joke—I had to work on turning around my energy and replacing bad vibes with good ones.

Remember, dilution is the solution to pollution. Very true. But the key to preventing this in the future is the awareness that Britney didn't do this to me; I should have limited my exposure or said: "I'm happy to help, however, no, don't send me everything that's been on your mind this week." After all, I'm her friend, not her therapist.

Just by being aware of the nature of viral energy and limiting your exposure to heavy energy, you can protect your good vibes. So, don't let others slurp and shoplift your presence. Get their straw out of your milkshake!

The Bottom Line About Humanity's Thirst for Power

Do you want to know how I ended up in the Loony Bin? It's a viral energy story if you've ever heard one. "All human beings have the capacity to experience a stressor that is so severe and so dramatic and so relevant to one's own sense of self that when experiencing that stressor, they can temporarily lose the ability to cope with it adaptively," Dr. Mitch Prinstein told me on a research call for this book. Dr. Prinstein is the Editor of the *Journal of Clinical Child and Adolescent Psychology*, and Director of Clinical Psychology at the University of North Carolina at Chapel Hill.

His words typify my own experience. My rock bottom was a negative virality collision—the perfect storm of violence meets empathy; the aligning of destiny's burnout stars. It was also the first year that I started noticing and journaling about the contagious properties of creation energy, including humanity's primal thirst for power. Most significantly, I became aware of the ways that the former impacts the latter.

I recall it was 2000 or early 2001. I was driving in my slick new silver Chevy Malibu with fancy gold detail on the tire rims. (I didn't know it then, but this leased vehicle would be repossessed in the dark of night in about two months.) A talk-radio station was on and they were running the news. "A five-month-old German Shepherd puppy was dragged behind a pickup truck on a Toronto highway yesterday. The owner, who tied the dog behind the vehicle, says that he was angry at the puppy for chewing his shoes. Other motorists saw the incident and numerous calls were placed to authorities. The puppy suffered severe injuries and the county Humane Society is considering the option for a two-leg amputation, yet sources report that, due to the extent of the wounds, euthanasia is most likely. Per Ontario law, no criminal charges have been filed against the owner, although he has been given a $500 fine," the news voice said, before moving to the next story. I pulled over to the grassy shoulder of the road, turned off my car, and cried.

Some time later, a petition was circulated by the Society for Cruelty to Animals and the laws were strengthened to provide Ontario judges with increased maximum penalties for the crime of "Cruelty to Animals" that equated to a ten-thousand dollar fine and up to ten years in prison. (Though, still today, this is just an upper limit *option* that is rarely handed down.) I participated in the petition, gathered signatures, and searched the depths of my soul to try to understand why anyone would want to hurt an innocent animal. What could be done to deter them from doing it again in the future? I knew that a stronger penalty was not the real fix and it wouldn't stop someone if they were inclined to abuse. I soon got a personal education on abuse, and I think that I got my answer in the end.

I had been dating a guy named Brad whom I loved more than he loved me. (Or more accurately, more than he was able to.) I desperately wanted him to love me back and I made excuses for much of his bad behavior. He was adopted and he feared rejection from women—a wound of which he reminded me each time I threatened to break up with him. But I didn't want to lose him; all I really wanted was to love the brokenness right out of him—that is, until I found him in bed with his nineteen-year-old neighbor. Yes, I actually walked into his house and caught them in the act. I ended it with him on the spot. This time I had no choice. I had gone to his house that night to tell him that I was pregnant. Instead, I left in a cloud of hurt and placed an ultrasound image on his kitchen table; the same table I helped him paint sky blue, just like his eyes.

Over the next two months, Brad drunkenly broke into my ground-floor apartment three times, with his violence escalating each time. It was that second time, however, that I managed to dial 911 while Brad had my phone cord wrapped around my neck, choking the breath from me. "Were you with another guy tonight? Who dropped you off? Do you think I'm stupid?" He yelled in my ear with the force of a lion. "If the police come, you'll be sorry, Penny."

The police did come, and I was sorry. The next week I had an abortion.

A few days later, Brad broke into my apartment again, this time through my bedroom window while I was sleeping. (He easily bent open the window bars that my dad had installed after the last incident.) I woke up to a real-life nightmare. In a blink I was on the hall floor and Brad had a fist full of my hair from the back of my head. He forced my left cheek against the tile and held me down with the weight of his chest on my back. I looked around for something to grab. I could feel the winter air barreling through the open bedroom window and I could see my sweet cat Sabrina watching with her frightened doe look. She's a cat that doesn't have a mean bone in her body. I had rescued her from a life on the streets and she too had been abused. I called for her to run. She did.

My next-door neighbor, Glen, called the police that night. He was my landlord; a heavyset fifty-something man who spent most of his adult life in a wheelchair because he was paralyzed from the waist down as the result of a gang fight when he was young. The day before, he told me, "If that son-of-a—" He paused and ground his teeth. "If that piece of work comes back, I'll crack him over the head myself with my baseball bat." Properly matched with his cheese-grater trucker cap, Glen carried that bat everywhere. It was always tucked into the arm of his wheelchair, with the handgrip resting across his limp right knee.

After that night, I spent the better part of a month interned in a psychiatric hospital. Yep, this is how I got *there*; it was the "depths of despair," a line that had always resonated with me from the 1987 movie *The Princess Bride*. Though hospitalization didn't cure my depression, it gave me a break from months of trauma. It was a solitary experience; patients mostly kept to themselves and blankly stared as though their spirits were traversing some other land. Maybe they were replaying their memories, or maybe they were just thoroughly dosed with Diazepam, Zoloft, and Paxil so they couldn't think at all. (After all, I guess that's the whole point.) For me, it was like a good long meditation. I wanted to know *why* some people hurt others. What kind of person would harm an animal? What benefit did Brad get from asserting his force over me? I believed with every cell of my body that there was more to it than what the psych ward doctors had explained to me. I could see it in their eyes, too; they knew that they didn't have the answers. I wrote my thoughts in my journal and I sketched out ideas where an energetically depleted person sucks energy from a less physically powerful being. A cycle was emerging and it had everything to do with viral energy.

To reference my milkshake analogy, a kink in a person's energy-straw will leave them starving to be energetically filled up. Some people are pinched off from life's magical force due to massive energy interference like their fears or a past hurt. Their unconscious self is a monster, an energy-empty monster, and it wants to survive. To do this it needs to find energy outside of itself. It becomes a predator and it finds vulnerable and easy targets. The monster is on level with the lower energies and this tends to affirm more of the same. They thirst for personal power and they want yours.

Remember, you can't live without personal power; none of us can. It's your energetic-presence. This is the vibrational level in which your being's energy resonates. It's the stratum of your personal energy and therefore the presence that you bring to your life and the life around you. It's part of the human experience to struggle for this energy source—that is, at this stage in our evolution. We are on the threshold of the era of our spiritual evolution. We are awakening to viral energy, and will ultimately be reunited with our sponsoring light energy, the mother of all light.

The pitfall for individuals like Brad and the man in Toronto with the puppy tied to the back of his pickup truck, is that the abuser has not learned a better way to gain light energy. For them, accessing low and heavy viral energy is learned and habitual. And so, for many people, a chronic depletion of power will manifest in animal abuse, then child and spousal abuse, or the abuse of power over a population. We've heard the pattern before but maybe we've never understood it from a spiritual truth. It's humanity's great thirst for power. We see it in our world leaders, religious establishments, industries, on Wall Street, in the slums, in the suburbs, and at our kitchen tables. It is the Energy-Thirsty Cycle of Abuse (ETCA). It's not to be confused with the standard cycle of abuse, which is: tensions build, incident happens, followed by reconciliation, calm, and it starts again—a cycle that moves in a circle. ETCA is different.

In the Energy-Thirsty Cycle of Abuse, individuals who are depleted of highly vibrating light energy will suck energy from targets around them by way of physical, emotional, verbal, or mental abuse. However, because this source can't and never will keep up the energy-empty's power source, they escalate their abuse over time in order to attempt bigger or lasting power rushes. Yet, no matter what they do, they cannot be satisfied or fulfilled because they are in flow with one of the lowest energy strata of "Indifference," "Ignorance," or "Hell." This cycle moves in downward devolution, inverting the transfer of power to a lower level. If caught up here, you are actually handing over power to the mother of all darkness.

Energy-empty people often abuse others not to take their power, but because they have an urge to get their frustrations out on them—they want to purge what feels so bad, essentially wanting to give it away. But this will never work. The thing is, you can't give away your energy vibration. By sharing it, you spread it virally, yet you do not "get it out." *In fact, you get more of whatever energy vibration you share.*

Be aware of the energy-empty. Through your awareness, you can break their power over you—it's both simple and magical. To put an end to abuse and negativity, we need to understand and put the phenomenon of viral energy to good use. Our Higher-Selves do not hurt each other, harm animals, cause war, or create discord with nature of any kind. It's time to find another way to get fueled. It's time to lift the curtain between wanting and awareness.

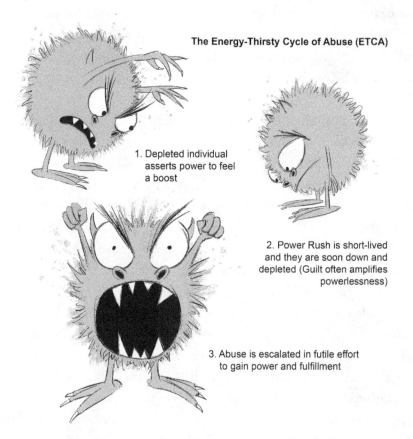

The Energy-Thirsty Cycle of Abuse (ETCA)

1. Depleted individual asserts power to feel a boost

2. Power Rush is short-lived and they are soon down and depleted (Guilt often amplifies powerlessness)

3. Abuse is escalated in futile effort to gain power and fulfillment

CHAPTER FOUR:

SEPTIC ENERGY

Stuck in Rage, Blame, and Envy?
Diminishing Them Minimizes You

I blame them. I do. I blame them for not supporting me. I am enraged that they chose their own interests rather than to be there for me, be a mentor to me, guide me, or present the options available to me to make myself a sustainable future. I envy what comforts and security they have while I struggle. I am enraged that they choose to tend to their own needs with little care for how lonely and alone I have been and still am. I am livid at their lame effort at love. I am livid that they just go on with their lives after they have defamed me to everyone I know, making me an outcast among relatives, neighbors, and family friends—deliberate sabotage to defer any guilt from *being cast their way. I deeply resent them for using me as a common adversary and fodder for gossip, bonding themselves closer together over the talk of my failures.*

I thought these things about the people whom I had blamed. You've thought some of them, too. They're more than feelings—these are our beliefs and the stories we tell ourselves: the stories that we are stuck being. But think of this: What about the good things that happened in your life? Who is responsible for the challenges that you faced and overcame despite the support that you didn't get from others (or perhaps motivated precisely because of it)? Somewhere along my journey, I realized that if I blamed others for my failures, then it was possible that I'd have to give them credit for my successes, and that just didn't seem fair. So, I decided that I would claim responsibility for both my failures and successes. Rage, blame, and envy had been draining my light energy. When I finally made the decision to let it all go, this empowered and enlightened me in a way that I never "got" before.

Catching heavy viral energy is not something that just happened to me, and it doesn't just happen to you. Watching your viral energy is about more than minding what you're marinating in—don't forget about that sauce of viral energy out there in the world, in your environment, and from the people with whom you spend time and share space. You are also a viral energy factory within yourself and you are always being the creator. All of your low emotions, energies, and actions work to minimize you—the person generating them.

Here's another low energy—jealousy. I once had a female mentor who ran an empowerment group for women entrepreneurs. She was very beautiful, smart, independent, and a role model champion for ladies in business; oh, how I had admired her. That is, until one day when I received a lengthy email from her, confessing that she had slept with my boyfriend. By that time, I had long been broken up with that boyfriend, yet she went out of her way to underscore that she had had sex with him while we were still together. She was writing to confess that she had been jealous of me.

(*What a mentor she turned out to be.*) I never wrote her back—I laughed one big HA! And deleted the message.

Jealousy between women is the Achilles Heel of the female species. Just think what women will create when we rise above jealousy.

And then there's reverse-jealousy, too. This is when we women don't respect the actions of another woman, would genuinely not want to be like her, and truly don't envy or approve of her…and yet we are fixated and overwhelmed with our distain and frustration towards her. (It's kind of like judgment, but with a twist; we have a vested interest or personal involvement.) It sounds like this: "I am fed up with her insecurities, vanity, and bad decisions. Doesn't she see how ridiculous, self-centered, and immature she is being? Are people really fooled by her nonsense and drama? She endlessly takes up other people's time for advice and yet she keeps repeating the same patterns and choices. I wish she would grow up, focus on something other than herself, and take responsibility for her life!"

It's sad but true: there are women for whom we have no mercy. Often times they are our best friend, a sibling, or even a daughter. We just can't tolerate weakness in another woman, especially if we're closely connected to her. Women have been acculturated to compete with each other, not because we're all biatches, but because of simple mathematics; there are more women than there are men. This means that there are more single women than there are single men. All over the world, more women are competing for fewer men, jobs, attention, and recognition.

But, please. Men are not jealousy-free; they're right in there, too. However, their jealousy is often called resentment. I had a client of my publicity business who was an actor and author; let's call him "George." He was soaked in talent, wisdom, and good looks, and his career was hot.

He wanted to get booked on OWN network's *SuperSoul Sunday*. I tried to make it happen, but I just wasn't getting any response from producers. It was as if there was some invisible block in the way, and it really didn't make sense because this guy indeed could have been booked on the show. A few months later, I got a call from George explaining that he resented Oprah for her fame and success. George felt that he was just as worthy of Oprah-level accolades and should be enjoying the same success. While he admired and adored her, he was also jealous of her. I immediately knew why we couldn't get him booked on the show. *Um, you're never going to have anything of which you're resentful—that's energetic rejection on steroids!*

If you're suffering from jealousy and envy, stop doing that. Yes, just stop, because it's your free-will choice to be jealous or resentful. Skip above doubt and don't seek to compete with others. If you're enraged with someone, step out of the hot energy until you can calm down. You don't have to engage anyone. You don't have to take the call. You don't have to stay for the fight. You don't have to multiply the hurtful words and actions. When outwardly projected, heavy viral energy minimizes *you*, not the other person. If you hear of the fortune of your friend, it should not take away from your joy. If someone else is smart or talented, it doesn't make you any less smart or talented. If you recognize that another is very beautiful, it doesn't mean that your beauty has dimmed. It's time to relieve your anger and jealousy. Keep close to you these words by Buddhist monk, Zen Shin, who said, "A flower does not think of competing with the flower next to it. It just blooms."

High Value Event Energy (HVEE)

Christmas. It's the most wonderful time of the year. So says the song, anyway. And it truly is. Thee. Most. Wonderful. Time. Well, that is, if you have nothing but love and peace in your life, family and friends with whom to be merry, nicely wrapped presents, and of course, a tree—especially if it's a big fat Griswold tree, complete with hand-strung popcorn and cranberry garland. Oh, and don't forget a warm and cozy Connecticut home, decorated and illuminated with all of the (pricey) cheer of the holy season. Also, you can't possibly have any financial stress or debt. And you definitely need plenty of holiday food and beverage spread out on long, elegant, candlelit dining tables.

But what if, God forbid, you are familyless, financeless, and festiveless at Christmastime? Maybe it's not so wonderful.

Special dates and holidays can trigger painful memories. Maybe for you, these dates have powerful energy associations that come far in advance and come with negativity. They hold tremendous viral energy called High Value Event Energy (HVEE). This energy has the power to create, and it does.

I have deeply rooted HVEE connected with Christmas Day. It was implanted from my first Christmas away from home as a stray teenager. These were the early days of leaving home and/or getting kicked out; it was a brief interlude when I stayed with old friends of my family, just before I became lost in the dark corners of strange buildings with stranger people.

That Christmas—I guess it was 1988—I stayed for a few days over the holidays with the family of my childhood best friend, Nicole Martin. I hadn't really seen Nicole since I was ten, because we had moved out of town. We moved back to town earlier in the year, smack in the middle of the ninth grade and I had very few friends. Nicole's family still lived in our former neighborhood, but our new house was now clear on the other side of town. Besides the distance, Nicole went to a public school and I went to a private school. We had all but lost touch, yet when I moved back to town, she invited me to the occasional house party with her group of friends—a rough pack of girls who smoked pot and were no strangers to trouble. Nicole had changed so much; no longer the nine-year-old bestie I had left behind.

The Martins celebrated the holiday (sort of), yet they didn't have any religious affiliation or set traditions. It was very different from what I knew of Christmas, having been raised Catholic. Heck, I would have welcomed a good Hanukkah, or an entirely non-religious family tradition in the spirit of *Christmas Vacation*—or even a happy Whoville Christmas. But the

Martins' Christmas Day didn't abide by any special rhythm and it had no defining purpose—it was short on symbolic moments that demonstrated a special occasion was even happening. On Christmas morning, the Martins had French toast for breakfast and then they opened their gifts—I awkwardly watched. After that, the family went about their business of things to do on a day off: Mrs. Martin did a bit of house cleaning, Mr. Martin shoveled snow from the driveway and tinkered in his garage, and Nicole and her younger sister tested out new clothes, books, games, and candy. I milled about like a stepchild, feeling out of place. I was sorely missing the Christmas that I knew. I was missing my family; the people to whom I was a child, and not a step.

Then, there was a knock at the door. It was my dad! Though I wanted to, I wouldn't telephone my family; I was way too proud. But like an answered wish, there was my dad. I was so happy to see him but I feared an unequal reciprocation and so I kept my elation under control. I was aloof; so was Dad, both of us standoffish. Or was it a standoff?

Mr. Martin, Simon, shook my dad's hand and they wished each other a Merry Christmas. When invited in for a drink, my dad refused, "No. I'm only dropping off these gifts for Penny because Joan asked me to. I've got to get back. Thanks anyway." Dad nodded at me where I stood behind Mr. Martin, handed me three packages and said, "Okay, well, take care then," and he left.

My heart sank, but I was still glad to see him and happy to get a few Christmas presents. It was a sign that they cared.

I tucked myself away in Nicole's room so I could open my gifts in private. What do you get your runaway child at Christmas? Was it going to be a token, or an offering with profound meaning?

The first was a soft package with twisted ends like a candy. I excitedly ripped it open. Socks and underwear. *Go figure.* Next was another soft package, folded and taped in my mum's trademark haphazard way. I had always preferred things in boxes with crisp wrappings and taut edges. This gift contained a scarf—one made for function, not style.

The last was a box wrapped in gold metallic paper with crisp lines like a professionally wrapped department store gift. It was even embellished with a red ribbon crisscrossed and tied in a bow. Of course, I saved it for last. This was the one that would say something. The grand finale of presents! I gently slipped off the ribbon, undressing it like satin from smooth shoulders, one corner at a time. Then, carefully, I plucked at the tape, trying not to lift the color from the foil paper. I slowly pulled up on the lid of the fine box.

It was a gorgeous clutch purse: the kind for use in the evening when you're going somewhere special. It was small and elegant. A jet black, beaded, twinkling, evening handbag! I rapidly drew it to my chest, closed my eyes, and hugged it close. I treasured it not because of its beauty, expense, or label, but because of what I thought it said about how I was valued. It was a woman's purse. It had the scent of home; the place I once dwelled that cradled the carefree days of childhood. My eyes welled with joy. My parents finally got me! (*They must have really put some thought into this gift.*) I was overjoyed, euphoric. (*Maybe this wasn't such a bad Christmas after all?*)

The next day—Boxing Day, as we call it in Canada—my dad telephoned over to the Martins. Mrs. Martin hollered out to me and announced that my dad was on the phone. I was happy to take the call. *What could develop today*, I thought? Frank Sinatra's "I'll Be Home for Christmas" was softly playing on the radio at the Martins' house. Perhaps, Dad was calling to ask me to come home. It might take some convincing, but I was open to it. I wanted to be asked.

"Hi, Dad," I said brightly.

He sounded a bit apprehensive, "Hi, Penny. Um. Yeah, I dropped off the wrong gift yesterday. I accidentally gave you a purse that I bought for Mum. I'm going to swing over and pick up the box."

(*It really was Boxing Day.*)

Dad never did come back. I suppose my parents decided the bag wasn't worth taking away, yet it was ruined for me just the same. I'm not sure what hurt more: my dad telling me that he was coming to take the gift back, or just not coming at all.

In retrospect, Christmas of 1988 was not even among my most painful and offensive holidays, yet it did—without question—set a trigger on Christmas. The holiday became my highest value event, preemptively loaded with heavy viral energy. Yet thankfully, since 1988, I have also experienced the best, most magical, romantic, and sacred Christmases of my life—by far.

To this day, Christmas and I have a love-fear relationship. Dates hold energy and I'm aware that December twenty-fifth is embedded with high value event energy. In fact, for me, it's a date that is supercharged with dangerously high voltage and comes with a warning label! I would love to tell you that I have reached a state of enlightenment and am not affected by such HVEEs, but that wouldn't be true.

As fate would have it, December twenty-fifth is my husband's birthday, so he has the polar opposite association with Christmas. For him, not only is Christmas *Christmas*, it is the most wonderful day of the year! It is the fusion of the two very best events for him and he has a lifetime of happy memories associated with this day. For Burt, it is easily, without question and without any hesitation whatsoever, an extra-special and wonderful day. Though he tries, this of course makes it hard, if not impossible, for him to understand my anxiety and doom over the date.

Maybe your HVEE is Valentine's Day, New Year's Eve, your birthday, or a death anniversary of a loved one. You can plan ahead of its impact and find what works for you to mitigate high value event energy. Don't wait for the day to come and have it be as terrible as you had predetermined it would. Defuse the power of high value events through your awareness. Know that it's not about the date, what you don't have, lost or found traditions, or lost or found love—it's about what it means to you.

I have found that resisting what is coming and is happening just plain doesn't work. HVEE is energy that comes around in a cycle: a repeating energetic block. Let it wash over you, feel it for all of its force and sting, stand in it, keep moving through it, and stretch your energetic-presence. Even. If. It's. Hard.

The Ties That Bind: Double Negative Relationships

Double negative relationships are when both sides are attempting to suck energy from each other, or when one side temporarily and willingly gives away their energy in an attempt to manipulate or curry favor with the other (and the other gladly takes it). These can be parent-child relationships, friends, romantic partnerships, or work colleagues.

With the double negative parent-child relationship, the trigger issue is often an identity crisis—both suffer from and act on a loss of power. They are starved for energy and power because their identity is in question. *Am I still a mother if my child doesn't need me anymore? How can I uniquely be me if my parents won't give me space?* But, these pairs can't entirely part ways; they have ties that bind, and they have to deal with each other. Are you in this struggle? Well, take a breath and give it time. Even if it feels like it will last forever, the parent-child identity struggle probably won't. Children and teenagers aren't often in a future or past mindset; they tend to think and act in the present. *I'm hungry. I want to go out with my friends. I want the car. I'm in love with so-and-so at school.* In particular, the future is not a focus or reality for most kids and teens. In fact, they will go out of their way to skirt the future by avoiding responsibility, even taking drugs to keep their mind on just one singular careless moment. On the other end of the scale, adults/parents remember the mistakes of the past and worry about the future. The parent-child relationship is a relationship playing out from very different perspectives and even in different times, yet thankfully, that gap will close.

Of course, it's not just young people who struggle with avoidance or identity crises. Many grown adults are confused beyond reasonable logic about their own identity. This confusion is a product of their doubts and insecurities. They have been unwilling to look inward to decide who they really are, and so they instead latch onto fragments and concepts of other people, claiming those identities as their own. While every single human being has a unique contribution to life, those who suffer from deep identity confusion have an overwhelming need to not only be unique, but to be better than and superior to others. Yet, they are so afraid that if they look inside themselves, they will (mistakenly) find that they are not talented, unique, or particularly exceptional, and so they instead set out, rather deliberately, to borrow identify from others. Those lacking a sense of self-esteem and identity are some of the most dangerous people around. They are passive-aggressive energy suckers.

Then there are romantic energy dynamics. In romantic relationships where *both* individuals are abusive to each other, both individuals are fighting for dominance and looking to the other as an easy and accessible source to gain personal power. These can be inherited dynamics that have carried over from other relationships in their pasts and are also frequently carried over from an abusive childhood. If you could see this couple's creation energy—*their presence*—with your eyes, it would look a lot like two straws forcing their way into a glass. Before long, much of that drink is wasted on the floor and both people are left thirsty. A depleted and unsatisfied person is the most volatile kind—this is the precise set-up for domestic abuse. Unsatisfied people need to regain and retain power and they'll find a way to get it, whether through physical force or enforcing guilt. These relationships are steeped in toxic energy. But all of the wishing in the world for a healthier balance will not overcome the root issue, which is mismanagement of contagious energy. Have you ever been a party in a double negative relationship? Sometimes you just have to go your separate ways. The match is not healthy and it's best to be apart, however, because you're likely an equal part of the problem, your energy-sucking ways will creep up again down the road. Before long, you'll be looking to stick your straw in the next unguarded milkshake.

Don't you really want to be happy? Don't you really want to find a companion with whom to journey through life? Wouldn't it be nice to have relationships that last? The good news is you can end the cycle of abuse through your awareness of the energy dynamic at play.

The truth is, with few exceptions, we're all energy suckers. We're all trying to steal energy from one another. In every interaction we have, we jockey for the most advantageous energetic position above one other. This is true from the most intimate personal interactions right through to larger and more complex relationships between nations. We also seek to steal energy by exploiting our environment when we use and abuse the natural world.

Not only do we continuously trade, negotiate, and steal energy from each other, we also steal beauty. And why is beauty such a commodity for us? Why are we so fixated on beauty? Because our inner selves know that to admire beauty—and ultimately *become* beauty—is the path to Heaven on Earth. Yet, in our constant state of searching to know what beauty is (or how to appreciate it with true love and sincerity), we instead take beauty from others. We steal beauty through judging and impugning the qualities in other people with whom we compete. As false evidence of our beauty, we do it by inexcusably and selfishly tearing fur from the flesh of animals for the sake of our own body adornment. We do it by copying the paths of others and parroting their beautiful contributions instead of digging deep to discover the unique beauty in ourselves.

These are examples of the ways we often misinterpret the beauty of the energetic ties that bind us to one another. In a way, we are all involved in double negative and codependent relationships. The trick is to drop the false face of power-jockeying and find the true source of energy, beauty, and Heaven.

The source of the empowerment that you seek is not hidden, it's not a secret, and it's not buried in ancient text. It's so accessible and so intrinsic to you that perhaps you just can't believe how easy the answer is. Maybe you don't trust yourself and so you'd rather ignore the obvious solution to your turmoil. The source of the energetic fuel that you need and desire is in the one place that we have been acculturated for hundreds of generations to never ever dare look, and certainly not speak of out loud. The source is not the sun. The source is not assessed by membership to a club or religion. It's not exclusive to the words of a wise someone from a foreign and distant land.

It's time that you start thinking differently. You will never ever be satisfied by seesawing power within a relationship. You will never really see, experience, or become beauty by ripping it from the dreams and backs of others.

You, my dear, are your source and savior.

The power that you want and need is in you. The great beauty of which to be in awe is in you. But don't hold it with a clenched fist because you're afraid to lose it. Share it. Circulate it. Through participating in this natural flow, you become part of Life's energy generator and you will always have enough. The more you share your presence and share light energy with others, the more you will generate. You are the creator of what you need and want.

You can fuel yourself from within rather than without. All you really want is to be seen and heard; you want a solid presence of your own—an internal vibe that is healing and self-renewing. Stop sucking from others; start building your own energy reservoir through sharing your light presence in sincerity, not in manipulation. Utilize the magic of viral energy for better relationships and a happier life.

Never Hide Cash Under Your Mattress: Circulate or Stagnate

So, how's your relationship with money?

Maybe you don't need to be wealthy at the moment (or ever), but it is perfectly reasonable to want to be financially safe, to not live in fear that you won't be able to get by, and to wish that debt wasn't a chronic issue and obstacle.

So, here's how you get financially secure. You enter into an agreement about how money will come to you and how you will honor it and utilize it. Yes, money is your friend, not your enemy. You don't have to cringe when money-talk or financial needs come up. Communicate with money like the resource that it is meant to be for you.

You must admit that you waste money because on some level you have learned to hate it. Look at how you've seen others go without. Look at how you have struggled with money. Money has never been your friend, has it? Well, I guess I will be the one to break it to you, because this was me too—money is a good friend to you, but *you* on the other hand have been a very bad friend to money. First of all, you spend money on things that you don't really need, and it's not always even *your* money—sometimes it's the credit card company's money, or some family member's money. So, if you don't like being in debt, stop creating it!

Okay, we've said that money (as with all resources) is available to you to the degree that you require it to live out your purpose and your spiritual evolution. Now, make a contract with Life regarding the resource of money. Write this down: "Dear Life, thank you for the money that flows into my life, my hands, and my bank account. I love the resource of money for all that I will create with it. Invest in me the financial resources to consistently match what I am and will become. I will do my part by always meeting my obligations and loving and respecting the resource of money."

Read this to yourself every day for at least three months. Your words and intention are energy units that will go viral and will begin to set your point of creation. Watch the magic start working for your financial freedom.

Once you've settled debt, you'll want to know how to prosper, right?

Do you imagine that the universe evolved from gas explosions to planets, from single cell organisms to modern man, all to just stagnate right here and forever freeze in development and no longer evolve? Scientifically, mathematically, logically, and spiritually, that would be an impossibility. Nope, the universe doesn't revolve around us. We are in a space somewhere inside it, not even in the center, and evolution is still happening and will continue to happen for millions of years to come. But if we want to be in play with those beings that evolve—and not be a species that becomes extinct—then we need to stay in circulation!

Perhaps you haven't given it much thought before, but in fact, all life must contribute a value or purpose, or it will become extinct. Everyone and everything must be utilized to stay in play, develop, and advance. More than just functionality, talent, and readiness, these must be put to good use to be supported by Life. *All* resources must circulate or they will stagnate.

If you stash money under your mattress for twenty years, the very same amount will be worth less over time in relation to the cost of living and the inflation of goods. On the other hand, money moved into real estate or other investments will grow or fluctuate at market value (whatever that might be); it's in motion inside the flow and the action of the marketplace. (Ironically, a synonym for "circulation" is "currency.") This is why the religious practice of tithing works for prosperity: it's a system of circulation. God is the architect of circulation and of all things under perfect order, including the magic of viral energy.

Yep, circulate or stagnate; it works the same way for all resources. In the body, blood must circulate, or it will stagnate. Without new atmosphere, even our breathing space will become unusable. During daylight hours, plants take in carbon dioxide and release oxygen through photosynthesis— nature's perfect lungs; moving and refreshing the planet's breathing air. What else, you ask? Think of static water in a pond. Stagnant water will grow algae and bacteria, making it unsuitable to drink. Sure, life is still present, however stagnant water is indeed landlocked, passive, and motionless.

This is also how it works for energy, your personal power, how you contribute to life, and the fuel for all that you create. When you sit on your talents and don't use them, as the saying goes, you lose them. If you allow your body and health to stagnate from lack of good use, Life says, "Well, he's not using it, let Us shift wellbeing to a form who will utilize it." Many people who have retired without redirecting their time and energy will tell you that they very quickly started to stagnate; their health diminished, and their joy dried up. But letting go of one thing doesn't have to be like that. You can choose to circulate your resources and energy elsewhere. When you share your light presence with others, your beautiful presence will grow, and your influence will expand. When you create with your resources rather than focus on what you don't have or have lost, you will be endowed with more resources, opportunities, energy, and creativity with which to create more. It works because of the magic of viral energy. Energy is contagious and it builds upon itself. It's sticky to itself that way!

Sometimes, we don't want to let go of our resources because we fear that we won't get any more. Are you a cheapskate who often lets your friends pick up the tab because you're stuck being broke? While they might be okay with this, it's holding you in a mindset that's preventing your abundance. Are you in a constant state of lack? Are you a packrat with boxes of stuff that you haven't needed in more than a year? If you haven't used it in a twelve-month cycle, chances are you don't need it. Chances are whatever it is that you're storing is getting more useless as time goes on. Saving or hoarding your resources shrinks and minimizes them; they further dry up because they're not being used. Life says, "Hey, if you're not going to use that, I am just going to redistribute its worth to a place where it can be used." You cannot just take without investing, or hoard and expect growth—or for that matter, expect that the standard will be sustained.

This is a good time to ask yourself, "What can I do to open the flow, mix it up, and bring in new resources and new creation energy?"

And it's not just your stuff, your money, your health, or your social life. Ask yourself, "Am I landlocked, passive, or stagnant? Do I need to take action to bring fresh water in my pond?" Maybe you itch for more out of your job. Maybe you've outgrown your town or some of your old friends who are keeping you frozen in bad habits. Do you feel stuck, bored, unsuccessful, or unfulfilled? If you're not growing over a significant period of time, and you feel like you're running on a wheel and getting nowhere, then you're stagnating. Perhaps it's time for you to bring in some new energy. "*How*," you ask? Take action and use the resources of your skills, talents, your ability to love and be loved, and your very presence. Imagine what you could become if you lived by the principle: *resources that do not circulate will stagnate, and resources utilized in motion will grow*! This shift could be a miracle in your life.

Look, you are designed to expand, to reinvent yourself, and to create numerous upgrades to your being. The cure for stagnation is circulation. Keep your resources in motion. This is what it means to spiritually evolve—circulate or stagnate; use it or lose it; be in play or be outplayed; evolve or become extinct. I think it's becoming clear now. Be more than useful, deploy your Selfness into action and you will grow, expand, and be an integral part of the human spiritual evolution.

PART TWO:

HAPPINESS IS SUPER, NATURAL

CHAPTER FIVE:

ENERGY OVER MATTER

The Cosmic Mind: Many Members, One Body

With the magic of viral energy, nothing is absolute and nothing is impossible.

Nature always has a way of revealing truth and magic. Observe birds as they fly together in formation—they turn, dip, and rise as one body. As though they are one organism, the entire flock moves at the very same instant with identical and instantaneous changes in their collective direction. Let's call this performance the experiential dance of viral energy. It's a magical dance, but the question is, how do they move together? What kind of communication makes that possible?

Birds of a feather fly in synchronized motion because they are tuned in to each other's frequency. Get this: it works the same for ten radio receivers as it does for ten birds.

Let's say you are having a big party and want to stream music throughout your house. If you don't have a multi-room sound system, you could accomplish this the old-school way and place a radio in the kitchen, another in the living room, and one on your patio, tuning them all in to your favorite dance music station. When the DJ at the broadcasting radio station changes the song, you can be guaranteed that all of your radio receivers will switch songs at the same time. The radio receivers throughout your house do not need to do anything fancy to synchronize their output because they're already effortlessly picking up on the frequency to which they are tuned.

Now, back to our birds of a feather. The exact same energy frequency phenomenon that makes radio broadcasting work also allows animals to sense the frequency of energy vibration. Animals see, hear, smell, touch, and taste, but they also have a sixth faculty or sense that perceives *energetic* stimuli from outside or inside the body. Their energy is in alignment—in pulse—with one another. What's more, animals of the same species share a "spirit body"—an energy body. The energy bond between them is an information transmission system that operates and responds as effortlessly as we breathe or blink. It's an unseen and unheard network of communication. Their bodies are in formation (order); their energy is information (communication). But it's not just animals; trees, forests, and all of nature communicate this way. And, you can too; you're just out of practice.

You are connected to and move with a great network of energy—the correspondence network binding all of Life. It is entirely possible that one day we will bypass talking and typing altogether and advance to energy communication. Mmhmm, and it's not that far off.

Have you ever heard of "thought communication," also called direct brain-to-brain communication or mind messaging? Some people are said to have developed this ability, and a number of scientific studies have demonstrated it. In 2014, an international team of researchers—some from the Harvard Medical School Teaching Hospital—successfully achieved brain-to-brain transmission of information between two people. But, get this: one person was in India and the other was in France.

Using a combination of an Internet-connected electroencephalogram with robot-assisted and image-guided transcranial magnetic stimulation—which, as the name suggests, uses electromagnetic induction to stimulate the brain from the outside—the team was able to communicate words from one human to another. (*This is big!*) Basically, they simulated innate functions that are hardwired in our brains, but are not usually activated.

It is rumored in folklore that some ancient civilizations were advanced in the use of telepathic communication between people and across distances, such as the legendary Lemurians of the Pacific coast of North America who communicated through their oneness with the Cosmic Mind. I don't mean "mind reading," as that suggests a sort of uninvited thought-theft. I'm referring to two-way communication achieved entirely through energy vibration, when two people are tuned to the same vibration and agree to transmit and receive information between one another.

In the book, *Lemuria—The Lost Continent of the Pacific*, published in 1931, author Wishar S. Cervé wrote: "To the Lemurians this sixth sense was not an extraordinary thing but quite commonplace, though they were conscious of the fact that its usefulness had been developed by their ancestors through practice and concentration and that it was a faculty more susceptible to development and growth than any of the other facilities which are common to the human race. We, today, are conscious of the fact that our eyes can be trained in seeing, as witness to the training given to an artist; or that our ears can be trained to hear, as is necessary with a musician; or our taste may be developed, as is true with those who are experts in the tasting of wine, for instance. We are likewise conscious of the fact that our muscles in any part of the body may be developed, or that certain features or functions of the body may be strengthened through definite effort and practice. With the Lemurians, the knowledge was handed down from generation to generation that the salvation of their race and the hope for mastership in the highest attainments of civilization depended upon the individual and personal development of this sixth sense."

Can we just pause here for a moment? Perhaps read that again before we continue.

It might be a stretch for you to believe in the supernatural abilities of highly-evolved ancient people from thousands and thousands of years before our time. (*Or maybe it's not a stretch at all.*) However, when we know that birds, dolphins, and lions can communicate through energy impulses, why is it hard to believe that you can, too?

While the animal kingdom and the plant kingdom continue to evolve the Cosmic Mind, humans continue to lose this unique communication ability as we move through generations. This is especially noticeable in the last two thousand years or so since we pulled away from communion with nature. Even so, we do still have it and we can cultivate it again.

Just think of all of the energy tuners that mankind has erected, including towering obelisks and temple spires, functionally designed for little else than to serve as antennae. Do you wonder why when meditating, some people posture their hands up to the sky with their thumb and index finger touching? Well, they are tuning energy by way of creating their own antenna. There is something in us as humans; this innate drive that just knows we need that energy. There is something so magnetic, magical, and useful to us about it. We want to draw it in. Somehow, we just know that we are part of it and it is one with us.

Have you ever called or emailed someone and the very first thing they say is, "I was *just* thinking about you"? You see, you're already using energy communication; you just don't believe what it is.

Let me further explain with this story from my own family history: My mum is known to have had a few significant premonitions over the years. Before he retired, her father was a farmer and had a small hobby fruit orchard. When my mum was young, her parents sold off a chunk of land to an elderly couple who built a cute two-bedroom home there. It was a white-sided ranch-style house with light blue shutters and awning that made it look nearly gingerbread-trimmed. As a young girl, my mum had always visualized that when she grew up, she would buy that house and raise her own family there. Sure enough, years later, she and my dad did buy it. So, when I was a little girl, we lived next door to my maternal grandparents.

One night well after midnight—I was about four years old at the time—my mum had a dream that her father was in trouble; she "saw" him having a heart attack. She woke up my dad and asked him to go next door right away and check on her father. He did, and my grandfather *was* having a heart attack. My grandparents slept in separate bedrooms, which was common for their "Cunningham generation" (a time of domestic-correctness exemplified by many TV families like the Cunninghams of *Happy Days*, when networks didn't show "suggestive" marital dynamics), and so, even though she was just down the hall, my grandmother had no idea what was happening with my grandfather. Yet my mother, who was hundreds of feet away, next-door in a separate house, knew that he was in trouble and knew what kind of trouble.

Because of my mum's real-time dream, my grandfather speedily got to a hospital and my parents had time to call together the entire family of seven children, some from a few hours' drive away. My grandfather died in the early hours of that morning, surrounded by his wife and grown kids.

My mum calls it a premonition, yet from where does the information contained within the premonition come? Was my grandfather sending my mum a message, calling out to her in the night, knowing that she was an open receiver? After all, it wasn't the first time that she had demonstrated this ability. While subtle and not discussed, my mum—*Joanie*—the youngest of the family, was known to be somewhat intuitive in her childhood.

Communication through energy vibration is the magnificent, ordinary, invisible, and automatic magic of viral energy. When solutions to problems pop into your head out of nowhere, this is an indication that you're a good receiver. When you're thinking about how beautiful garden tulips are, and then someone brings you fresh flowers, this is an indication that you are a good sender of information—a transmitter, if you will.

It's fun to practice developing this ability. When you discover how to work with it for the highest good of all, you will become the power to fulfill your dreams.

Crowd Energy

"The energy of the crowd is insane. Twenty-thousand people. It's the biggest jolt of adrenaline. It's very hard to explain. You know the old story about the woman lifting the car off her kid? It's in that realm. You can actually hurt yourself and not know it," said the late great Tom Petty in a 2006 interview with Esquire magazine on the feelings associated with performing on stage.

The power of just one person's energetic-presence affects others. Indeed, each of us has an energy field and vibration, and when you put energies together, you get a very large energy field. At a concert, political rally, mega church, or dance club, a powerful concentration of energy from the collective presence of a great number of people—especially when the majority are vibing at a similar frequency—can actually turn events, moods, and outcomes.

The home-team advantage in sports is a well-known phenomenon, and you've very likely felt it for yourself. When the majority of people in the stands of a sporting event are passionately supporting one team, projecting all of their energy and attention toward their team's hopeful victory, you could say that the population is energy-homogeneous (of the same kind or nature; congruent). That's pretty powerful stuff. If you were feeling down, sluggish, tired, and blah, and then you were suddenly dropped in the middle of the home-team crowd of a professional league football game, even if it was not your team, your sport, or your town, your mood funk would very likely dissolve and be replaced by the powerful energy of excitement in the air all around you. It might take a few minutes to feel the effects, but it won't be long before the change begins. That's the power of the home-team advantage and for the players, it's a magical viral energy high. And it's a high that's not reserved for players or fans; anyone can significantly benefit from more frequently opening up and letting in these environments rich in light energy.

On the other hand, there are times when, rather than being energy-homogeneous with the energy around you, you should practice being energy-homeostatic (maintaining a condition of balance or equilibrium within your being's own energy, even when faced with external heavy energy). In terms of the latter, think of the energy of a crowd like the temperature that is outside of your own selfness. The human body has a marvelous ability to remain temperature-homeostatic for a duration of time, no matter the outside temperature. When you go outside in the winter and it's below zero degrees, your internal core temperature (which is about 98.6 degrees Fahrenheit) might drop a few degrees—even several degrees—but because of your body's ability to keep homeostasis, your internal temperature (for the most part) is maintained. Rather than equilibrate (become a state in which opposing forces or influences are balanced) with the frigid outdoors, your body temperature will guard you, for a time, from freezing. Again, this is the body's ability to remain temperature-homeostatic for a period until you change environments, like re-entering the warm house.

Comparing this now to your being's energy-engine—you can train your energy field (a.k.a. your "spirit body"—your energy body) to be energy-homeostatic with light energy, if you choose.

Sometimes there's no way to escape an environment of heavy viral energy—you're soaking in it and that's just life, so you'd better have an understanding about how to remain energy-homeostatic. If you work at a large debt collection agency, in a factory farm or exposed to the wholesale slaughter of animals, in a combative political environment, or within the bowels of certain government agencies or corporations, you may be marinating in the heavy crowd energy of stress, fear, and tension on a daily basis. Maintaining your light energy can be challenging to say the least, but just as your incredible physical body has the ability to remain temperature-homeostatic, your incredible energy-body has the ability to remain energy-homeostatic, and you can achieve this by being selective of what you choose to be in energy flow with (what you are being). For many people, it's easier to let heavy energy in than it is to block it out. For other people, it's the exact opposite; they more easily stay in a light energy vibration no matter what is happening around them. It all depends on your thought habits and how you tend to see the world. You could say it is an attitude, a perspective, or an intention. This is key, so I repeat it for special emphasis: *it all depends on your thought habits and how you tend to see the world.*

Anne was forty-three years old and single, though she didn't want to be. She had difficulty being around couples because it reminded her of what she didn't have. Weddings were particularly challenging, and she avoided them if she could. When one of her best friends was getting married, she had no choice but to attend the wedding. But she *did* have a choice about whether or not to let in the light energy—the joy of the wedding experience. She could barely stand to look around the ballroom of couples embracing in the glow of romance, so she sat at her table most of the night and made a point of not dancing or mingling. *I'm not going to let this insufferable wedding get to me*, she thought. And she didn't. As expected, she had a terrible night and suffered through it with a wall clenched around her heart. Despite (and in spite of) the light energy of the crowd, the uplifting beat of the music, and the love filling the room, Anne's internal energy was not affected. She didn't want to let it in, and so she didn't. Another friend of the bride named Sue, also a single woman of the same age, had a very different experience at the wedding. Sue was a little melancholy to find herself still single and wished that she had a significant other, or even a date for the wedding. Since she attended alone, Sue decided to have a good time with some old friends and hoped to meet a few new people throughout the day. She did both—she let it all in and had a wonderful night.

Ask yourself, do you want to be an "Anne" or a "Sue"? I suspect that if given the choice, you'd rather be happy than miserable. And so, as far as viral energy is at play all around and inside you, the goal is to be unchanged in the presence of heavy crowd energy, and to be enlightened and equilibrate in the presence of light crowd energy.

The energy field of a crowd in synergy can change your mind, change your energy-body, and even change your history. Start deliberately creating.

Nothing is Absolute: The Incredible Breakthrough to Possibilities

A relative of mine who is in the medical field recently said to me, "I think in absolutes. I can't operate in abstracts." While I can appreciate their belief system, the only absolute in life is that there are no absolutes. And by the way, the opposite of "absolute" is not "abstract," it is "possibility."

Dr. Beau Lotto, a globally renowned neuroscientist at the University of London, also a Visiting Scholar at New York University and head of the Lab of Misfits in London (an experiential research lab comprised of leading neuroscientists, artists, and technologists, whose mission is to understand why we perceive the world the way we do, and apply that understanding to helping others to see differently)—studies psychological mechanisms of perception and says, "Only through uncertainty is there potential for understanding."

Bestselling spiritual author, Marianne Williamson, said, "Old Newtonian physics claimed that things have an objective reality separate from our perception of them. Quantum physics, and particularly Heisenberg's Uncertainty Principle, reveal that as our perception of an object changes, the object itself literally changes."

No matter who you are or what you believe to be true based on your current knowledge, you live in a universe not of absolutes and certainties, but of possibilities. Even mathematics and geometry are not absolute; in fact, they are far from it. But this idea isn't mine and it's not even a new notion.

To help dispel the misnomer "absolute," here's an example that can be easily understood once you've heard it: Let's look at triangles—a basic and simple shape that's easy to visualize. What most of us believe about triangles is what we've been taught in school: no matter what shape a triangle is, how long and short its sides, or what angle each of its interior corners make, the sum of its three angles will always be 180 degrees. (*Wow, that's cool! But, wrong.*) Now, imagine this (it's mind-opening when you do): Let's say that you are marking off land to be used to create a dog park and that the area is to be in the shape of a triangle. Plot out the outline of its perimeter on the ground. To make it simple, use an equilateral triangle, which is one that has three equal sides and three equal angles. Make each side 100 yards long. Now, measure the three angles. They will be sixty degrees each, together totaling 180 degrees to make up the triangle. If you drew an isosceles or scalene triangle, the result would be the same—a sum of 180 degrees for the angles of your triangle.

Okay, now let's say that you decided to make your triangle even bigger. (*Here's where it gets really interesting.*) You plot out a perimeter of triangle sides that are 1000 miles long. (Or just imagine a triangle of straight lines running from Los Angeles to New York City and then to Miami and back to Los Angeles.) Now, measure the three angles. Magically, they are greater than a sum total of 180 degrees. But how is this possible? This is not what you've been told. You've been told that math and geometry are absolutes that follow laws and can guarantee certainty.

So, do you want to know why the larger a triangle is, the greater the sum of its angles? The answer is intrinsic to the fact that nothing (and no thing) is absolute. The answer is that the angles of a triangle were never absolutely 180 degrees. They vary, because life, the world, and the universe are not two-dimensional.

As you draw out a large triangle on the ground, the ground bends past the horizon, wrapping around the bend of our globe, stretching and warping the angles of the triangle's shape, affecting how it comes together, and changing everything that we thought we knew. It's not noticeable in smaller triangles—unless you are able to take measurements on the quantum level—and hardly noticeable in triangles even as large as the sides of an Egyptian pyramid. Yet, in actual fact there are no absolutes, only fields of possibilities when you open your scope of awareness. In our limited understanding, what appears to be a straight line from Los Angeles to New York City is not a straight line at all, and what appears to be a straight line from New York City to Miami isn't either. Of course, what appears to be a straight line from Miami back to Los Angeles is also not a straight line. All three are *bent* lines with a sum total of varying degrees. And it doesn't stop on Earth. While this phenomenon might seem as though it is derived from the fact that the Earth is round, in actuality it has to do with a greater reality: the curvature and possibilities of everything.

Let's take a look at gravity as an absolute. A fairly certain scientific fact, don't you think? Not so fast.

In the fourth century BC, the Greek philosopher, Aristotle, enlightened us to cause and effect: there is no effect or motion without a cause. In his system, heavy bodies are not attracted to the Earth by an external force of gravity but tend toward the center of the universe because of an inner gravitas or heaviness. He was a smart guy and that theory held for a long time. Until it didn't.

It was during the seventeenth century that Galileo found—counter to Aristotle's teachings—that all objects equally accelerated when falling. Hmmm, was *this* the new absolute?

But then came along Sir Isaac Newton, the mathematician and physicist whom we hail as having discovered gravity in 1687 BC. Newton's law of universal gravitation states that every mass attracts every other mass in the universe, and the gravitational force between two bodies is proportional to the product of their masses and inversely proportional to the square of the distance between them. But Newton only had a piece of the puzzle. His theory was not accurate and yet to this day, most of us have internalized that iconic image of an apple falling on Newton's head, and so our inquiring mind just stopped right there with the belief that Newton cracked the mystery of gravity. But, not quite. (*I'm almost to the point and it's worth the walk down history's memory lane in order to explore absolutes.*)

Next, the metaphorical baton of gravity was passed to scientist and mathematician Carl Friedrich Gauss in the early nineteenth century, who then handed it off to his pupil Bernhard Riemann. Together, their insights led to the idea that space is bent. (*Whoa, now this brings in a whole new perspective!*)

Finally, building on what Gauss and Riemann theorized, Albert Einstein came up with his theory of general relativity, which he developed between 1905 and 1915. It described what we perceive as the force of gravity to be in fact a geometric property arising from the curvature of space and time, or spacetime, and it's the theory that science currently upholds. Even still, most people don't understand what it is.

To break it down: Gravity works because the space around the Earth responds to the presence of the Earth. In the presence of matter and energy, this geometry can evolve, stretch and warp. Otherwise said, the added possibility called Earth actually alters space. Imagine, little old us in this big universe, altering space and time? Today, many scientists describe the universe as moving from order to disorder, however, the magic of viral energy says that it's moving from possibilities to more possibilities.

Space is malleable; everything bends and adjusts to variables. You are one of those variables and you can initiate change in your reality. Your presence alters outcomes. *So, what will be the impact of your presence? What will you create?*

Do you remember what quantum physicist Dr. Fred Alan Wolf told me about the bar magnet and iron filings? He said, "The mind is a process and it's related to what is happening at the level of what we call the quantum field of reality. At this unobservable invisible level of reality, we are dealing with a field of possibilities, not a gathering of physical objects. Changing the field of possibilities changes the pattern of behavior."

Even that which was once considered as fact evolves as we grasp the next discovery. This begs the question, what's next?

Whatever we create is next. Whatever you create is next. There are always more questions to be answered and then re-answered again, furthering your understanding. From this, of course, becomes even more possibilities.

There is one question, a loose end so to speak, that we *have* answered. It's the question posed in the eighteen-hundreds by astronomer William Herschel and his brain-pack of stargazers: is our galaxy everything?

To answer this, the groundwork was set by the 1893 discovery of "variable stars" made by Henrietta Swan Leavitt, a female American astronomer at Harvard. Variable stars provided a key for how to measure distance in far space, and to determine what was inside our galaxy and what was beyond it. This key was then used in 1923 by American astronomer Edwin Hubble when he tackled the question using the famous Hooker Telescope on Mount Wilson near Los Angeles, California, and calculated that the Andromeda nebula was really the Andromeda *galaxy*!

We now know—thanks to the open minds of many people over many hundreds of years—that yes, indeed, there are hundreds of billions of other galaxies besides our own Milky Way galaxy. At long last, we can observe that we are not the sole galaxy in existence.

Everything is out there. All possibilities are present. Everything does exist. If you can imagine anything at all, it exists somewhere in space and time. So, dream big—the biggest that you can. Audrey Hepburn said, "Nothing is impossible, the word itself says 'I'm possible!'"

You can discover your idea or create it. Nothing is too big, too late, or too absolute, unless you see it that way. All energy bends to the presence of possibilities—whatever it is that you dream of for the highest good of all. Say it is so and for you, it will be.

Original Doubt: The Story of Your Soul's Eden

There is a massive forest of aspen trees in Utah's Fishlake National Forest that stretches over 100 acres. It was discovered that the trees of this forest share a root system, which means they are not separate individuals at all; they are one single genetic individual with thousands upon thousands of stems. These stems have a life cycle: they appear as individuals living above ground, then they "die" and other units sprout in their place. Scientists call the organism Pando and have documented it as the largest organism on Earth. When any stem experiences health, disease, or drought, the whole of the organism is affected.

You see, *we* are Pando. We are awakening to the strange, beautiful, interconnected, and magical nature of life. It's all materializing in our lifetime, right now. Our species is moving away from the drive and need to forcefully steal power from Earth and Her creatures, resources, populations, and individuals, toward the utilization of the energy from our collective internal enlightenment: the free-will sharing of energy. As empowerment replaces force, we will no longer live from the perspective of dominance or struggle for the upper hand over any other. When we understand and practice this shift in understanding, we will stop inventing ways to excuse how we often treat others, and we will recognize the ways we foolishly dominate nature, stripping Earth of her resources. When we acknowledge that our efforts to gain the upper-hand are counterproductive and against everything that we were made to be, we will illuminate darkness, awaken to the illusion of separateness, and be the enlightened One.

Some divine beings have tried to tell us about our power—our connected and contagious energy—yet we're still in doubt. So, here it is again: we are made in the image and likeness of the Creator. The divine One gave you a powerful directive: "Love your neighbor as yourself." It's the Golden Rule, but do you know why?

Before time began, Life chose to slow the vibration of consciousness-energy and therefore manifested itself into minuscule units of form; all to create the unending cycle of the birth and rebirth of Creation. Separating into countless units means that each unit had a vastly reduced energy field, all the while still sharing the same content and operations within the body of the Whole. You are one of those units. Life is not only in us; we are part of Life—one organism, one body. (*You are being Life right now, so you might want to start believing it.*) However, it's not a sin that we don't know everything that there is to know about the connectivity of Life; it just means there is much to discover. Consider this: the intended translation of "original sin" is original *doubt*—a lack of faith in our Oneness or the belief that we are separate from the whole of Life.

Your highest purpose is to unite with Life. Your wondrous opportunity is to consciously create. Your monumental challenge is that you are essentially operating in a state of limited access because you don't recognize that on the level of energy, everything is entangled. All of Life is interconnected through viral energy. Just like Pando's roots, our unborn souls are interconnected; and just like Pando's stems, so too are our born souls. As souls born into physicality, we cannot "see" our Oneness because it is not a visible connection; it is a palpable awareness.

When we are born, we "sprout above the ground" as individuals. It's at this moment that our connection to the Whole is forgotten and we begin our original misunderstanding: believing that we are on our own and that our survival is a solo project (or the real project). It's as if we look at the stems around us and immediately decide that we need to procure the most resources for "self." We want to be better and more successful; we want the best and the most. And with this fundamental and original misunderstanding, we disregard the wellbeing of all other stems. All of this must happen for the physical experience to exist: our physicality is a slowing of Light into matter in a realm of relativity. We must first forget in order to take on the journey of remembering. It is our ultimate joy to experience our Higher-Selves and remember our Oneness.

Sincerely ask yourself and your Higher-Self these questions: Is it possible that your first "wrongdoing" is not a sin at all, but is to doubt that you are still fully tethered with the Everything? Is this the inception of all "evil" thoughts and actions? What if you knew for certain that you are sharing one body with the trees, oceans, and air? Would you knowingly choke out or pollute yourself? And what if it was a certainty that you are one with all people of all kinds, nationalities, ethnicities, and religions? Would you create war with yourself? Would you loathe and fear yourself? How about if you had a divine guarantee that you are one body—one Life—with dogs, cats, and dolphins? What about if you are one Life with cows, chickens, lambs, and pigs? Would you farm yourself in filthy factories and slit your own neck? Or, would you have others piecemeal the unpleasant tasks while you demand the supply of your own flesh? Would you experiment on yourself, infect yourself with diseases, and cause grave self-harm simply to make product-marketing claims? What if everything that you did unto Earth, other people, and animals was exactly and equally done unto you?

Doubting that you are part of the whole of Life results in dense energy blocks such as hatred, guilt, rage, resentment, judgment, jealousy, doubt, fear, greed, and disease. Behaving as though you are disconnected from Life creates heavy energy and "sinful" actions which are bi-products of your fears and doubt. Unlike the aspen of Pando that is under perfect natural order, *you* have the free will to perceive yourself as separate if that's what you choose. But, the truth is, you are One with Life.

No longer be in doubt about the roots of your misery or your happiness. Starting today, you can live like Pando. Imagine if our world leaders operated by this truth. Heck, imagine if our religious leaders did. Wait for it—imagine if *you* moved past this barrier of separation and truly stepped into who you are as One with Life. What would happen if you put aside your original doubt?

We are Pando. Even though our connected roots are not visible from "above the surface," we are one body. Do you believe that you (or any of us) truly get away unscathed by the harm that we do unto others? No, we do not. All of these attitudes and actions create energetic bi-products that obstruct the Light—they are dense energy masses: tumors. We wonder if we'll ever find a cure for cancer, all the while we are creating tumors within ourselves and our planet from the buildup of both physical obstructions (i.e. pollution and resource-stripping) and energetic toxins (i.e. the heavy energy of some of our intentions, thoughts, and actions).

Sucking power through force or abuse will not sustain an individual's energy needs. Stealing beauty by taking it from another life can never make anyone truly more beautiful. Taking resources that have been prescribed to be shared cannot satisfy the drive for abundance. Yet, until now, humanity has been conditioned to accept all of this as common practice and what's worse, we are ignorant to the fact that any unit (stem or person) that's disadvantaged, left untreated, or harmed results in suffering for the whole organism.

Can you imagine if we lived in total harmony with all of Creation? There wouldn't be any lack, loneliness, cruelty, murder, theft, poverty, jealousy, judgment, or greed. Is it probable, if not provable, that if we moved with life as one organism—one shared and permeable energy field—we would attain Heaven on Earth? Yes, of course it is.

So much of what we have learned needs to be unlearned before we can move to our natural state of unobstructed light energy. It's an awakening and it has already started. Humanity's original sin is not that we are all born impure or weighted with the errored karma of a mythical first woman and man whose wrongdoing was so vile that a purification ritual is now required for our souls to have a hope in purgatory of reaching Heaven. Nope, our original sin—our first forgetting—is the doubt and unknowingness of who we really are as One with Life. It's doubting that we too are Creator, and forgetting that we are truly powerful, empowered, and worthy. It's doubting that we are as vulnerable as the most vulnerable in our midst, and doubting that we are as good as the very best among us. All of this is a misunderstanding that we chose, and we now have the consciousness to choose again. It has been a collective sleep-state from which our enlightened souls are thrilled to wake up and to create ourselves anew.

CHAPTER SIX:

WHAT YOU WANT, WANTS YOU

What if You Didn't Get What You Wanted?

I didn't choose not to be a mother. Well, in a way I suppose I did. I chose not to be a single mother. I chose to wait for true love before I chose to try to get pregnant. I dreamt of a little girl named London. However, my "window" has passed and I didn't get to have a child of my own, which means that I won't have milestones and family around in the same way that others do.

Life is real. Sometimes the milk spills and you can't put it back in the bottle. So, cry about it if you want to, and then move on—because it's time to.

I have a dear friend who is in her early fifties and she's never been married; not yet, anyway. While she faithfully believes that she will be married one day—because she wants to spend her life with a committed companion and marriage is something that she desires—at the same time, she knows that there are life moments that she can't get back. She shared with me, "I can never go back and get married *young*, like other people. It's too late for that." Now both of her parents have passed away and she won't physically have them at her wedding someday. And she too will not have children of her own.

So, what if it's too late for you to get what you wanted? What if a great loss, circumstance, tragedy, or simply the passage of time has taken away your options?

I believe that I've been a mother, perhaps hundreds of times, in my previous lives. Or a father for that matter. And I'm sure I will be a parent again—in another lifetime, that is. Shortly before she passed away, I had a reading from renowned psychic medium, Elizabeth Barron, who told me this: "Your life's purpose is not about those things. Your life's purpose is to write and to share your knowledge and your presence with others." Because I truly believe this, it gives me some comfort. (*Maybe in my last lifetime I was a mother to fourteen kids, and when reviewing my life, I said, "That's enough already! May I please have my next lifetime be about something else, pleeease?"*)

It also gives me comfort to think of parents who sincerely wanted to be a parent and *were* able to fulfill that dream. Even though it is not my experience, I'm happy that it's someone else's experience. I can see it that way because I believe that all of life is One Life; I believe that each of us have and will experience all expressions of creation. I want for others to live in deep happiness, just as I want it for myself. I want others to be successful, healthy, and abundant in all ways. I've learned to be very happy for the joy that others experience.

Get this—when you truly believe that we are all connected, the creation energy of joy that you have for others eventually circles back to you; *what you want, wants you.* Nowadays, I think of it this way—maybe my London is a piece of writing that encourages many, or a work of art, or some other creation bearing her name.

I have saved a fortune cookie message for many years that reads: "We are here to create not merely survive." It's always what you didn't create that you regret the deepest. Cast off the smallness of focusing on what you didn't get. Free yourself of it. Instead, get in the energy of what you can create now. What's your London?

The Return of Love Suspended (And Other Open Doors)

Have you ever dreamt of a job-change and then received a surprise opportunity? Or broken up with someone, yet still can't part ways? Or reunited with an old flame, seemingly out of nowhere? (*I have.*)

Doors open to what (and who) you think about. Thoughts hold energy and that energy tends to connect with other energy on the same vibration. Here's an example: if you're unhappy or bored in your job, chances are that before long you will—by your choice or not—become devolved from the job. Conversely, if you deeply desire better work hours, projects, and experiences—and you imagine, from a place of excitement, what that would look and feel like—it's quite possible that you are *energetically* opening a portal to an opportunity that will soon come knocking.

Relationships work like this, too. When you have someone on your mind, consistently and often, don't be surprised when they turn up on your phone or doorstep. I've had three engagements and one marriage. (*I'll try to simplify this, as it does get complicated.*) My third engagement resulted in the marriage to my husband, Burt. Before this, right in the middle of dating, we had a two-year break-up in which I became engaged to my ex-boyfriend from a decade previous. This didn't last long, and we broke it off a few months later. I then returned to Burt who truly had my heart all along.

Oh, the first engagement, you say? A rookie mistake at twenty years old.

I have had some experience with love suspended and getting back together after years of separation. The bottom line is, on each of the occasions when I had been reunited with someone from my past, I was consistently thinking about that person and fueled by deep emotion. They then turned up or were "open" when *I* turned up. This kind of thing happens when two people have each other on their minds.

Here's a cute and sweetly benign story about a woman (whom I know) and a man, both in their seventies, who connected out-of-the-blue five decades after they were high school sweethearts. Nancy (seventy-three) was going through some old memory boxes and came across a set of baseball cards belonging to John (seventy-four), an old boyfriend from fifty years earlier. This was the first time she had thought of him in decades. She wondered what ever happened to him and if he missed his cards. Five days later, Nancy received a letter from John. He said that he had thought of her and just wanted to say hello and hoped that all was well in her life.

That's some of the magic of viral energy: if it gets entangled, it might always be entangled, even across time and great distance.

Knowing how the magic of viral energy works—how your thoughts are energy units that can be picked up by receivers tuned in to that same frequency—you will want to mind what you think about from now on.

Put the magic of viral energy to good use when you want to dial-in a fabulous new job, fresh new experiences, or a soulmate from your past or future!

Mansions of Your Mind

There is a deeper consciousness emerging inside you. It's like that feeling that you get when you leave the house and sense that you're missing something. Can you feel it? You are about to remember something that will make your heart ache with joy. It will come back to you as warm sun on your face. In a reality more real than this one, you knew it very well. It was the song that you sang to yourself like the one a mother sings to her newborn baby. Yes, you love it that much. It was the gift that you chose when you had your pick of any under the stars. You've been so occupied, but you're ready for it now. What you're aching for was conceived in your soul and will soon be born in your mind.

Now, please do this visualization with me. Let me take you on a journey to remember:

See yourself walking through a beautiful seaside town. Each home is more striking than the last—some are contemporary with tall windows and clean architectural lines, others look like grand lodges made of timber and stone, others still are ranches with brown and white painted horses grazing along wooden fences that stretch past the horizon. It's dawning morning and sunshine floods into barns and bedrooms alike. You begin opening doors and taking a look around.

Now, you remember that you're looking for a dear child about five years old. Search the mansions of your mind. What else do you notice? You're not exactly sure what the child looks like, as the faces of people are fuzzy like in a dream, but also like in a dream, you somehow still know each person by their presence. You have no doubt that you will recognize the child when you find them. You keep looking, not in anxiety or desperation, but in untempered excitement.

Just now, down a long hallway of high ceilings lit with chandeliers, you see the child at a distance. At first, you slowly approach. As you get closer, you begin to run towards them, arms outstretched. Your smile is wide as you drop to your knees in front of the child and scoop them into your chest. The child giggles with joy and you hold them so close that you can feel their heart beat against your own. You notice that your heart and the child's are beating together at the same rhythm to the point that they're indistinguishable. You want to look into the child's eyes, so you ease your embrace and, holding the child safely with your hand on their back, you look into those familiar eyes—now you remember their color and how they sparkle! So beautiful. So unguarded. So expectant.

Looking deep into the eyes of your child, like through the doorways of their soul, you ask them, "Precious One, what would you like to do?

And who would you like to be? For so many years I had forgotten how I love you so. At long last, I have found you in the mansions of my mind. I know your heart as my own. Whatsoever you want, you can create. Whatsoever you can think of, you can create. You are so cherished, so wanted, so intentional. Never forget that. You can do anything. Tell me, what would you like to do? Who shall you be? Oh, what a joy it is to be you, becoming."

Open your eyes.

Finding your purpose in life is a great joy. It's the greatest joy! Your purpose and your soul are synonymous. One beat.

Your purpose should be cherished. It is you becoming your true self: your Higher-Self.

CHAPTER SEVEN:

YOUR DEFINITIVE GUIDE TO AFFIRMATIONS

Your Breathtaking Agreement With Life

The big question on your mind is the same question that mankind has pursued for thousands of years: Why am I here? And, what's the meaning and purpose of my life?

On this topic, psychiatrist, neurologist, and Holocaust survivor, Viktor Frankl wrote a best-selling book titled, *Man's Search for Meaning*, first released in 1946. The book details his experiences as a concentration camp inmate during World War II, as he survived imprisonment at Theresienstadt, Auschwitz, Kaufering, and Türkheim. This led him to discover the importance of finding meaning—even in life's most brutal circumstances—and therefore a reason to continue living. While interned and suffering the worst horrors imaginable, Frankl held a vision of his purpose. As a doctor, researcher, and also a captive, he conducted his own study and concluded that holding a belief of one's distinct purpose—including an envisionable future plan—had a connection to and a great deal to do with whether or not a prisoner survived to fulfill their purpose. In *Man's Search for Meaning*, Frankl points to research indicating a strong relationship between "meaninglessness" and criminal behavior, addiction, and depression. He famously said, "What man actually needs is not a tensionless state but rather the striving and struggling for some goal worthy of him…the call of a potential meaning waiting to be fulfilled by him."

I can't imagine a better case study on the importance of life-purpose and success at "life," and hearing of Frankl's outcome should probably fuel excitement about *your* purpose.

During my miserable years, from fifteen to thirty-four—and yes, it's a long time to be miserable—I had never thought of my purpose or intentions in life. I didn't even know what that meant. I suppose my day-to-day intentions were no more than rogue thoughts like, "I want to be loved; I want everything now; I wish for all animals to be safe from cruelty; I want maximum reward for minimal effort; I want world peace; I want others to respect me and think well of me; I want to be happy." When I was happy, I was a joy to be around; when I was empty, lonely, or broken, I was uncompanionable. For many years, I did not connect the inner intentions that I carried through my life with the circumstances and events that I would experience.

It was in 2007, following my own personal rock bottom, that I actively made a decision to change everything, beginning with the very meaning and purpose of my life. I started to read all that I could find on self-help, spirituality, and new age philosophy. I journaled, asked myself big questions, and sought answers. Finally, I began making the connection between my thoughts and what I was manifesting in my life.

I asked myself, "What am I most passionate about?" That was clear: I am passionate about healing the systematic and epidemic planetary, human, and animal suffering at the hands of humans. I had always believed that our Higher-Selves do not hurt each other, harm animals, or cause war and discord with nature of any kind and so I decided that this should be the beginning of my personal mission statement. It was suddenly evident to me that my foundational intention is: to make a positive difference for our planet and in the lives of others by inspiring the Higher-Self.

Once I spoke these words out loud and wrote them down, things started to fall into place and to serve my mission.

So, how about you? If you are wondering what your "purpose" is, here's a hint—for Life to magnetize the resources and opportunities to you, your purpose will be something that is of use to others. Instead of asking, "What do I want," ask yourself, "What will I *create*?" You are intended and designed to create. And, imagine this—you picked what you wanted to create *before* you started this life. You chose your purpose.

Have you had a vision board for five years—or fifteen years—yet still haven't manifested what you want? Do you write down your intentions, dreams, and affirmations, but can't get them from the page to passion-in-motion? You hear a lot of talk about vision boards and positive affirmations, but maybe you've been approaching affirmations—and what you want out of life for that matter—from the wrong end. Maybe you need to start with why you're here.

Your soul's ultimate purpose is always your soul's spiritual evolution. Even before the very moment that you took your first breath, you began the journey to awaken to and fulfill a breathtaking agreement that you made with Life; a contract of what you decided you wanted to contribute to humanity's evolution, and your own.

If you knew for sure that you have an essential purpose that you set out to move towards, would you spend your days straining, stressed out, or checking tasks off a list? No, you would not. Would you waste your energy and your presence on smallness unworthy of your life's true purpose? No, you would not. If you could see the contract that you have with Life—your Breathtaking Agreement—how would it read? If you could remember what it was, what would it be?

Your life's purpose is what you create it to be. No one, not even God, needs you to be what you do not choose, and what you choose to create in this life does not have to change the world (but it can). Your agreement is "breathtaking" not because it needs to be awe inspiring; it's breathtaking because it is *why* your soul chose to take your first breath and every one after that until this moment.

Life already knows Itself as Almighty; She wants to experience Herself as a fashion designer, a grocery store clerk, a scientist, a janitor. If you are a janitor, be the janitor that Life would be. Design and create with the passion that Life would have. Conduct scientific experiments in accordance with how the Giver of Life would do so; do no harm to any of your creatures. Give the customer service that Life would give, wanting and embracing the experience of serving others. Be the parent, child, or spouse that the Creator would be. Even if you experience trouble, loss, or hardship, experience hardship as Life would; as God would. Then, if you're satisfied with that experience, choose another one. Be in every moment of your life as though you specifically chose it for the joy of being it as Creator.

Let your passions and talents point the way. Look for Light. (Keep in mind that Light is the opposite of confusion.) Write it out. What would you contribute to Life if you could do anything? What would you create?

Here's a helpful template for your "Breathtaking Agreement With Life." It's a contract, remember, so you have to write it down. Fill in the blanks with your passions. What do you want to create and contribute?

Write, "Dear Life, I am choosing this life incarnation again and with renewed energy in order to…I choose to share Life and happiness through my gifts of…My intention in this world is…My unique contribution is… Please help me to use my life to…Show me the signs and bring me the people, resources, and opportunities to fulfill this, my agreement with You. Sincerely and with love and Light, (sign *your name*)."

If you choose, you may tweak it over the next few days, weeks, or months—it is your contract, your choice.

Robin Williams said, "No matter what people tell you, words and ideas can change the world." You see, the sky is the limit!

Once you've finished your contract, fold it up and put it in an envelope, seal it, and place it wherever you keep important paperwork. (Or, you can frame it and place it on your wall, as I have.) Even if you don't look at it again for a year, it is in motion. The magnetism of Life and the great magic of viral energy will do the rest, provided you do your part—take action and steadily move in the direction of your intention with sincerity and reverence for your Breathtaking Agreement With Life. This is the most powerful force at your will and from this, all that is meant for your life is born.

Here's my own Breathtaking Agreement With Life:

"Dear Life, I am choosing this life incarnation now, again, and with renewed energy in order to make a positive difference in the lives of others by inspiring the Higher-Self in all of us. I choose to exemplify and mobilize passion and compassion through my gifts of sharing inspiring messages, channeling wisdom from Higher-Self, and openly sharing my light presence with others. My intention in this world is to advance humanity's spiritual evolution because I believe that our Higher-Selves do not hurt each other, harm animals, destroy Mother Earth, or cause war and discord with nature of any kind. My unique contribution is to open minds and enlighten people to expansive new concepts such as the magic of viral energy. Please help me to use my life to help heal our planet and

Her people, plant life, wildlife, and domestic animals in peril by inspiring change in the hearts of all of us who are indifferent or in denial. This is my spirit's deepest motivation and my impetus for choosing this life. Show me the signs and bring me the people, resources, wisdom, and opportunities, to fulfill this, my agreement with You. Sincerely and with love and Light, Penelope Jean Hayes"

If You've Ever Said, "I Am Fat," Read This

Be on purpose about what you tell yourself. You're better than some of the ways that you talk about yourself.

My typical mantras used to sound like this: "I am not thin enough; I am lonely; I am broke; I am depressed; I am bad; I am overwhelmed; I am not appreciated; I am tired of this; I am lost; I am too old; I am undeserving; I am stuck."

What I have learned is that all of these statements are affirmations.

Words command Life to create something.

Life doesn't know that the story you are telling yourself is not fact and it's not what you want. It only knows that you said, "I am lonely," or "I am fat," and so Life will affirm it and turn the energy of your words into form. You will get what you proclaim. Of course, it works the same for, "I am sad; I am unworthy; I am poor," and so on. Negative statements are affirmations, too. They are toxins in your creation energy.

As a contemporary theorist, I have developed my own ideas on this. I've also spoken to experts and physicists on the matter, but I wanted to get an academic voice on this topic, so I spoke with Dr. David Burns. Dr. Burns is Adjunct Professor Emeritus in the Department of Psychiatry and

Behavioral Sciences at the Stanford University School of Medicine, and he's also the author of the bestselling books *Feeling Good: The New Mood Therapy*, and *The Feeling Good Handbook*.

Here's what Dr. Burns had to say when we discussed some of mankind's lowest emotions: "Depression and anxiety are really the world's oldest cons. You're fooling yourself but you don't realize it because your negative thoughts seem as valid to you as the fact that there's skin on your hand. It doesn't dawn on you that you're involved in this gigantic and cruel hoax. The very moment that you change the way you are thinking, and you see that those negative thoughts aren't true, the negative feelings will disappear. We create our own reality in every moment of every day. It would be interesting to know how to measure it, this 'viral energy' that you call it—to test it scientifically would be really fun, because it is almost mystical."

Dr. Burns and I talked about the things that we tell ourselves, including our "I am" statements. He added, "It is certainly a fact that when people are in a happy mood, it's infectious and you feel it right away. When you feel 'hot,' awesome, or happy, it is a vibration and people can pick it up from ten or twenty feet away. They want to be with you. And if you're in the 'I'm no good' mode, everyone wants to reject you. When you get down or anxious, people are kind of turned off to you. You see it in business, in dating, and in every application in life."

Dr. Burns is one of the country's top experts on mood therapy and his advice is clear: watch what you're telling yourself! I'm going to testify to this here, because it worked for me. So, if you think your self-talk or social talk about yourself is a show of modesty, rethink that; your happiness and success in life is on the line and this is no time for self-critique (even if you're intending to be slightly humorous and facetious). Instead of your usual self-deprecating mantras, try telling yourself this: "I am blissfully happy; I am abundant; I am fit; I am a genius; and I apply my wisdom." (I have been telling myself this last one for years, yet it's not originally mine...)

Many, many years before he was rich, famous, and living the life of his dreams, Dr. John DeMartini (author of the book *The Breakthrough Experience: A Revolutionary New Approach to Personal Transformation* and well-known cast member in the film, *The Secret*) met an old man who changed his life.

At the time, John was a vagabond surfer living in Hawaii who couldn't read or write. He was told his entire life that he was mentally impaired and would never amount to anything. Yet, he had dreamt of so much more and so, when he met the old man, he asked for advice.

The man told John to say these words and to repeat them again and again, and really mean them: "I am a genius and I apply my wisdom. I am a genius and I apply my wisdom. I am a genius and I apply my wisdom."

Today, Dr. John DeMartini travels the world as a highly sought-after speaker and motivator. In fact, as six-degrees-of-separation would have it, John drew a smiley face in pen on the tip of my right index finger at a talk in Vegas given by *Chicken Soup for the Soul* co-author, Jack Canfield. We sat next to each other in the front row. The finger drawing was some sort of exercise that the audience was asked to do; John was up next to speak.

I believe that John *is* a genius, but do you think that John truly believed he was a "genius" when he first began speaking the mantra? No, he did not—until one day he did.

You'll know when it's real—you'll feel it.

I AM are powerful creation words. In fact, they are the most powerful creation words in existence.

Get this, "I am" appears in the Bible 719 times—508 times in the Old Testament and 211 times in the New Testament. God himself and to himself is known as the great I AM: "I am that I am." "I am the Light of the world." So, take it from the most divine, I AM is supernatural!

Indeed, there is a miraculous order to Life. Life responds to your free will. Life is both in order and taking orders. Life wants for you what you want for you.

Make a list of ten powerful I AM statements. Even if they don't feel real, write them as you want them to be. Post these on your bathroom mirror or any place where you will read them often. Say them out loud daily, then make a copy, fold it up, and place it your wallet. And while it might not happen overnight, you can expect magic and miracles in your life. Life (big "L") is moving into order!

Eight Areas to Accelerate Extraordinary Abundance

You've heard the saying, "God is in the details." Well, magic and miracle are also in the details.

Consider and dream about what abundance means for you in each of your eight areas of abundance. Your life is not just about what you *do*, and your life is not just about what you *have*, want to have, or have achieved. To be abundant in one area, you must practice abundance in all. After *all*, what good is financial abundance if you're unhealthy? And why cram your life with social events if you don't also have joy within your own home or spirit? Be clear about what you want in all areas of life and a path will be cleared.

Here are your Eight Areas of Abundance: Spiritual, Physical, Social, Familial, Occupational, Vocational, Financial, and Mental.

Spiritual Abundance: To maintain a healthy mind, think about incorporating practices into your life such as prayer or meditation. Perhaps cooking, writing, or quietly sitting in nature is your spiritual practice. Think outside the box to find that which will give you peace of spirit and keep you balanced.

Physical Abundance: It doesn't have to be hard work. Do you like to walk, run, bike, go to the gym, do yoga, rollerblade, or swim? Then do that! However, physical abundance is not just about staying fit and active; it's also about taking care of your body—for any of your dreams and goals in life, you're going to need your body! Pamper yourself with a relaxing bath, book a massage, get a pedicure. Eat well and balanced and be mindful of where your food comes from.

Social Abundance: How do you socialize now and what would it feel like to you to be abundant in your social life? Would you like to entertain more in your home? Do you dream of more time spent breaking bread with family and friends at a restaurant or picnic table in the park? Do you enjoy stepping out to socialize and meet new people? How would you like to spend the holidays, and with whom? (Here's another great example of how your eight areas of abundance need to be equality nurtured—because without financial abundance, it can be hard to maintain the social abundance that you most desire.)

Familial Abundance: How about family life; what does that look like to you? Is it just you and your beloved dogs? Do you have or want children or grandchildren? Do you have or want a partner or spouse? How do you want to communicate and interact—in a healthy way—with your parents, siblings, or children? What would the benchmark look like in those close relationships?

Occupational Abundance: This is what you do for a living; the way in which you make your money. This area can be heartache if you don't feel content with what you do every day to provide for yourself and your family. Really think about what your perfect work and perfect pay would be if you could choose. If you desire a new job, imagine it in your mind and create it on paper exactly the way you dream it to be. If you don't know what it is that you want, you likely aren't experiencing it yet.

Vocational Abundance: Did you think that your occupation encompassed everything you do for a living? Nope. When it comes to your vocation, think about what you would do if you could do anything, whether you were paid for it or not. Think about what you loved to do when you were a kid. Your vocation is often in line with your talents or passions. Maybe yours is painting, entertaining others, fostering cats or dogs, volunteering with veterans, journaling, building furniture, fixing things, advocating for the environment, or some other cause.

Financial Abundance: What does financial health and abundance look like to you? Is it stability, security, the ability to help others? Where are you lacking and what are your themes of lack, stress, "less," or "not enough" that repeat and cause you to suffer? Now, recreate in your mind what financial health and abundance is for you.

Mental Abundance: Mental abundance can sometimes be satisfied with a practice of physical abundance like exercise or sport to burn off charged emotions. However, mental wellness and abundance is a little more—it's also the way that you satisfy your curiosity with continued learning, stretching your mind, exercising your potential, and continuing to flex your beautiful brain power. What's thought provoking for you—philosophy, contemplating art, debate, education? What have you done for your brain lately? And, what will you do?

Seven Tips for Affirmations That Work!

When I was single, I wanted to meet and marry a man who was chivalrous, who opened doors, and helped me with my coat. And so, I had a photo pinned onto my vision board (it was from a perfume advertisement, I recall) of an elegant woman stepping out of a car. Under her stylish stiletto was a man's crisp white dress shirt covering a puddle. A firm male hand was openly extended towards her as she leaned forward with eyes locked on his—no concern for the puddle.

I held out for a man like that, and then I married him.

Affirmations are tools for you to actively manifest your goals, dreams, and heart's desire. Olympians, professional athletes, titans of business, military special ops, celebrated actors, and artists—all have used them. Even the Bible offers tips on visualization: "Where there is no vision, the people perish," (Pro 9:18).

Now, it's your turn to declare what you really want.

So, what exactly are affirmations? Affirmations can be spoken, written, or visualized. They are present tense proclamations to you and to all of Life. Affirmations are commands to Life to create something. They can be

I AM statements (but they don't have to be). They can be derived from your Eight Areas of Abundance or your personal mission statement. They can be a prayer spoken or written in the present tense (e.g. "Thank you for the resources to fulfill my purpose."). To work, they must serve your life's purpose. You decide what you want to be, do, and have, and you ultimately determine what you tell yourself.

Okay, so what are affirmations *not*?

Affirmations do not work in the negative, such as, "I am not alone; I am not fat." They are also not spoken, written, or visualized in the past or future, for example, "I will be a bestselling author." They are not a list of things to do; if it feels heavy it's not going to work. They are not accomplishments that once reached are no longer relevant, such as, "I want to lose ten pounds; I will meet my soulmate this year." Affirmations are not egocentric aspirations like, "I want to be a star; I am rich; I am a millionaire." Now, here is a really big hint: if you need resources such as money or influence to fulfill your life's purpose, then create your affirmations around the purpose, not the payout.

There's a recipe, so to speak, for doing affirmations, and there's also magic to it! Here's what I have learned and know about positive (and negative) affirmations, as well as tips to finally get what you truly desire:

Clean Up Your Daily Vernacular: Affirmations can be as simple as what you tell yourself all day, every day. "I am" are the most powerful creation words in existence—they command Life to create something. You're a powerful manifestor; mind what you say.

Get Clear About What You Want: When you know what you want, Life starts to move the resources, people, and opportunities your way. The clearer you become, the clearer it shows up. Masters of karate succeed in cracking a board in half with their bare hand by aiming past the board. By doing so, they chop *through*. Aim far past your goals by seeing them far past anything that you can imagine reaching. You see, when your dreams and goals are foggy and unfocused, what shows up is unfocused. Daydream about it. Visualize it. Really see it in crystal clarity.

Get It On Paper: It can help to write your affirmations down. Do this only when you have time to make it a relaxing and inspiring experience. If you need help to get in the vibe, first try meditating or practicing yoga, or just get yourself a nice cup of tea and enjoy it. It's supposed to be fun; after all, it's all about you! Here are some of my favorite written affirmations, one or more for each of the areas of my life that I choose abundance. Some of my affirmations can be used by many, and some are personalized to my journey yet will still give you some good ideas.

- Spiritual Abundance: "I am a powerful creator." And, "I live surrounded by the extreme beauty of nature."
- Mental Abundance: "I am a genius and I apply my wisdom." (*Thanks, John!*)
- Financial Abundance: "Life is moving the resources, people, events, and opportunities to me in order to fulfill my purpose."
- Vocational Abundance: "God, use me to help animals in peril by inspiring change in the hearts of all of us indifferent or in denial." And, "I am and have everything I need to make my inspired dreams come true."
- Occupational Abundance: "I am an author who inspires others and my books enrich and enlighten millions of people around the world, enlightening them to their Higher-Selves."
- Familial Abundance: "I am married to my gorgeous funmate." And, "My family are my best friends, and my best friends are my family."
- Social Abundance: "Our home is alive with family and friends and we have the space and time to entertain, experience love and create memories."
- Physical Abundance: "I am fit, toned, and my body is in perfect alignment."

    ☙ ...And one more because it's fun, and when it comes from a pure intention it's very powerful: "What I want, wants me."

Supercharge It With Images: This is where a vision board is handy (or a vision scrapbook, or a Pinterest page—whatever works to help you visualize your inspired dreams). Pairing your thoughts and dreams with photos snagged online or from magazines really helps you to visualize what it looks like in detail. After all, a picture is worth a thousand words. Match your images to all eight of your areas of abundance and synchronize them with your affirmations. Be clear about *why* you want what you want. Instead of asking, "What do I want," ask yourself, "What will I create?" When choosing photos of your dream home, for example, dream of the home that fits what you will do and be. If you will create your inspired work from your home, make room for office or creative space. If you want to host a lot of visitors, then be sure to have guest bedrooms. Don't wish for a big house; visualize and magnetize to you the home that fits your inspired dreams! (Tip: Photos of beautiful empty homes are just beautiful empty homes. Choose photos that include a happy family, entertainment, pets, food being prepared—whatever abundance looks like to you.) Beginning in 2005, I had placed my vision board where I couldn't miss it—on my bedroom wall directly in front of my bed. Every morning and night I would lie in bed and gaze at my board of powerful images containing all of the abundance that I wished for with sincerity; it filled me with excitement. The images that I had thoughtfully selected helped me to really see and feel all of the areas of abundance that I desired in my life.

    Proclaim It To Claim It: Tell people about it. Make yourself accountable to your goals by sharing your intentions. There is a power that comes with speaking your intentions and affirmations out loud to others. Your words go up like bursts of creation energy at large, and are echoed back to you in another's voice. Then, it starts to become more real to you.

Get Emotional About It: Emotions are magnetic and they speed up the manifestation of your goals and dreams. If your affirmation feels like a task that you want to tick off your list of accomplishments, it's not an affirmation that's going to work well for you. When choosing tools to help you manifest your dreams—whether they are I AM statements or glossy magazine clippings—choose something inspiring that makes you feel something. Choose what is meaningful and exciting to you. Rather than imagining what your choice in a partner would look like, or how much money they will make, or what they do for a living, ask yourself, "How do I want to feel?" Perhaps you want to feel adored, supported, and part of a team. Whatever it is for you, choose visualization images that make you feel something wonderful!

Take Action Through Choice: It's not going to jump off your vision board or your notepad; you must take action. Your action could be to take small steps in the direction of your goals, or your action could be a quantum leap. In either case, just keep putting one foot in front of the other. "A journey of a thousand miles begins with a single step," so says Confucius. In both scenarios, you will be faced with choices every day and all you have to do is pick the one that serves your personal mission statement and the agreement that you made with Life. For your affirmations to work, your words and actions must be congruent with what you have said you wanted to do, be, and have. What do you really want? Do it now.

How to Believe Your Affirmations (Pssst, Just Be Life)

I had a million-dollar check from Oprah Winfrey in my wallet in 2007 when I was pulled into secondary inspection at the Detroit-Windsor border. Certainly it was the check that alerted the U.S. Customs and Border Protection officer of my intention to illegally do business in the United States. (*Very naughty, indeed.*) Or it might have been my nervous demeanor when I drove up to the officer's booth, entering from Canada in a Canadian plated car with an abundance of clothes—perhaps too many—for a long-weekend holiday. I had made this border crossing perhaps hundreds of times before, having lived for thirty years in the border-town on the other end of its bridge. However, I had never been asked the question that I was asked on this day by this border officer: "May I see your wallet?"

I confidently passed him my wallet, as I had nothing to hide, totally forgetting about the million-dollar check folded up and signed—*Oprah Winfrey.* The very check that had been in my wallet for about three years. The check that I had made and signed myself—quite authentic looking I might add—as a visualization tool for when I would be a bestselling author, a popular public speaker, and in business in some way with Oprah. I left it loose in my visualization as to the exact work I'd be doing with Oprah; maybe it would be a series of inspirational seminars, perhaps a publishing partnership of sorts, or an educational television event. All I knew is that I had some future business with Ms. Winfrey, or so I wished to manifest by affirming it with this play-check in my wallet. And while I thought it to be obvious that it wasn't *really* a million-dollar check from Oprah, my story made no sense to the U.S. Customs and Border Protection. Try talking to them about affirmations. (*Yeah, they weren't into it.*)

The next five hours went like this: naked strip search, then sitting alone in a very cold box of a room while customs officers scoured my laptop for evidence of illegal earnings, followed by a three-on-one interrogation on what I *do* for a living, ending with my being turned back to Canada.

After this event, I had been blacklisted at the border and denied entry back into the U.S. for the next four months. It was during this time that I obtained a Visa to live and work legally in the United States, and I (of course) refined and defined my affirmations. (*But, come on, I have to laugh at myself here: My visualization tool was so realistic and effective that it got me strip searched! I have a sneaking suspicion that I'm a rather powerful manifestor.*)

Now is a good time to recap what Dr. Fred Alan Wolf told me: "Quantum physics says that the observer (*that's you*) affects reality. Therefore, if you can change how you go about observing what you call life, you can change the reality that you're living in."

Quantum physics has proven that through our individual perspective we have the ability to change our own reality. This is precisely why we do affirmations—to decide what we want and then affirm it to ourselves until we can really feel it, believe it, and manifest it.

Still, believing our own affirmations is the hardest part. (You know that.)

But, did you know that at the quantum level, it has been proven that the tiniest bits of all energy move in a wave (unseen) and that they only appear as a particle (matter/materialized/manifested) when they are observed? So, for any energy "pop"—say the pop of an idea—to manifest into form, it must be observed, noticed, seen. It's a strange thought, right? It's kind of like: What came first, the chicken or the egg? How can you have an egg without a chicken, and vice versa?

How can you see something *before* you can see something? How can you believe your affirmations *before* they are true?

The law of attraction—which is a principle of the mechanics of matter and energy at the quantum level—states that first you must believe, and then you will receive. You might remember this explained in *The Secret* film and also in numerous writings throughout history. It's the believe-receive formula of manifestation, which states that when you believe something (say your affirmation of what you want to do or be), and if and when you believe it truly, deeply, and fully, then you will receive it. But the caveat is: you must believe it *first* before it becomes manifest. You don't need me to tell you—*this is a tall order*! Because when you don't have what you want, or can't *see* it happening, it's hard to hold a belief that it's already true. It feels like a lie because in reality, it's not yet true and you *know* that it's not yet true.

So, what's the *other* secret—the untold key—to the law of attraction's "believe-receive" principle? How can you believe your affirmations if they're not yet true? *Hmmm...*

What if we switched two letters in the word "belief" (the "e" and the "f") so that it became "belife"? That is, "be Life." And—while you might prefer to say God or Lord, consider just for this purpose using my favorite name for the Creator, which is "Life" with a capital "L." What I'm getting at—*which is the key to believing*—is to just "be Life," or you might say "be Creator." And *how*, you might ask, does this help you to believe your affirmations?

Your happiness and your success are not found in what you want, but rather in what you will create. You are here to create and you have a purpose. *Be* your very purpose for manifesting into this life. Be confident that you have a purpose to add something to the evolution of humanity; the Creator created you to fulfill your purpose. Life wants for you what you want for you.

And so, let's revise—and *complete the code for*—the law of attraction's believe-receive formula of manifestation from "You Believe, Then You Receive" to "You Be Life, Then You Receive." (Or you can think of it specifically as "You Be The Creator, Then You Receive.") Who's "The Creator" in you? Why, my darling, She's your Higher-Self! Be that. Fully step into you; you as Creator. Be *that*, and you will receive what is meant for you and what you need to fulfill your purpose.

When you know with total sincerity that you are not just pretending, but rather you're a human, being the Creator that your Higher-Self set out to be—when you know that you *are* your Higher-Self on the journey of becoming—then you should quite effortlessly and with conviction believe in your powerful and divinely inspired affirmations.

You are a powerful manifestor. "I am _____ (fill in your dream)." Tell yourself, "What I seek, seeks me." Re-visit your Breathtaking Agreement With Life; it's not just what you *do*, it's what you *are*. In your heart-of-hearts, you already know this to be true. Your heart-of-hearts knows who you really are and it's not the person who makes mistakes, fails, hurts, and struggles, but it's the Selfhood that your soul *is* and knows to be. Trust in this; Be Life Itself, and Receive.

You see, that visualization tool that I carried in my wallet was not about receiving a million dollars; it was an affirmation to myself of my purpose and my usefulness to others with regard to my talents, intentions, and contributions. What really happened that day at the border—*by the magic of viral energy*—was that, over time, I had affirmed to myself through several visualization techniques that I had a purpose in this world that would be of benefit to others. Getting detained at the border was the impetus (*the force or energy with which a body moves*) for me to start a whole new chapter in my life with opportunities beyond my dreams.

When you remember that you are in an agreement with all of Life— that your purpose is a precious remembrance and that Life is moving the resources to fulfill that agreement—it then becomes much easier to believe your powerful affirmations.

You believe by being.

CHAPTER EIGHT:

RECALCULATING

Are You There Yet?

I returned home again for a short stretch when I was nineteen, before moving out for good into my first real apartment (where I paid rent and everything). One night, my dad was up late having an asthma attack. (He was sick with asthma since his mid-twenties.) I sat in the living room with my dad, both to keep an eye on him and also because we liked to philosophize and debate life, love, and even death.

"I know we are supposed to believe in Heaven, but I don't know what I believe," I opened the conversation.

After a pause, Dad took a deep breath and began speaking in a slow and soft tone. "I want to tell you something that I haven't told anyone in many years. Heck, the only person I have ever told this story to is your mother," he started. (*He had my attention.*) I didn't say a word and he continued: "It happened when I was in my early twenties. You were a baby. It was back when I was in the hospital for the worst part of two years. On this night when I arrived, the doctors on duty had had enough of me. They mocked me a little and joked to each other, 'Here's *that guy* again….' They put me on a gurney and rolled me into an old examination room at the end of the hall. I guess you could say that the room was out of service for some time. It seemed like they thought I should just snap out of it," he said as he wheezed and took in short gulps of air. "I was there only a few minutes, when all of a sudden I was looking down at a frail man who was lying still in a bed. I kind of thought the guy looked familiar. Then I recognized that it was me; I was looking down at my own body from above. And just then I knew that I was dead, although I had no emotion at all about seeing my body like that. What I knew as myself was still aware. My consciousness was exactly the same as it was in my body, but I had no pain and no concern at all for the outcome of the scene beneath me. Then a nurse came into the room, saw that I was breathless, and urgently called in two doctors. I saw her facial expression and even heard her gasp. I floated at the ceiling and overheard the surprised doctors say, 'He's dead!' Just like that—they used the word 'dead.' They were in a panic and started to discuss what their story would be about my death. They discussed it at length and I listened, but I had no judgment of them whatsoever, or even sympathy for myself. I knew I was dead, but I had no regrets, no hard feelings or disappointment. I was certainly thinking in the very same way I am now but had no concern of earthly things at all. I was already detached. It was already behind me," he plainly told me. (*All I could do was blink and wait for more.*)

Dad continued, "Then my awareness shifted to a power and presence far greater than the events in that room. At the ceiling of the room a light opened up and I was instantly enveloped in a warm, golden-yellow light. I noticed that the light was coming from not just an opening, but a swirling vortex. Without effort, I moved into the light. I could see it was very bright and it felt warm on me."

I nodded again and kept quiet to hear more. (*Wow. He thought, saw, and felt!*)

"Then, *voom*! Just like that, I was traveling at great speed going up on a forty-five-degree angle. It was a rotating current. It appeared like a tunnel and there was a light at the end. It turned slowly, drawing me in quickly like I was being pulled by a magnet. Around me were the 'walls' of this tunnel or 'vortex,' made of a smoky grey-black, gaseous cloudy mass. I was moving towards a powerful light radiating a bright golden glow coming from a doorway—an actual doorway—at the end of the tunnel. It was total peace, love, and pure contentment. There was nowhere else that I wanted to be, and simply nothing to be wanted," he gushed like a boy in love; not at all typical of the vernacular or expressions my dad typically displayed. "I wanted only to completely move into it. I knew that if I could just get through that door, it would be Heaven. My goal was to get through the door."

"Did you?" I asked as if I couldn't wait another second to find out what happened.

"No. Instantly and without journey or ceremony I found myself back in my body. Back in grave pain," he was visibly saddened at the remembrance. He was sad that he couldn't stay there. Wherever "there" is. He was back in that chilly hospital room. "Now I was surrounded by doctors who suddenly seemed happy to see me." He stopped for a moment and then said, "Some people who have not had the experience themselves will say that it's caused by a chemical reaction in the brain at the time of death. That's all crap. I know exactly what I experienced and it's more real than what we know here on Earth. I came back to finish something. God's plan for me had not yet played out." Those last words struck me hard and then lingered in the room.

Neither of us had noticed when dad's asthma attack quit, yet now he was freely breathing. I too was transformed and sat stunned. A whale of an epiphany washed over me—I could run away from home, but I couldn't run away from my purpose.

For me, the testimony from my father was more than enough proof of life-after-death. From that day forward, I believed it without question. And I wanted to search for proof that I could share with others, beyond the thousands or millions of firsthand accounts throughout history of near-death experiences (NDEs). The knowingness of our spirit living on beyond the body changed everything for me—I mean, everything! There was now a greater purpose to it all. Life is hard and until that conversation with my dad, I had struggled with the burden of finding life's greater purpose and making it worthwhile. Now, I was eager to share my new excitement with others and to find further proof of Spirit for those who wouldn't accept a secondhand account. I knew that I needed to reconcile the spirit's travel with science, and though I was just nineteen-years-old, my curiosity and need to soak up more on the subject was insatiable. I wanted to—no, I *needed* to—understand how the soul journeys and why. So, I started reading.

I have discovered that many answers to my deepest spiritual questions can be found in understanding the nature of energy, physics, and quantum mechanics. Spirituality and science speak different languages, yet often are not at odds after all. So, if you're a science-buff who might balk at stories like my dad's NDE, just hold up before you dismiss the idea of the movement of the soul—or you may call it "consciousness" if you like—outside of the physical body.

In theory, you (your selfhood, that energy pattern that is your consciousness) could teleport around the globe because your energy is a unique presence like a fingerprint. (*You would not be far off track to think Star Trek Transporter here.*) You see, there is your body, and then there is your unique energetic self. In the quantum field, teleportation has already been done. (Yes, seriously.) It was the first decade of the twenty-first-century when researchers quantum teleported light particles (photons) a distance of thirteen kilometers; then ninety-seven kilometers; and in

2011, European researchers quantum teleported protons from one island to another—over 143 kilometers apart—between two Canary Islands. (*Yep, it has happened.*)

How it works is that they can move the particle from one place to another by copying its energetic information (that energy fingerprint), then they pop it to another far-off location by borrowing the energy patterns of entangled twin particles—one at the start location and one at the destination. That's the simple version. (*Look, I didn't make this up, I'm just giving it to you in easy speak.* And if you're interested, this twinning is called "Quantum Entanglement.") Once copied, the original form falls away to nothing but dust, and poof—the particle has jumped from one place to another in an instant! Yes, quantum teleportation is not only possible—it's done.

Just like those wanderlust particles, the essence that is you is energetic information, or energetic intelligence; not a physical form or body. Let's call that energetic information your "spirit." The virality of energy says that your spirit can, and does, move from dust to dust. As described in my dad's near-death experience, even without our physical bodies, we still have life, intelligence, consciousness, and feelings akin to physical sensations.

So then, what's the point of the journey in this body? Somewhere along the way, all of Life decided that we wanted to slow down our powerful energetic Selfhood in order to experience our potential—what we would create. Only through your doubts and fears do you discover and decide who you are. Are you strong when tested, persistent through challenges, brave even when you're afraid? Do you embrace the path that you chose? What is it that you will create in this body, in this life? How will you impact Life on Earth? How will you experience the love of Earth, both Her physicality and her soul? How will you contribute to mankind's spiritual evolution as we journey to Heaven on Earth?

Well, I suppose that you wouldn't know if you directly jumped to the destination. So, rather than ask if you are there yet, or wish for the struggle to be over, explore the purpose of your journey.

New GPS Navigation for Sleepwalkers

You might have been raised and acculturated to believe that it offends God when you mess up. Those ideas were implanted very early on in human evolution and have been passed down—until now. Not long after early mankind turned grunts into first languages, the idea of multiple gods was invented. This gave mankind reasons as to why it rained too much or not enough. Early humans knew *they* had no power over the weather and so they wanted to attribute power elsewhere. Much later in our history, the rule of one God became popular. The Egyptian pharaoh, Akhenaten, was the founder of monotheism; this cleared up allegiances to other figureheads and placed him as the direct and only bridge and access between God and the people. (Rather handy, actually.) Yet, whether one or many, we have become exceedingly comfortable with the idea of a deity controlling our fate and dishing out punishments when we've disobeyed or sinned.

But today, we are at the precipice of a new era in our evolution. We are just now starting to move from power-based thinking to creation-based thinking. We are entering an age when science and spirituality agree to a partnership, consequently evolving religion as we know it. The need to have power over others and to control resources will soon fade and we will be governed and fueled from within. We will stop hurting others and harming our environment because we will know that these actions are counterintuitive to our goals and success as a species. Nowadays, we call those negative actions, "sins."

Here's an analogy that explains the truth about **God's Position on Sin**. Imagine that you're in your car and you've decided to drive from Chicago, Illinois, to Salt Lake City, Utah. It's just under a twenty-one-hour drive if you don't take a break, or the scenic route, or get lost. So, the very first thing you do, before stopping for coffee and gas, is set your GPS. It's quite a journey, so thank goodness you have your trusty navigation system.

When you take a wrong turn and get off track (or sidetracked to buy a coffee or lunch or to take a break), your **GPS** doesn't shout, "You idiot! Now look what you've done!" It only says, "Recalculating," as it illuminates another way.

Well, Life kind of works like that, too. Maybe you've been sleepwalking through life and have no idea why you are where you are. Maybe when you make mistakes, you're very hard on yourself. How about when you have *really* messed up—when you've ruined an opportunity, waited too long, hurt somebody, or been guilty of a wrongdoing? Now, consider this: all choices lead to different roads with the same ultimate destination; some are just longer routes than others.

Let's take it further. Our "mistakes" are often just choices that are not judged by the Creator—at least not in the way that we have come to think of as the dreaded "wrath of God"—but are expressions of free-will which might delay your soul's destination while creating your soul's evolution. Some choices don't even delay your destination. While they do have cause and effect, like everything in life, they are simply your chosen journey and not a sin. Let's look at the topic of so-called "sexual sins" as an example: How young is too young? Is sex before marriage a minor sin, a social-taboo, or an action that could get you sent to Hell? Who gets to decide this—why should anyone have the power to suppress the sexual energy of another as it pertains to their own body and selfhood?

Then, what about expressions of selfhood that have nothing at all to do with sin, mistakes, or even choices? To be clear, let's separate the topic of sex from the topic of gender identity, including same-sex relationships, transgender, and nonbinary self-identities. After all, who are you to say how someone else should relate to and express their selfhood? The only body that you have domain over is your own.

It's hard to let go of being the watchman over other people's journeys, huh? Certainly. Yet, once you start living this way, you'll find it's a mindset (or a *soulset*) that's very enlightening. Now, instead of focusing on others' journeys, let's talk about *you* and what you see as your wrongdoings. In addition to your own sins, there's also the self-righteous judgment that you project towards others. This heavy viral energy may be weighing you down, but is it too late for you to be the person that your soul intended?

Maybe the word "sin" is too intense for many of your actions, judgments, and mere hiccups. Instead, think of "sin" as a catchall for your poor choices, wasted time, hurts, and mistakes of all kinds—your wrong turns.

Your GPS always works the exact same way; it can be counted on. No matter how many times you get turned around or take a detour, your GPS calmly says, "Recalculating," in the same steady tone, and once more suggests another way to get you where you said you wanted to go.

But guess what? You still have to decide on a destination, declare that destination (if you want to go places, don't keep it to yourself), make directional choices, choose speeds and routes, push the gas, and actually turn the wheel. Yikes! Wouldn't it be easier if your life was predetermined, or determined by an outside source? Easier, maybe—but that's not free will and it isn't how it works. Your GPS is always available and patiently ready to guide, but you must take action, put one foot in front of the other, and even take some chances.

After all, if you take the long-road for a while or get turned in circles by making poor choices (or by stagnating and not making choices at all), you can always recalculate. And while you might lose some time, you gain a journey to your heart's desire. Let your intuition be your best guidance system. Intuition is the living mind of God installed in you, to get you where you declare you want to go. If you listen, your intuition will give you the answers to your questions while on this journey. Program your GPS to "Highest Soulset"—it's like the endless potential of your brilliant mindset, but better! At every choice, automatically check in with your soulset: your higher voice, your Higher-Self. What does your gut instinct tell you? Practicing automatic writing is also helpful: Write down or type your question, then write the answer. Don't think on it too long; just freely write whatever comes to you from your soulset rather than your mindset.

You will get "there"—to your purpose that is—no matter how many detours you take, over how many lifetimes you travel, and whether or not you take the scenic route. And you *can* get there from here.

The Crossroads of Providence Street and Action Lane

I was helped by a clerk named Adam when I visited the local Department of Motor Vehicles office to get a new driver's license after Burt and I moved from South Carolina to Florida. Although the office was crowded and noisy, Adam was cheerful and so I asked him if he enjoyed his job at the DMV. Adam told me about his father who had been a residential roofer, working construction jobs his whole life, until he recently died at just sixty years old before he even really followed his true dreams. Adam explained that he would be sure to follow his dreams, "God willing," and that his job at the DMV was not his true passion; "God willing," he wanted to be in broadcasting. I then mentioned my background in television, and Adam opened up even more. While he had spent a couple years researching various career paths and universities for his broadcast journalism dream, he didn't see the opportunities lining up quite yet. He figured that it wasn't the right time to move on his dream, and "God willing," it would happen soon. Finally, I said, "Adam, God *is* willing. Just by giving you the dream and the passion, God is willing. But you have to take action and make it happen."

Are you waiting for a divine answer to your problems or questions? Do you believe that things in your life will work out "as they should," because you are not The One making the plans for your life? Are you praying for a result or a change in your circumstances, though not doing the work or taking the action to get it?

In the dictionary, the definition of "Providence" is: "The foreseeing care and guidance of God or nature over the creatures of the earth; God, especially when conceived as omnisciently directing the universe and the affairs of humankind with wise benevolence; provident or prudent management of resources, prudence; and foresight, provident care." Okay, so it's clear from this definition that Providence is another beautiful name for God, and it is also what God *does*.

Here's a great parable by an unknown author that exemplifies the crossroads of providence and action: While out to sea, a large boat became shipwrecked and there was only a single survivor. This man prayed and asked God to save his life. Soon thereafter, another boat came by and offered the man some help. "No thanks," he said. "I'm waiting for God to save me." The people on the boat shrugged their shoulders and continued. As the man became more deeply concerned, another boat came by. Again, the people aboard offered this man some help, and again he politely declined. "I'm waiting for God to save me," he said again. After some time, the man drowned. Upon reaching Heaven, the man asked God, "Why did you let me die? Why didn't you answer my prayers?" God said, "I sent you two boats!"

Providence is yours to tap into, but it still requires you to take action. And when you have taken action, you then have to also take the opportunity. Sometimes you are in disbelief when a great opportunity comes along—you're not sure if you should jump in and accept it. Why? Because it seems too good to be true. (Or, because—maybe, just maybe—an even *better* opportunity is coming?) And yet, I bet that if you really stopped and thought about it, the opportunity didn't come out of thin air; you have worked towards it, put energy out in its direction, and now something has shown up to answer the call, so to speak.

Your search for meaning, purpose, and true love has brought you to the crossroads of Providence Street and Action Lane. Perhaps that intersection is another way of saying that God helps those who help themselves. Providence Street and Action Lane is an exciting place to be. You need only put your energy into the latter—that's the beauty of the crossroads.

Is Someone Undermining Your Dreams?

Towards the end of the medieval period—or middle ages—undermining was a method for bringing down a castle's curtain wall by digging a tunnel under the surrounding protective wall. The tunnel would then be intentionally collapsed, compromising the fortress walls and foundation below the tower or castle itself. Trained soldiers called "sappers" did the undermining. (Sounds like a fitting name.) And by the way, these tunnels weren't dug overnight; if you were undermined, it was going on for a long time and it went unnoticed. However, if the king became aware of the sappers' undermining, he would rapidly stop it and fortify the wall.

To undermine a person is kind of the same thing—to compromise one's protective deflector shield. Today's definition of undermining is: "To damage or weaken (someone or something), especially gradually or insidiously."

So, here you are. It feels like the bottom fell out again. Some sapper (or Stage Five Energy Sucker!) has attacked your dreams and left you feeling deflated. If you're ruminating over what happened, stop doing that. If you're crying over the fight, or blaming someone else, stop doing that. If you can't take any more, stop taking any more.

The undermining of your dreams, goals, milestones, and beliefs is negative and heavy viral energy that you don't have to let in. Think of it like this: if someone were trying to hand you an apple, maybe one with a big fat worm in it, and you didn't care for the apple, you would just wince and say, "Thank you, I'm going to pass on the offer."

Or, let's say that you were enjoying a day in the park, just sitting on a bench in the sunshine. You notice someone scooping their dog's doo-doo and placing it in a bag. Then, rather boldly, they walk right over to the bench where you're seated and attempt to hand you the steaming bag of their dog's poop. Now, *I'm just guessing here*, but I bet you would not hesitate to say, "You can keep that! I do *not* accept it."

You need not accept undermining any more than you would accept an apple with a worm or a hot load of doo-doo. The same response works very well: "I do not accept that."

As it relates to your dreams, undermining often comes from someone whom you were hoping would—finally—acknowledge your accomplishment, support your goal or passion, be proud of you, and validate you in your journey. It's important for you to know the difference between healthy feedback and foundation-shattering undermining. Some people just don't have a clue how to support you or your dreams, and they are often a family member or close friend. If you really peeled back the onion, you might find that they are either jealous of your dreams, in fear that they are losing something because of who you are becoming, or fearful that your choices are putting you in peril in some way. So, that's what's going on with them; it doesn't need to be your experience just because it's theirs. If it doesn't feel good, you don't have to internalize other people's beliefs or their opinions—you can plainly choose not to accept it.

When others attempt to undermine you, let them know that the jig's up and you're not having it. Keep your dreams sacred from those who are unable to support your vision.

Disallow these sappers to steal your power simply by letting them know that you don't accept undermining. You will regain your foundation and avoid the same old implosions of your past.

In responding to sappers, keep in mind that undermining is often a battle over power and who will come out on top. Don't wish to undermine their energy in return; each side thinks they are right and undermining the sappers will not get you closer to what you want and need. You see, it does not serve your empowerment to enrage others with your response. An emotion-based response lets the other person win because they're taking (sapping) your energy and they know it. Let's practice some responses to those who attempt to undermine you. As we try these out, also note that when facing a sapper in your life, leave out the word "but"—it's a word that has a way of stirring the pot that, trust me, you don't want to stir. You can use these replacements to the word "but": "yet," "and," "at the same time," or "still." Here are several suggestions for ways that you might respond to a sapper in order to safeguard your creation energy and fortify your foundation:

"While I appreciate you wanting to provide feedback, *at the same time* I don't accept negativity around the matter of my dreams, and so I am not in a place where I will internalize other people's doubts and fears."

"We have some areas of our core beliefs that are not exactly aligned with one another, *and* that's okay. I will not argue with you on what's so foundational to who you are, and I do not engage with any attempt to disempower my beliefs either."

"You might not agree with me and I know that this is hard for you. *Yet*, I'm not asking for permission about what I choose to create."

"I do not accept anyone's attempt to undermine my dreams or accomplishments."

"It feels as though you are trying to disempower me. I had hoped that you would support my dreams. *Still*, with or without your support, I know that I am serving my highest and intended purpose."

"I admire your passion for what you believe in, and *yet* I have to tell you that it comes off as insularly. I have my own ideas and experiences that support my beliefs. I think it's okay that we respectfully agree to disagree."

"I'm sure your intention is to be helpful. *Yet*, what I'm hearing is about your own beliefs and ideas, which are wonderful for you. *At the same time*, I am going to follow my truth and I have every valid reason to know that I am on the right path."

You can cut off the access that energy-sappers have to you. Take responsibility and acknowledge that this didn't exactly happen overnight; you've let other people undermine you in the past. They might believe that there is a weakness in you at which they can chip away. Not anymore. Disengage their access to your creation power. Stop emotionally reacting to other people's doubts and fears. Do not accept being dejected from your own dreams, and practice a thoughtful response to those who would, even if unwittingly, undermine you and your vision.

The Upper Hand

Fundamental to the human experience—the way that we have created it thus far— and systematic throughout our culture, is the (false) driving belief that we get our personal power (creation fuel) from others by taking it from them. We want to get the better of others before they get the better of us, so we try to disempower them by stealing their momentum, confidence, beauty, energy, and resources. That's right—not many of us are exempt from a desire and effort to gain the upper hand over others, and we do this through force, violence, intimidation, withholding (love, attention, time, or information), righteousness, ridicule, and outwitting. It's a struggle for dominance that is going on inside you and all around you. It plays out both in grand schemes and everyday trifling.

For my dad, the early 2000s was a time of inner-corporation battles and jockeying for power and dominance. The company that he dearly labored for had been his own—he started the business years before and later sold it to an international corporate conglomerate that kept him on as the Vice President. From the moment he relinquished the reigns, Dad fought to maintain his way of doing things. Some newcomers wanted him out entirely, and perhaps wanted to unseat him as the figurehead of the company. One man led this charge and Dad says that he perceptibly and tangibly felt the *energy* of this work-nemesis "like a wave" of heaviness or denseness coming towards him as the man approached from across a room. The power-struggle between the two was palpable and in time, my dad was out, and the other man assumed his role.

Attempts to undermine are customary in the corporate world and political arena, but rehearsal starts young.

After trying on more than a dozen formal dresses with great excitement, sixteen-year-old Alice picked out a lovely floor-length pale-yellow gown for her prom. It was the dress of her dreams and a little more expensive than her parents' budget, so Alice gladly paid a third of the cost out of her own savings from her part-time job. To her, it was well worth it. She was so thrilled about the dress that she decided to post a sneak peek photo of herself in the dress on her Instagram. Within moments, her post received dozens of "likes" from friends and classmates, however something shadowed Alice's joy. A close friend snapped a screenshot of Alice's post and reposted it to her entire social network with the caption: "Have you ever seen an uglier prom dress?" Alice was devastated; she cried for a solid day and then returned the dress. There was a period when she and her so-called friend didn't speak, but they eventually talked it out and made up. The two girls were so similar in their appearance that people would often ask if they were sisters, or even twins. To Alice, the cruel act was inexplicable; as for her friend, it was unexplainable. For the magic of viral energy, it was a clear case of seeking the upper hand. In the end, Alice changed her outlook and decided not to acquiesce to her friend's embarrassing criticism—she went back to the store and entirely with her own money, she re-purchased her dream prom dress; the very same one.

Our need for the upper hand is created from our fear that we are less, or could become less, and so we believe that we have to make ourselves more than others. Every one of the world's problems would instantly cease if we stopped seeking the upper hand over others. All of the war, turmoil, starvation, hate, fear, oppression, want, jealousy, envy, blame, perfectionism, greed, pollution, and using and abusing, are all by-products of our need for the upper hand.

Dominance is perpetuated even in many religious traditions. In the Old Testament of the Bible—the King James Bible, the English Standard Version, and the New International Version—God said, "Let us make man in our image, after our likeness. And let them have dominion over the fish of the sea and over the birds of the heavens and over the livestock and over all the earth and over every creeping thing that creeps on the earth," (Gen 1:26). (*Oh, the pain that word "dominion" has caused.*) Other versions of the Bible use the words "reign" and "rule" as opposed to "dominance."

Yet, how do you know that God said those words in *any* of the many versions? The contents of the Bible, particularly the Old Testament, began as stories told by word of mouth thousands of years ago, and were passed from generation to generation. Eventually, these stories were chipped into stone and then translated into Hebrew and some Biblical Aramaic, then into many languages and versions. Though, none of these versions was "The Bible" just yet; they were countless scrolls scattered around several countries, by several religious sects. It was at the First Council of Nicaea, in 325 AD, that early Christians convened to decide what to include in the first edition of what would be "The Bible." From then until modern times, the Bible has undergone many language translations, allowing further opportunities for the Word of God to receive subtle variations due to the range of meanings in comparable words from language to language.

In Genesis, chapter one, verse twenty-six, the words "dominance," "dominion," "reign," and "rule," are a few that were selected from the limited words available in the English language to communicate what God intended way back when. At present, we are not only stuck with the word "dominance" in many of our religious teachings, *we like it*—it gives us a free pass for much torture, cruelty, and imbalance that we thrust upon the animal kingdom, the environment, and the earth herself. In fact, condoning and perpetuating the mindset of dominance has been the primary source of all pain and turmoil that mankind inflicts on each other, too. It might help to consider that the original word used by God, the Creator of all of Heaven and Earth and the whole of the natural world, was indeed for us to act in accordance with creation through "guardianship" (the position of protecting or defending something), or "stewardship" (the job of taking care of something)—"And let them have *guardianship* and *stewardship* over the fish of the sea and over the birds of the heavens and over the livestock and over all the earth and over every creeping thing that creeps on the earth." I believe that these words are much closer to the intended Word of God. After all, how could anyone possibly make an enlightened case for a God who would create animals and the natural world, only to turn them over to be harmed, hurt, bludgeoned, and poisoned at our impulse or for our gluttony or greed? Not—A—Chance. To say that this is God's intended directive is nothing short of blasphemy.

When we *get* this, this one shift in understanding, we will end all of our suffering. When we *get* this and no longer invent ways to absolve our backwards practices and beliefs, we will be in balance and at peace. When we *get* that our efforts for the upper hand are worthless and against everything for which we were made, we will become the enlightened ones.

PART THREE:

INTERFERENCE: IT'S YOUR CALL

CHAPTER NINE:

THE MAGIC OF GREAT RELATIONSHIPS

The Naked Truth

Well then, do you want to know how to find and keep a true-love relationship? Here it is, sans sugarcoating: stop BSing yourself and others about who you are (and what you want). And I say that in the nicest possible way, because who you are is really great!

Monica was a serial live-in girlfriend. She had several long relationships and got close to marriage more than once, yet the relationships would inevitably end because the men just couldn't see themselves marrying her.

One man even said it very clearly: "Every time I go to propose, there's just something *off*."

Monica was a good person and a great catch, but she was very focused on manipulating her guy into marriage. She wanted him to see her as light-hearted, fun, and morally and intellectually superior. She played the role of what she *thought* would enamor her boyfriend, yet glimpses of another side of her seeped out here and there, leaving him feeling that something was "off." Monica was holding pieces of herself—all of what she believed to be imperfect or less desirable—in contempt.

Maybe you know someone who is an amazing catch, yet they just can't seem to turn dating into a commitment. They're always going on first dates or stretches of a few weeks or months of dating. But then, they report that "it just didn't work out"—the other person was just not for them. And maybe you know someone who tends to have relationships that last even a year or more, and then they still fall apart. (*It could be that that person is you.*)

In nearly every case like this, the primary issue that keeps someone from the stability and love of a long-term relationship lies in the fact that they refuse to let suitors see the real them and/or they are not being honest about what they really want in a relationship.

Dating is very confusing these days. There's an entire population of single people that are much more concerned with swiping left or right than they are about organic interactions, how they engage with people face-to-face, and what energetic impressions they're giving off. Dating culture today has morphed into the popular acceptance of "hooking up" in place of traditional courting.

More often than not, people don't go on traditional dates anymore because women have bought into (and have actually created) the new norm of ladies paying for dinner or splitting the bill. *Before you freak out about women's liberation, read on...*

It all started with our desire to be taken seriously, to be in control, to be treated equally, and to live in fairness. These are all fabulous and necessary advancements in gender roles, however, what ensued was colossal date-night awkwardness when the dreaded check arrived to the table. Men didn't know if women truly wanted to pay as a stand of equality, or if they secretly wanted the man to insist on covering the check as a show of care and chivalry. Women felt that they were doing the modern and expected gesture by paying, then later felt less than revered whenever a man accepted the offer. (I've informally polled dozens and dozens of women from different backgrounds and of various ages, and what they tell me—even the most independent of women—is that in their tender and yearning-for-love hearts, they feel devalued when men don't put up a fight at check-time and provide for them.)

And so, romance was replaced by discomfort. The more men were convinced that women wished to pay for dates (or go "dutch"), the more men pulled back from their inclination to be caretakers. The more confusion and discomfort that grew (Who pays? Who drives?), the easier it got to drop dating and romance and go directly to sex. As it got easier to dismiss serendipitous "meet-cutes" and instead online shop through dating apps and platforms that offer drama-free ways to find exactly what you're looking for—including custom ordering a mate from their hair color to their income level—the "dating" process evolved and completely negated the wondrous magic of a chance spark or energetic connection.

All of this has created a dating culture in which men no longer get to wine and dine and chase and court women (which they love to do, by the way), and instead of working to earn the "rare diamond," it all became too easy for men, and therefore unfulfilling. Like it or not, here's the bottom line: a man imprints on a woman to the degree to which he has to invest time and attention (and even money) into earning the woman's affection. It's just the way it is. But nowadays, we're all lying to ourselves and to each other about what we *really* want.

So, who will drop the pretense first? Perhaps now is a good time to start being honest about what you would *really* love in a mate. Though let's be clear (in case you didn't get the inference)—your happiness in a relationship has very little to do with who pays for a dinner date and yet has everything to do with being true-faced.

To get what you wish for, you need to own what you want.
Whatever that is for you.

For as many decades as we've had images of humans and their interactions projected on "silver screens" and "boob tubes," we've had the inclination to measure ourselves against those characters of fantasy. With the emergence of social media, the last couple of decades have seen us epidemically mirroring our idols in such extreme ways that our culture has descended into a self-image and selfie tailspin. Many women (and men too, yet women are particularly vulnerable) claim perfectionism (well, somebody's version of what a perfect woman should be) or some other persona that allows them to disown their true selves and separate from genuine closeness with anyone for fear they expose their real imperfect selfness. In the end, many women would rather run from the relationship than let the other person see who they really are. It's like they're in a leaky boat full of holes and decide to swim from life raft to life raft (person to person) in a search for dependable buoyancy (unconditional love). Yet, unconditional love is only possible when you're being true to yourself. I know so many women who announce that they are a "perfectionist" like it's a badge of honor, as though aligning themselves with the word "perfect" somehow makes them perfect. In truth, striving to be perfect is energetic self-sabotage.

Today, perfectionism is almost like a disease and it's affecting younger and younger women and girls more than in any previous generation. I wondered if this is something that girls do only to themselves and each other, or does society as a whole perhaps play a role in this fixation on female perfectionism? I asked Dr. Stephen Hinshaw, Ph.D., Chair of the Department of Psychology, University of California, Berkeley, and author of the bestselling book, *The Triple Bind: Saving Our Teenage Girls from*

Today's Pressures. He said that girls are now expected to be excellent at everything and this has set up unrealistic expectations. It is the accidental backside (negative effects, basically) of encouraging girls to realize that they indeed can do anything they want to do, and somehow, we are accidentally sending the message that girls should be able to do *everything*, perfectly.

Perfectionism is in actuality a fear of loss, failure, and rejection, and so a perfectionist wants everything to be and stay perfect. They tend to see other people's lives as better and pristine, unspoiled by failures, loss, and bad behavior. A perfectionist feels at a disadvantage when they have behaved badly in front of someone else, especially if they are dating them. They believe that being above such moments is their armor. Yet, life is about personal evolution, and so perfectionism is operating in a falsehood; it's the perfect lie because no one is perfect.

It's okay to fail a test. It's okay to have a bad day or even to behave badly. It's okay to burn dinner and follow it up with a meltdown. It happens. It doesn't mean that the person you're dating will dump you. (And if they do, trust me, they weren't in it for the long haul anyway.)

Years ago, I had a boyfriend break up with me after I had a weekend-long meltdown while we were on vacation. I recall that I was very hormonal and acted like both a jealous nut and a spoiled brat. He broke up with me right there in the hallway outside of our hotel room. To add insult to injury, I went home alone while he stayed the last two days of our vacation on his own. He was actually a great guy whom I admired and respected, and so I was devastated by the loss. Now, years later, I can see it much more clearly. Sure, at that time I still had a lot of maturing to do, but the truth was, he just wasn't the one that would unconditionally love me.

But how do you decipher the difference between your insecurities and your standards?

My friend Katie moved in with her boyfriend, Andrew, whom she had been dating for six months. Andrew had a group of friends that included both men and women: two of his girl friends regularly called and texted him with no boundaries whatsoever regarding the commitment that he had made with Katie. By Andrew's own admission, one of the girls had previously been his "movie-and-snuggle-buddy-on-a-drunk-night friend"—that is, before he met Katie. The steady contact to and from these other women had been tolerable to Katie in the beginning of the relationship—to clarify, she believed she had no choice but to tolerate it—however, since she and Andrew had moved in together, Andrew's steady contact with his female friends had Katie feeling insecure. She started polling her friends for advice and each and every girlfriend (notably, all single ladies) had the identical feedback: be a "cool girlfriend" and let it go unchecked. They said things like, "You can't tell him who to be friends with," and, "Today, there's no such thing as a true gentleman or a fairytale romance," and, "Everyone has friends of the opposite sex; you have to accept it. Guys like cool women, not jealous women."

Uh…no. Ladies, that kind of advice is the biggest lie around, and the worst part—it comes from other women! A strong woman knows that she has a right to voice her deal breakers. Playing the role of "cool modern girlfriend" will only get you "cool modern singleton."

As for Katie, despite the bad advice from her girlfriends, she let Andrew know that his communication with girl friends and old snuggle-buddies felt disrespectful to her. Andrew understood and admitted that if the shoe were on the other foot, he wouldn't like it either. When Katie finally communicated her needs and boundaries to Andrew, he very quickly decided that Katie's happiness was tied in with his own happiness. He got his other relationships in order and gave Katie the respect she needed, and that anyone would want.

Most often, people do what they want to do and if no one complains, they'll keep doing it. But, when it comes to love, men fall in love with women who have standards. The thing is, by not being your true self no one can really know you. Where true love is concerned, the only fairytale is the one that you try to project with a "cool" version of you that doesn't really exist. That's the big lie that has infected the current population of actively dating individuals, and it won't get you what you want. In actuality, there is no such thing as a successful lie, or even a successful cover-up or misleading omission. Lying can confuse at best, yet on a subconscious (energetic) level, other people always know when your words—even your best appearances—are incongruent with the truth. (If you're feeling insecure in your relationship, your insecurity is not hidden from anyone.) In fact, it won't be long before lying is obsolete. As mankind evolves to higher levels of consciousness, the intention to deceive does not have the desired effect and is therefore rendered useless. So, don't waste your energy; just be you, with all of your imperfections and "uncoolness."

As William Shakespeare rightly declared, "To thine own self be true." Claim your worth, just as you are. You don't have to accept guilt or be a hiding place for someone else's insecurity and doubt. You don't have to be perfect, or *try* to be perfect, or look perfect. You don't have to deploy a faux-you in order to insulate yourself from experiencing loss. Life responds to the quality of your true presence. It's only when you drop the facade that you truly open up to the love that you want.

Water Will Always Seek Its Own Level

Here's an interesting phenomenon: water will always seek its own level. It will trickle down rocks and slopes and rush to meet itself in a pool beneath a waterfall. It's not merely a gravity thing; even when suppressed on each side of a barrier such as a dam, water will forever press to resolve misalignment. (By the way, you are about sixty-five percent water.)

Cameron, a beautiful and successful realtor, visited her dentist's office and because her regular doctor was away, she had her checkup with a new dentist on staff. He made quite an impression on her. She felt like they had a "cosmic connection" (her words, not mine). So, she later did a little social media recon and learned that he was single. She returned to the office a few days later with thank-you-baked-goods for the office staff and had directly addressed a second prettily wrapped bundle to the cutie doctor, whom she was hoping to see again. He came out to the waiting area, thanked her for the banana bread, they spoke for fifteen minutes, and before she left, she gave him her business card with contact information for the second time. She fully believed that her "I'm Available" sign was clear and that he would soon be calling her for a date.

But he never did call. In fact, two weeks later, Cameron "popped in" to the dental office yet again (you've never seen teeth so clean), wearing her "sure-thing" body-hugging skirt and sweater. But when she passed her prey—*I mean, dentist*—in the hallway, Doctor Cutie deliberately avoided her. And while Cameron's phone number had already twice been hand-delivered like a hot pizza, Doctor Cutie just wasn't moved to dial, text, write, or contact her in any way. Cameron will likely never know why. That's just life and you don't always get to know why. But my guess is that she and Doctor Cutie were simply not on the same energy stratum.

Look, if someone wants to get a hold of you, they will. Period. To get a mate's attention, you don't have to make yourself as convenient as Uber Eats or parade yourself around wearing a pink tutu like a dancing bear. (Da dadada dada da da da!) Reality check: bears shouldn't dance; it's unnatural and it doesn't work.

I've been that dancing bear more times than I can count. I once dated a guy who had never before been camping and because I was a practiced outdoorswoman, I coerced him into a weekend camping trip. I believed it would bring us closer together, and so even though he expressed that he wasn't entirely comfortable in the great outdoors, I pushed for the adventure. This trip was definitely not car camping; it was real backwoods-style where you have to hike out a mile or so just to reach your campsite. I had all of the equipment any camper could need or want in my repertoire; therefore, I took care of packing every last bit of gear from the sleeping bags to the aluminum pots to the morning coffee and even the food for forty-eight hours of what was a miserable experience—mostly for him. I pitched the tent without any help while he took inventory of the rattlesnake nests nearby and searched for a number of other perilous creatures including ticks, which seemed to be of tremendous concern to him. I thought the trip was all good fun; he did not. He called me a week later to say that he had found a tick embedded in his butt crack, and by the way, he was breaking up with me. He gave me the best line that I've ever heard when being broken up with. And I mean it; it was truly a great line. He said, "I just don't feel it in my heart." *Well shoot,* I thought, *I can't argue with that!* We were simply not on level with each other.

I've probably experienced at least one of every kind of dating experience, including the infatuations with great promise (and promises) that just don't work out. Have you ever wanted someone who was just slightly out of reach? I have.

A number of years ago, I went to Hawaii with one of my best friends, Federica, for the wedding of her twin sister. After the wedding in Maui, we all flew to Oahu for the second half of the week. Another bestie of mine, Lisa, flew in from Canada and met up with me in Honolulu. She had rented a red convertible Mustang and we explored the island from Pearl Harbor to the North Shore. We ended up at a beach bar just in time for sunset over the sparkling Pacific Ocean. I recall that reggae music was playing and high flames from tiki torches dotted the blush-colored sand. Most of the bar was open-walled and guests overflowed from the under-roof area to the southwest-facing patio. The best part was (and this rarely occurs at any bar, anywhere) there were a few more men than women. Yippee!

That night, I met a man who was like a unicorn among men. Paul was very handsome with jet-black hair and green eyes. He was kind and intelligent, and he carried intriguing nobility about him. He was beautiful in every way and he seemed as dazzled with me as I was with him. We talked the night away and then he called a cab and safely returned my friend and me to our hotel. He had written his name and contact information on a cocktail napkin from the bar and when we were departing the cab, he placed it in my hand, looked deeply into my eyes and said goodbye. The next morning, I looked for the napkin, but it was just gone. Once we flew back home, I searched the Internet and couldn't find any phone number or email address for Paul. I only found some old news articles about his family, but nothing on him. Even so, I definitely didn't forget about him.

Then, a month later, I saw Paul's name in my email inbox. He somehow found me. From that day, we had a two-year long-distance romance, entirely through email love letters. But sadly, our lives were too different and there was no way to logistically make it work. I had moved from Canada to Tennessee and was busy trying to build a business from nothing. He was busy saving the endangered wildlife of his island home and managing various work projects. We ended our communication and carried on with our very separate lives.

I did see Paul one more time about four years later on another vacation to Hawaii. We held each other for two half days and one full night, talking about everything and listening to the late March rain hit the metal roof of his seaside cottage. And that was it. I could tell you a dozen reasons why it couldn't work between us—our religions and political views were completely unmatched, for starters—but the one reason that could not be overcome was that we were just not meant to be together in the real world. I called him a few days later from my house in Nashville and asked if he thought we could make it work, and when he hesitated, I said goodbye to him for the last time. And I meant it. I was ready to move on and I did.

Later that summer at a Country music honky-tonk in Nashville, I met Burton. Oh, Burt was everything that I had been hoping for in a man. Our affection was even more intense than anything I'd ever known, and much more real. Our love was deep, natural, and unguarded. Over the years, we've had our ups and downs; we even broke up twice before getting back together and then getting married. There are plenty of things that are not perfect in our life together, yet our equally matched love for and dedication to each other is not one of them. After dozens of relationships and heartbreaks, I finally know what it is to be in "true love."

When the fit is right and you're both on the same level, you'll know it. But if you're not on level with each other—for reasons that you might never know—it won't quite line up. It's a funny thing about unicorns—you can't really take one home.

Be Willing to Move On

I know, I know, I know. You don't want to hear that maybe it won't work out with so-and-so. You want someone to tell you how to get him to fall madly in love with you; how to become her number one priority; how to get him to claim you as his girlfriend; how to get them to come back to you; how to get her to be more attracted to you. However, it doesn't really work like that. You must be willing to say goodbye, although let me preface that by saying I don't believe that any advice from me or anyone else will bring you to see the reality of your relationship until you're ready. And that's okay. Author and Tibetan Buddhist, Pema Chödrön said, "Nothing ever goes away until it teaches us what we need to know." That's true, and it's also true that whatever is out of alignment will eventually go away.

Maybe your relationship has ended or is ending and you're hurting. Or maybe you've been single for way too long and you're lonely and weary from being on your own. It sucks to be alone, and yet you've been told by society to be as strong as oak, independent, and that you don't need a partner or companion. Frankly, that's ridiculous. You already know that to be alone is not what you want, or you wouldn't be reading this.

Maybe the trick is not to be strong as oak, but to be strong enough.

When my friend Natasha's landlord sold off her rental house and she needed a place to live, she ended up staying with her boyfriend for a while. But "a while" turned into seven years. They never took the relationship to the next level, they never shared money or bank accounts, and while she wanted to get married, Natasha's boyfriend was never going to one-day stumble on his undying love for her like tripping on a crack. "*Oops, I just fell in love with my girlfriend! Crikey, that came out of nowhere.*"

I said to her, "Pardon me, Natasha, while I'm a bit blunt, but please, get over your obsession with avoiding emotional pain and rip off that Band-Aid!"

Word to the wise: in the event that you haven't noticed, most men don't like to hurt women's feelings. A great number of men find it easier to just go ahead and do what they want to do and wait for you to eventually dump them. So, maybe you think that you've *never* been broken up with, right? Newsflash: this *is* being broken up with, just passively. Maybe now is a good time for you to start standing your ground. You deserve so much more, and if the two of you are meant to regroup and reunite, you will. Trust me, it is impossible for you to lose a guy who loves you with sincerity; not in ten days and not in ten years. Heck no. Any man who truly loves you will chase you, fight for you, and even if you break up with him, with utter certainty, he will move mountains to try to earn you back—if he truly loves you.

Being taken for granted happens to men, too. Scott is a man, divorced with two children, who was in love for more than five years with a woman named Heather. Yet, from Heather's perspective they were just friends. She got a lot out of the friendship: Scott was her beck-and-call-guy, her go-to companion when she didn't want to be alone, and he was endlessly reliable for errands and household fixes. Sounds like dating, right? Of course, that's what Scott thought (and hoped). Heather, on the other hand, was never going to install him as her boyfriend. She knew that he was wonderful in every way, but he didn't make her heart flutter. You could say that she was using him, but the reality is, he let her. Heather repeatedly made it clear that she only wanted friendship from Scott, but Scott found hope in her carrot-dangling and not in her words, and so he ignored every bit of evidence telling him to move on.

It sucks to be alone—that is, if you don't want to be alone—and so you sometimes make compromises with yourself in order to stay in a relationship that's not really working for you. Is it the fear of being alone, lack of self-respect, inability to accept rejection, a primal need to win, or some strange pride gained in martyring oneself for the cause of togetherness? Sure, perhaps one or more of these thoughts and patterns could apply. And that's what they are: habitual patterns of thoughts and actions. (Maybe you are just *used* to being treated as *less*.)

While this next one sounds like an urban legend, I can assure you that it's a true story because it happened to one of my closest girlfriends who I'll call "Sarah."

For over a year, Sarah had been dating a guy named Jake who was good-looking and charming, yet by his own choosing, he was living a life of *less* in every way. He had fixer-upper skills, yet he didn't value his things. His house was in a state of total disrepair: floorboards were rotting, light bulbs were out in most rooms, the roof leaked, and because of the constant dampness, there were mushrooms growing from his kitchen ceiling. (Yes, actual upside-down hanging mushrooms.) In the crisper bin of his fridge were vegetables (as best as Sarah could tell) that were so old they had liquefied into a pool of green syrup. Dirty dishes and clothes were also scattered everywhere throughout the house.

Sarah was such a clean person, fussy even, and so it would follow that she was repulsed by the filth. She cleaned Jake's house on several occasions (to the degree that she could without a bulldozer), but Jake would let it go back to "normal" in no time; he simply didn't take care of his house and his standards were very low all around. It was painfully clear that he also didn't value Sarah's comfort and happiness; he didn't take her out much in public, wouldn't call her his "girlfriend" in front of his friends, and only made time for her when it was convenient for him. Sarah certainly wasn't getting much out of the relationship, but she somehow didn't see it or didn't want to. She thought Jake was very attractive and she had hoped that he would realize how great she was for him. And (surprise, surprise), she had hoped that she could change him.

After spending the night at Jake's house—her first overnighter in a while—Sarah woke early in the morning needing to go *Number Two*. She very rarely went Number Two in any place that wasn't her own apartment's bathroom, and she definitely did not want to go at *Jake's place*, but she had no choice—it was coming. Trying not to wake Jake, she slipped out of bed and tiptoed across the creaky wood floor to the upstairs bathroom.

Holding everything in until she reached the bathroom, she quietly closed the door behind her; relief was imminent.

She turned to face the toilet and what she saw was a waterless, orange-ringed, out-of-use bowl. "Oh no," she whispered to herself, "it's dry!" She looked around for a solution to this dilemma. There was a small plastic wastebasket. *Hmmm*, she thought, *could I?* But there wasn't any time to think so she squatted into the little wastebasket. Then, after using the last few squares of toilet paper from the end of a roll that sat on the countertop, she opened up and flattened the empty cardboard tube and placed it on top of the contents of the wastebasket as if she was covering a murder. Now, she had no choice but to dispose of the evidence. *Should I take it home*, she asked herself; *just flee with it now?* She eyeballed the screenless crank-window that was to the left of the toilet. Sarah slowly opened the window, and exactly like the elderly Rose DeWitt Bukater plopping the Heart of the Ocean into the Atlantic, she tossed the pail and all of its contents two full stories down to its final resting place.

In light of that experience, Sarah realized that she and Jake were just not suited for each other. (*Ya, think?*) She stopped dating him and never addressed what had happened to his wastebasket.

The truth is, everything that you are getting—*including all of the crap*—you are getting because it's what you have access to in your viral energy stratum by way of the level and vibe of your energetic-presence.

The treatment that you get and give in a relationship, plus your level of closeness and openness, as well as the depth and sincerity of your love, are the standards that together make up your personal "relationship culture." Keep in mind that before they met you, the person that you're dating had their own relationship culture, too: what they are used to, what they like, and how fast they move in a relationship.

After a while, you can allow yourself to be acculturated into the other person's standards; this could be a good thing and an upgrade, or not. On the other hand, how the other person operates in a relationship might be at glaring odds with your standards and it would serve you well to be aware of it rather than become absorbed into it.

Decide on your preferred relationship culture and then more easily make decisions based on those standards. Having the genuine love relationship that you want means practicing not always getting what you want (or *think* you want at the time), even if it requires a breakup to "enlighten-up" for true love. By stretching in this way, you become more, you expect more, and you get more.

Quantum Entanglement (Otherwise Known as Karmic Love)

First of all, karma is not a bad thing and it's not penance or punishment. Karma is not about learning a lesson, either.

Karma is exactly the same as your presence—the sum total of creation energy that your soul is being.

Your soul has an exciting goal of reuniting with the whole of Life, and each lifetime is a spiritual evolution for your soul journeying towards that state of enlightenment. In karmic relationships, your soul and the soul of another choose to journey together through several, perhaps many, lifetimes. These are souls with whom you are connected in a quantum entanglement by mutual choice. You reappear in each other's lives in a variety of relationship arrangements. Sometimes you are the mother to the other, other times you are their father, son, sister, wife, or husband. As you look at each of your significant and long-term relationships, you can be sure that you are in a quantum entanglement with those souls.

Karmic relationships are not a one-hit wonder like you would think of a "soulmate" as being your singular cosmic connection. Your soul has many mates. These souls journey as a system, not only for their individual soul agendas, but also for a collective mission. Basically, they have business with each other. Their agreement is to bring light to the evolution of both souls. Often (but not always), this path to enlightenment is endeavored through circumstances that are challenging and that offer resistance. Your soul and the soul of the other knows that resistance can strengthen and reveal much about who we are and show us much about who we are choosing to become.

Separate from karmic love, a quantum entanglement is a different experience. This is when two (or more) energies share common realities, even across great distances of time and physical space. As far as romantic relationships go, some karmic lovers will be in your life for a period of time, until the work of both souls is complete. This may take several lifetimes, or it may come full circle in a single lifetime. Either way, as painful as it might be to be together (or apart), prior to both of your incarnations in this lifetime, your souls knowingly chose to experience a journey together. There are no mistakes or coincidences here, but that doesn't mean that the relationship is "healthy" or "fulfilling," it just means that your soul hasn't yet evolved from the experience. It's so important to understand that a bad or abusive relationship does not need to continue simply because your two souls may or may not be working through a growth process or path to enlightenment. Simply choose to complete your karma together and in doing so, the goal has been achieved: in that choice, you create your enlightenment.

But, guess what? Your soulmate is no myth. That beautiful, steady, genuine, lasting love that you dream of does exist. You will recognize true love by these three criteria of a soulmate:

1. You and your mate never seek to overpower or undermine each other;
2. You grow together (not stagnate, deflate, or outgrow each other) and your continued togetherness will fuel the evolution of your souls;
3. Your relationship will be a secret to none and a beacon of light for all.

That is the formula for a true-love relationship. By those three criteria, you will recognize your soulmate.

You will have concerns and hesitations about your mate, sure. That's normal. These might be sizeable challenges such as: he drinks too much; she's deeply in debt; they are a nag about household stuff; he sometimes has a negative outlook on life; your religions are different; your families don't get along; you don't like his mom; you don't even live in the same state (or country); you're not sure if you share the same vision for the future; she doesn't know what she wants to do with her life. While you might decide that these concerns are too much for you, none of these topics identifies if the other person is or is not your soulmate. Ironically, circumstances and experiences like these are ideal scenarios for greatly beneficial karmic loves as you stretch to meet in middle ground.

Maybe you're dating someone and would like to get a sense of your future potential together. Or you are in a long-term relationship (even living together or engaged) and you're *still* not sure if they are The One. Using the all-important "Three Criteria of A Soulmate," here is a yes-or-no quiz to help you recognize your soul's mate:

1. Does the person with whom you are in a relationship promote your strengths and encourage you to become your best and Highest Self?
2. While you've been in the relationship, have you consistently grown as an individual and feel a sense of forward movement in your life?
3. When in public together, are you proud to be associated with the other person and are you eager to introduce them to others as your significant other?
4. Do you feel confident that your mate is trustworthy and faithful?
5. Are you supportive of the other person's personal goals without any fear of losing them to their dreams?
6. Rather than simply saying, "This is Jane," does the person with whom you are in a relationship introduce you with a title such as, "This is my girlfriend, Jane," or "Did you meet my partner,

Jo?" or "I'd like you to meet my husband, Tom?" (There is one exception: they have forgotten the third party's name and are simply trying to avoid a formal introduction.)

7. Is your mate a jealous person in general or often jealous as it relates to you being around other people?

8. Do you feel that you and your mate keep having the same fights or are locked in a cycle of hurt-regret-makeup with each other?

9. Would you prefer that your old boyfriend (or girlfriend) not know that you are serious with your new boyfriend, because you would rather not hurt the former's feelings?

10. Have you noticed that before you were with your mate, you were truer to the real you, or simply freer to be you?

If you answered, "yes" to all of questions one through six, and you answered "no" to all of questions seven through ten, then the person you are with could be a true love, perhaps even your soul's mate. Any other combination of answers points to a relationship that is serving a purpose for a time, yet maybe not forever. Tough love? Perhaps. But if what you want is to identify a healthy, mutually beneficial, and forward-evolving relationship, then you now have a clear guide. True love means not struggling for power with the other and not fighting for the upper hand. True love's primary function and goal is to grow the spiritual evolution of the soul, helped along by the relationship or directly because of the relationship.

You have karma with anyone and everyone with whom you are journeying in your life. Karma is the currency of energy that you have earned and that you take with you in this life, and even before and after this life. Your soul's true mate will be evident by how your two souls individually evolve as a supernatural function of your togetherness. And when you find it, you will experience the beauty and magic of love's quantum entanglement.

CHAPTER TEN:

NO ANSWERS, ONLY CHOICES

You're Not Unhappy; You're Just Empty

I t was New Year's Eve of 2006. With 2007 on the horizon, I was on my bathroom floor holding the side of the tub; a familiar place. For some years, I had spent so much time wailing in anguish on bathroom floors, especially after every fight with my parents when I was younger. Truth be told, it went on far beyond my youth, through devastating breakups and losses of all kinds, where I'd sometimes vomit in grief until only bright yellow bile came up. But now I was too empty even for that. I held the white metal tub, eyeing it for what it could be used for.

The last time I had remembered feeling secure in life was at the age of ten, before our family began to move around shadowing my dad's work opportunities. As an adult, I had yearned for one person to call my own; one person dedicated to me no matter what. I never got that with my family, and my friends could only be present so much. I wanted a partner in life like most other people had: a loyal spouse, or a sibling with whom to share a fierce and unbreakable bond, or a parent for whom I was the apple of their eye. I had friends and family, but I was nobody's treasure; I was no one's "person."

What I did have was a fresh breakup. I loved Jack, my boyfriend of the last two years. He had a broad white smile, salt-and-pepper hair that gave him an air of distinction, and a hint of pedigree that matched his natural confidence. Though he was not famous, he had a celebrity presence about him, and he lit up every room that he walked into. I believed that Jack loved me too, but I broke up with him because I wanted more than he could offer. He had already been married and was still scorned from his divorce. I couldn't understand that. All I knew was that I needed just one person who would be mine; someone who would commit to being my partner of his own volition. Jack couldn't be that person for me; he wasn't ready for it. So, I broke up with him. I often did the thing that hurt because I thought that it was the right or best thing. Then I suffered for it.

Two weeks later, it was New Year's Eve and I was alone. It's so hard to be alone on holidays, especially the ones that are custom-made for coupling and romance. My friends had plans that night; everyone was coupled up. Jack had called to say, "Well, we're both alone tonight, we might as well hang out," but I declined in a show of female strength and defiance for all that I had already told him that I deserved. I wanted him to claim me; to fight for me. I wanted stability and someone who wouldn't leave me or easily let me go. And, Jack was a super guy, so there was also that fear of whether or not I was ever going to find someone as good as him. The clock was ticking, but not my biological clock. It was the clock that reminded me that I was approaching my mid-thirties and so many of the "good ones" were already taken. And who wants a *bad one*, right? (*Was this my last great opportunity for love and I blew it?*)

Though, it was more than just lost love that had me in a heap on the bathroom floor. I had struggled to pay my bills, squeaking by paycheck-to-paycheck—that was me. I remember times when my friends invited me out to dinner and I either couldn't go, or I went and ordered just a bowl of soup and one glass of wine. I recalled when just a month earlier, seven friends and I dined at a five-star restaurant in downtown Detroit—when Detroit was hot and still embodied much of the Motown glamour—to celebrate three of our birthdays, mine being one of them. I ordered the soup and a glass of chardonnay. Imagine my anxiety when the check came, equally split eight ways, divvying up several bottles of champagne and wine, appetizers, entrees, and desserts—all that I had purposely not partaken in. I should have just spoken up. I should have told my friends that I would get my own check, but I didn't. Rather, I added my credit card to the pile (calculating in my head the likelihood that it would be declined), simply because I wanted to be included with my peers and not draw attention to what I couldn't afford. This only got me further stressed about my bills. On top of it all, my job was crap, too. Right from the start I knew that I was a medium-sized fish in a very small pond, which was fine in itself. However, over time I became weary of pandering to the big fish while violating everything that I believed in just to try and make my ripple mean something. I knew that, even at work, I was a fish out of water.

If I had had a theme song it would have been, "Here I Go Again (on My Own)" by Whitesnake. I was tired of having to start over again. I was depressed and exhausted by it, but it was more than that. By this night—a night that was supposed to signify something wonderful and special and celebratory—I was suicidal. I was thinking: *how can I go through this again?* Really. *How can I go through this again?!* I was angry and helpless at the same time. *How can I start another year completely alone, heartbroken, not over Jack and now having to think about who else is left out there for me, while also feeling stuck in my unpurposed job and unhappy all around? How can I do what I want to do without the right education, money to turn my many ideas into my own business, or the support or resources of any kind to up and change occupations?* And it was my hometown, too. I felt that my dreams didn't live there and I resented how the town held me in a certain role just by way of been raised within its borders. (*But maybe it was only me holding myself back all along.*) I didn't let myself be who I truly felt I was, because I believed that other people wouldn't let me be more than I had been—little Penny, a local face of public relations, the inspirational speech-giver at the annual beauty pageant, the rep for my company at every community event, and the Vanna White of presenting scholarships and donations around town. Don't get me wrong—my job started as a great gig, but I had outgrown it. At annual reviews, I would ask for succession plans that never came, and so my boredom grew. In short, I was unfulfilled and yearned to advance and to be acknowledged for "all-of-the-more" that I felt inside. I believed that my town wouldn't be able to "see" the more in me, and so I was getting very claustrophobic of my future outlook.

There's something about that age range between twenty-nine and thirty-five that can really mess with a person's perceived outlook; that is, if you are not already settled and successful, *which I was not.* There is an inherent pressure in that block of selfhood that is a relentless and powerful force—a cultural pressure, albeit self-permitted, of comparison to others who are established in their careers and happily married off. And if you're not all those things, then what's wrong with you? (*Because, there must be something "wrong" with me that has me crying on New Year's Eve whilst others are celebrating, right?*)

As I sat cradling the bathtub, I thought about all of the different ways that I could kill myself. I could slit my wrists. Although come to think of it, I didn't like blood. I couldn't imagine doing that; I didn't even have a sharp knife or a straight razor. And, how do you do that? How do you take a knife to your wrist and *actually* do that? That first press into your flesh—how do you do *that*? And you can't change your mind; there's no going back from *that*.

I wanted somebody to knock on the door and to save me from my "overwhelment," and to just be there with me. I wanted companionship. It was New Year's Eve, after all. It's harder to be alone on New Year's Eve, or Christmas, or a birthday; harder than on any other day or night.

I also thought about hanging myself, but I was living in an apartment at the time and I couldn't find a place to do it; the logistics of it weren't easy. There wasn't a ceiling hook or anything; I couldn't figure out *how* to hang myself. Again, it's not exactly an easy thing to do and it was something that I had obviously never done before. It's not like riding a bike or carrying out a task I had done many times before. *How long would I be choking*, I thought? *How long would it take?* I was already having a tormented night and a miserable year; now would I have a painful death, too? No thanks, it would just bring more pain to the pain that I was already feeling.

The best that I could figure, the easiest way to do it would be to asphyxiate myself in my car. The problem there was that I didn't have a personal garage in my apartment building; it was an underground, shared garage. It wasn't even an enclosed space. The entrance and exit ramps were both open and so air flowed right through the one-level underground garage. *Well, maybe I could still do it there*, I thought. I saw something like it in a movie. I could rig up some sort of a hose from my tailpipe and thread it through one of my car windows, plugging the rest of the window crack with rags. Then, I would just sit there, run my car, and hope that no one came along to stop me. That was the tricky part because there were plenty of other vehicles down there even late at night, including one on either side of my car. I even went down to my car space to assess my chances of privacy and to do recon on what I needed. *I can do it*, I encouraged myself, *as long as nobody stops me.*

As I surveyed what could later be the scene of my suicide, I took a look at the fuel gauge. *Oh no, I don't even have gas in my car!* To make matters worse, I had less than twenty dollars in my bank account. (I also recall that night I had attempted to make myself feel a measure better—mid all-out-meltdown in my New Year's Eve self-imposed-solitude-tragedy—

by attempting to order a pizza or Chinese food, but when I called in my order, my credit card was declined. I had limited out of that option.) *It seemed I was always running on empty*, I mused. This night was typical, I had less than an eighth of a tank and the gas light was on. I didn't know if that would be enough. What would happen if it wasn't? Maybe the engine would sputter to a stop and I'd be brain dead, but alive. What a pathetic suicide attempt that would be. This asphyxiation option surely presented some challenges, but I hadn't yet ruled it out.

And then, I thought of my cat; Sabrina was eleven at that time. What would I do with her? My parents were not interested in taking me in; I was lonely and struggling to get by financially, yet my parents offered no invite to return home (they didn't want a thirty-three-year-old kid at home and in retrospect I don't know that I blame them). If they weren't going to take me in, then they definitely weren't going to want my cat. It was then that I realized I had no one who would take Sabrina; no one to whom I could will her guardianship. Could I bring her into the car with me and off us both? Maybe the gas would last long enough to kill her but not me. I couldn't imagine how absolutely awful my life would be without her. And, could I do that to her? Well, no. I couldn't do that to her. The idea entered my head and left just as quickly. I couldn't murder my beloved cat. But then what? Could I leave her behind? How long would it be before anyone came to check on me and therefore found her? Days, even a week? It likely wouldn't be until after the holiday break when I didn't show up for work. No one would come looking for me until maybe it was too late for Sabrina, too. They were awful choices.

As my mind ran my exit options, I also wondered what would happen at the moment of death. Would I be swallowed up by demons? Tortured for eternity? Would I have a fate much worse than the life I was currently living? I've heard that the body eliminates all waste at death. *Would I crap my pants?*

"Please help me. I'm so alone," I whispered to myself (or perhaps to God, or whomever or whatever could possibly stop my grief). I wanted the pain to end and I could not think of a way for it to get better quickly enough. My heart ached. It actually ached with fear; fear that I would never be happy; fear that I would be that old spinster that never got married; fear that I would lose my job and not be able to get by; fear that I'd be stuck in my comatose job another day; fear that I would not make it through the night alone.

Yet, I did make it through that night. A distant spark of hope for something more both sustained and haunted me, yet I somehow fought to pull myself up off the floor and then I wrote in my journal, "I am going to drill through the rock of this tomb and tell you all how I did it."

That same year, I took an inspired leap and soon changed everything, starting with the very meaning and purpose of my life. I needed to inject new water in my stagnant pond, and so I moved from Ontario to Nashville, Tennessee, and began to follow my dreams and explore my own potential for the first time ever. My journey has been years in the making, yet from the moment that I risked letting go of all that I knew in pursuit of my dreams, I was happier and felt more alive than ever.

I never forgot that promise that I made. In openly talking with many, many people, I can report that all people have the capacity to suffer depression at different times or under overwhelming circumstances. Sure, life can be easier when you have the support of others, or strong faith, or some other centering affect, but no one is immune.

This might be news to you (or maybe not): people who suffer depression or feel suicidal don't want to die. I know, it sounds very counterintuitive, doesn't it? If you haven't felt depressed then you don't know what I mean, but if you have, then you understand. When I was suicidal, I did *not* want to die. I did not want to slit my wrists or hang myself. I didn't want to suffer the pain of dying. I didn't want to never see my beloved cat again. I didn't want to leave this world, but I did wholly want out of my circumstances.

Please have compassion for the depressed and suicidal because it is not "the easy way out." There is nothing easy about suicide or having to contemplate suicide. There is nothing easy about feeling like you have no choices in life. There is nothing easy about that. Nothing. People who are suicidal (or have taken their life) probably don't want to die; they want out of their current circumstances. They want to wormhole to a different existence; to that dream they had for their life; to an evolution of themselves that feels at home. They just can't figure out how to do it, how to get there, how to make it happen, and how to be happy. *How. To. Be. Happy?*

While some surely are, most forms of depression are not a mental health crisis, but rather they are a *spiritual* health crisis—a suppressing of one's spirit. Going forward, the fields of psychology and psychiatry will begin to address it in this way. To be very straightforward and to make no mistake, this *spiritual health crisis* has no association with religion or the constructs of religious traditions. This crisis is a deep inner restlessness for meaning and purpose—a no-middle-man knowingness of our own power to create and of our true selfhood and Higher-Self. Today, the widespread (and more common than ever before) *spiritual health crisis* experienced by so many is not a "bad" thing; it is a sign that we are aching and ready for the depth of Life available to us.

But, how will we respond to this outcry from our youth, our community, and our own friends and family? How will we support each other in our spiritual evolution as we connect with our Higher-Selves?

The cure for unhappiness is fulfillment. The pharmaceutical for hopelessness is engagement in a meaningful purpose. I'm talking about the planetary pulse towards the metaphysical, a new-consciousness, and the deep longing for a return to our natural inclinations that our species is currently experiencing. We, as a whole, are at the precipice of a spiritual health crisis. What is most fascinating about this crisis is that it's a flashlight to awakening. When we finally get tired of the status quo, we seek. Humanity's present-day spiritual health crisis is an opportunity and an invitation to awaken and evolve.

"God, Are You Listening?"

I had an opportunity to receive advice from a well-known spiritual teacher and she later sent me a recording of our session. She gifted me with so much wisdom and many insights that have since proven to manifest in my life. In listening back to the recording, I noticed that there was only one thing that she repeated more than once. In fact, when I counted, she repeated it seven times. She said, "You need to be meditating. You create with the Creator, and so to serve your purpose and realize your dreams, you need to be meditating." Again and again she told me this. I had periodically meditated for a number of years, but today I meditate as a practice and I have experienced meditation to be a form of communication with Life; it's a portal to receive inspiration, grace, wisdom for my writings, and to be renewed.

You might have heard the saying that prayer is asking and meditation is listening. That's a great way to think of it. And yet, a prayer doesn't have to be about asking, it can be about thanking. Perhaps a song can be a prayer, or an answer to one. And meditation doesn't have to be about listening, it can just be about creating space; the lack of thought opens us to "inspired thought," which is Life's perfect order coming through.

Sometimes when I'm alone, I talk out loud to the whole of Life—the omnipresent force that you might call God. I say to Life, "We're in this together, I'm going to need some more help. I'm struggling and need the people, resources, and opportunities to come to me, because I can't always find them myself. I made a breathtaking agreement with You. I'm here by my choice. Please use me for good. I can't do this on my own. Thank You for engaging all of Life to help fulfill my agreement." (Sounds a bit like a prayer, huh?)

Asking is the easy part, yet it can still be a challenge for you to remember to plug into Life and all of the resources available to you. Here's a formula that I have found cannot fail to work:

1. Speak out loud what you desire with sincerity. Verbally release your fears and doubts and recreate your words into passionate love messages.
2. Then, be open to the signs, answers, and opportunities.

3. Use every question or crossroad, all day and every day, to make choices in the direction of your goals and purpose.
4. Take action.

It might surprise you from whom and where the answers or encouragement will come. The other day I said out loud to Life, "I sometimes find it hard to believe that I deserve all of the good things that are happening lately in my life. I have difficulty trusting that it won't all just disappear and turn to rubbish again. It's hard to forgive myself for things that I've done in my past, the time that I have wasted, and what I put my former self through. Sometimes I feel guilty for the happiness that I feel today, when the person that I was before had hurt and been hurt so much. It's strange to let go of the fight. I am now choosing forgiveness, fulfillment, and success in my purpose. Please show me a sign that I am worthy, and that if I fully embrace who I am today, I'm not abandoning the girl I had been who had so greatly suffered."

Then I mentally moved on. I let it go and gave it up to Life to sort out. I put my Apple earbuds on, queued up my favorite music station, and left for my morning exercise routine.

The very first song that played was one that I know well and must have listened to a thousand times. And yet, I had always visualized it speaking to a romantic relationship, an old flame. I've watched the music video, too. I had never thought of its story in any way other than the way Adele had likely written it to a former boyfriend (*or, maybe not*), until this day when I heard these words from a completely new perspective—no man, no old flame; just me and old me... (I'll paraphrase the lyrics as I heard them.)

Hello, Old Self
I was wondering if after all these years you'd like to put the past in the back seat

Hello, are you hearing me?
I'm dreaming about who I used to be when I was younger and
searching
I've forgotten how it felt when I had no foundation under my feet

There's such a difference between me and old me
And a million miles apart

Hello, from the other side of years of hurt
I must have cried a thousand times
But those who've hurt me don't have power over me now
In my true and Higher-Self I've made my home

Hello from the other side
I know I can say that I've earned my freedom, so hard I've tried
I'm sorry that my younger self had to go through it all
But it doesn't matter now, the past doesn't control me anymore

Get Rid of Space Holders (You're Just Not That Into Them!)

My dad once told me that if my closet was full of stuff I didn't like but I didn't have the money to buy new clothes, then what I needed to do was give away the clothes that I wasn't using. "The 'Vacuum Effect' will fill in the void," he said. I assumed it would work on everything—because I was young and idealistic and believing—so I tried it on *everything*! Since I first heard of it, I've now used the vacuum effect on my closets, bad choices in friends and mates, and for new and exciting jobs. Dad was right: it works. Even if you don't know from where the resources, people, or opportunities will come, start by making room in your life for the new by creating a void in place of the old. Then, let the magic of viral energy do the rest!

My dad didn't make up the vacuum effect; he just applied it to the clothes in my closet. (Although, I do think that a more precise name for the vacuum effect would be the *void-fill effect*.) It works marvelously to move energy, people, and things. A void will naturally be filled with what's around it and accessible. It is a certainty.

Interestingly, the vacuum effect has been studied by scientists on feral cat populations. Evidence indicates that "removing feral cat populations only opens up the habitat to an influx of new cats, either from neighboring territories or born from survivors," says AlleyCat.org. "Each time cats are removed, the population will rebound through a natural phenomenon known as the 'vacuum effect.' The vacuum effect is a phenomenon scientifically recognized worldwide, across all types of animal species."

It's kind of neat to know how spatial voids work in nature, and it's handy to understand when wishing to manifest new clothes or shoes, yet its power is much more magical when put to the right use. Think about it—why not use the vacuum effect to your benefit to create a life of happiness for yourself and others?

When it comes to clearing out what's not working and creating the life that you truly want, do not avoid creating a void; embrace the void!

I've known a few "space holders" in my life: relationships that were going nowhere, jobs with which I was unhappy, and even influencers whom I had outgrown. I had clung onto some of these space holders for way too long. I didn't think it was hurting anyone to keep them around until what I really wanted fell at my feet. (*Ha! Was I wrong.*) Guess what? My dream job, soul mate, and true friendships didn't manifest until I created the space for them.

But, not so fast there, Hoover. As you create a vacuum and nice spatial void, clearing out your negative friends, users, boozers, losers, and some genuine sweethearts whom you're just not that into, also take a look at yourself and the quality of your own viral energy. If you don't improve your energy quality you will only suck in fresh new space holders; more of the same to match your energy—*born from the survivors*, to put it in feral cat terms.

Ever go to a good restaurant or coffee shop and notice how fast an empty seat is filled? Just about as soon as a chair is vacated, it is occupied again. But what about a restaurant with a bad reputation, poor quality food, and bad service? Not so in demand, right?

In this analogy, the restaurant or coffee shop is your energy presence; a product of what you chronically and typically "marinate in," such as the energetic influence of the people with whom you surround yourself, plus your environment including the battery of influences from television, news, your work culture, and all that is around you. If your coffee shop feels good and elevates others with a great product and service, your seats will be occupied, your cash register full, and vacancies will immediately be filled. On the other hand, if your restaurant consistently allows unsatisfactory products, lackluster service, and is sweeping garbage under the rug, it will be devoid of visitors, cash flow, and quality.

If you are experiencing repeated low-quality romantic partners, uninspiring work opportunities, and friends who consistently take rather than fill you up, then you need to look at the sum total of what and who you surround yourself with and what you energetically give off. You need to audit your viral energy.

Ask yourself: if I were to create a void today, am I in a pattern and environment that would give me more of the same or something similar to what I have now (which isn't working)? Keep in mind that a void will naturally be filled with what's around it, nearby, and accessible.

Jonathan was in a job for eight years that he didn't enjoy. He butted heads with his boss on a regular basis, his assignments and projects had become boring and unfulfilling to him, and he felt overworked and under-appreciated. One day, on a whim, he applied for a similar position at a different company. To his surprise, he got the job with ease, and in no time, he slid right into work at the new company. Within four months, Jonathan knew that he hated the new job as much as the old job. The faces at work were different, but the problems and unfulfillment were the exact same. He didn't much like his boss, the work was both busy and boring, and he felt trapped and frustrated.

If your new job is just as joyless as your old job, consider that you created the same experience, again. Yes, you created it that way based on *your beliefs* about what you need to be happy, how bosses treat you, industry norms, and how work should be hard.

Before you make room for something new, get your viral energy right by getting your thoughts and beliefs right. Decide what you would really love to do and be. Then, use the vacuum effect phenomenon to create a void-fill that enriches your life with what you *really* want.

Why Don't You Just Pick What You Want, Already?

Know what you want or risk getting a mixed lot. Here's a true short story that I like to call, *Don't Ask and You (Still) Shall Receive.*

One very lonely day, Vickie (forty-one), who had been single for two years, prayed to her deceased mother to intervene with God for a favor: "Just a date with a man. Please, just get someone to ask me out!"

Well, the next night she got a call from a friendly acquaintance that she had met some weeks earlier. He asked her if she wanted to grab dinner with him and she accepted. During dinner, she became agitated because there was no romantic connection, and this was not what she had in mind when she made her supernatural request. Inside, she was annoyed with her mother for messing up and sending her this man-friend instead of her soulmate. Frustrated, Vickie excused herself, stepped outside, and cried out loud. Then suddenly, she had a new thought and burst into laughter. "You're right, Mom! I only asked for a man," she said to the sky while wildly laughing, "I didn't specify what I really wanted!" She laughed and laughed, and she didn't care who saw her; this was a big moment of realization. "You got me, Mom. Next time I will ask for my soulmate!"

One year later, Vickie got engaged.

Life wants for you what you want for you. Your history of relationships, jobs, and other life experiences point you to your preferences. Each of your exes brought qualities and traits into your life, some qualities you appreciated and others you rejected. Use all of your past relationships to create a guide for that which you are looking, including exactly what you must have in a partner, and what you will never again accept.

And while you're picking what you *want*, go ahead and pick what you want to *do*. What would you do if you could do anything and get paid for it? What's your "paid fun"? What truly makes your spirit sing and brings you excitement and a deep sense of purpose? Look at what your past positions and roles have to show you about your preferences. Some jobs were a bore. Some jobs were rewarding. Rather than seeing the job as a singular experience, separate out the tasks and responsibilities into "like" and "dislike." Make a list of what you would truly want if you could define your paid fun. Take some time to detail what you would love to do, or more specifically, what you would love to *be*. Then spend a few minutes each day thinking, feeling, and planning on it. Marinate in the energy of your paid fun. The neat thing is, your paid fun wants you as much as you want it! All you need to do is be in the flow of it; that is, be on the viral energy level where all those things, people, and experiences exist that you want. What you want and dream of, including your dream job, paid fun, and divinely designed work, might not be found in the viral energy stratum in which you are currently residing. Remember, if you are not seeing it in your life, chances are you are not sharing the same energetic space with it! Put yourself in the path (flow, stream, current, stratum) of what you want by using the knowledge and magic of viral energy to work in your favor.

So, where are you in developing your skills to manifest your goals and dreams? A very easy test of your power to manifest is to choose a number that you'd like to see pop up. Tell yourself that it's a sign, and that when it pops up, you will be reminded that you can and are affecting the quantum field of reality. (*Whoa, cool! And yes, my dear, your energetic output and presence can and does affect reality.*) For me, the number twenty-three is my number. It's my birthdate and it's an affirmation from my Higher-Self to myself that I am on track with my mission (my birthright). I see it everywhere. I'm not exaggerating when I tell you that I see it, on average, about three to six times a day. I see it on clocks, on TV, as street numbers, in license plates, as taxi cab numbers, you name it. Two-digit numbers work well for this. One-digit numbers are too easy, and three or more are too specific. However, 11:11 is a special number to which many people are connected. Some say that the number 11:11 is the number of masters. It happens to be my dad's special number. My cousin Janine's number is thirty-three. It was the age that she was when her mother died, and they had agreed before her death that it would be their number of remembrance. Once you pick a number, especially one with some meaning to it, you will start to see it often. Certainly, the Spirit World has a hand in it; for all intents and purposes, you and Spirit are one organism. Although, the plain and simple reason for the appearance of a chosen number is that you chose it. (And, you can do this with much bigger signs and symbols, too!)

When your number pops up, it's a message from you, to you. And the message is: *what you believe is so*. You see, twenty-three pops up for me in relation to the meaning that I have assigned to it. It is not only confirmation that my purpose is on track; it's proof that I'm creating what I choose. And, so are you.

CHAPTER ELEVEN:

ARE YOU ABOUT DONE STRUGGLING?

Why Are You Making Life So Hard on Yourself?

You are so hard on yourself. You have enrobed yourself in doubt and guilt as if they were warm blankets because somehow they comfort you. Even when something great comes along, you don't trust it; you feel it's too good to be true because your doubt and guilt won't allow you to believe that you deserve it. Because of this, Life agrees with you. You're creating what you're experiencing; you're a very powerful manifestor.

And so, the big question is: how do you stop the struggle and start getting more of what you want? While you absolutely must take action to get on the right path (and perhaps to even get "there" quicker), the magic of viral energy is effortless. Viral energy is working even when you think you are not doing anything because you are resonating at a vibration, which, as we discussed in chapter two, is also known as your presence—your energy attainment within the consciousness-energy strata. It's important to remember that the energy shared within your stratum-flow is the fuel for all that you are creating and then experiencing.

Sometimes I am not particularly positive, and my presence isn't always as enlightened as I would like. I'm the kind of person who might not look as overjoyed as I feel and since I'm human, I'm not always overjoyed. Like most of us, I have ups and downs, loss and hurt, and passion and bliss. However, even when I am stressed, sad, or not the positive person for whom anyone would expect good things to happen, great opportunities and synchronicities do miraculously happen, seemingly out of nowhere (and rather often). When I want to share something really awesome, I call my cousin Janine and say, "You're never going to believe what just happened." I then fill her in on the exciting news or opportunity, and she always says something like, "UN. FRICKIN'. BELIEVABLE. Shut up! Of course this happened to you! Incredible things always happen for you!"

So, how—when I'm not a bubbly and effervescent Mary-Poppins-type—do these awesome experiences and events continue to come my way (and in a big way)? More importantly, how can *you* manifest great experiences and events even when you have bad days, negative experiences, and undesirable feelings?

The power lies in your energetic-presence and has much less to do with your mood or the polarity of your thoughts on any given day or in any given week. You see, in spite of myself sometimes, Life is upholding its promise to me, nudging me towards my purpose and bringing me the signs, people, resources, opportunities, and sometimes the courage, moxie, stiff upper lip, and magic to journey towards fulfilling my end of my Breathtaking Agreement With Life.

Have you ever unwittingly devolved yourself from a job, relationship, or opportunity? (*I have.*) Deep down, could it be that you were not in sync with it? Did you believe that it didn't fit you anymore? Did you speak negative affirmations of complaint or criticism, only to soon be surprised when you lost the job, relationship, or opportunity? Well, you weren't as passive in the cause-and-effect as you might think. (And by the way, the devolving of an association, commitment, or heavy weight is sometimes the best result for you.) In not sharing the same energetic level as the job, relationship, or opportunity, you devolved it from your life. You have a strong ability to manifest results in your life.

But what about the times when it's *not* in your best interest or the interest of your personal and/or spiritual growth to become devolved from a relationship or opportunity? Yes, you sometimes remove yourself from those, too; but why? This happens because you are so powerful that you create two specific energies that exist to undermine your goals: doubt and guilt. These are the most creative of all low emotions. (Remember that *both* light energy and heavy energy have the power of creation.) Doubt and guilt are powers that multiply. When you feel in doubt or guilty, you tend to say and do more things about which you can feel in doubt or guilty. Maybe you know what I mean and have experienced the multiplying effect of heavy energy. It goes like this: you are feeling down about an interaction with someone that didn't go as you had hoped, or something bad that happened for which you are at cause. You are feeling awful about what happened, and in addition to that you fear that your negative feelings will attract more bad experiences or loss to you. You are now feeling and building doubt and guilt on two levels.

Doubt sponsors more doubt, guilt likes more guilt. Why? Because the energies of doubt and guilt, like all energies, are catchy multiplicators. But what's so special and powerful about the energies of doubt and guilt in particular? Well, it's you! You are the X factor. (You are a powerful creator.)

Jeff was a person who had done everything right in life. He was a good son and friend. He did well in school and worked hard to grow in his career, always making the right moves at the right time. He had recently started dating a great woman, Shannon, who brought even more stability and peace into his life.

One day when driving home from work, Jeff's phone rang and he mistakenly answered it without using the hands-free option. He was distracted for a moment and rear-ended an SUV, sending all five of its occupants to the hospital. For the most part, everyone was okay, thank goodness. However, several months later, two people who were hit reported that they suffered whiplash and so they sued Jeff and his insurance company.

Not only did Jeff feel terrible about what he had caused, he also felt tremendous fear and doom around being sued and all of the unknown repercussions that come with it. Jeff couldn't see that he had already taken responsible for his mistake. Just by having auto insurance and accident coverage, he had preemptively covered the expenses that might result from an accident. Jeff didn't understand that the victims who were suing him were not doing so to prove that Jeff was a bad person or a criminal, but to cover their medical costs. Because he habitually welcomed guilt into his being, he felt comfortable punishing himself. He even fell into a depression over it. The weight of the *idea* of legal action against him was paralyzing and he feared that his negative emotions would bring to him more negativity and bad events.

Maybe you've heard that the law of attraction states that like attracts like, and so if you're in a bad mood, in a negative space for a week, in a huge fight with someone, or experiencing a meltdown, then you believe you're going to attract bad things to you. Guess what? That's not how it works. (*Well, it's not the full story anyway.*) Yes, your emotions and thoughts do have the power to attract more of the same, however, your point of attraction is much bigger than that. The Universe didn't design things to function in a way that would mean bad life events would be attracted to you just for the sake of matching how you feel because you're having a miserable day or are in a hormonal funk. No; that would be cruel. The law of attraction works on your current vibration and—news flash—that has a minimal effect on what you create and then experience. The law of attraction only tells part of the story and the magic of viral energy completes the book.

Your magic is working even when you're not vibing with positivity and pure joy. But, why? Because it is your *energetic-presence* that is the creation-point of all that is yours and coming your way. (This is a good time to go back to Chapter Two for a refresh on the Seven Consciousness-Energy Strata and the definition of "Viral Energy Presence.")

Thank goodness your energetic-presence is not just your current vibration; oh, it's so much more than that—it's your vibration baseline. Your presence is where your power lives; it's the clarity or lightness of your soulset—*there's that word again*! You could say that your energetic-presence is your "soulset"—and it's a product of these three factors:

1. Your soul's chosen purpose;
2. Your deep inner intentions; and
3. The degree of light or heavy energy that you let in from your environment and from the people with whom you spend the most time.

Your mindset cannot override your soulset. Your emotionset cannot override your soulset. Great opportunities and happy events are not stripped from you because you've been in a foul mood, are on your period or hormonal for any reason, are fighting with someone, have a head-cold and are feeling miserable, or have been in an accident (even if you're to blame). "Bad" things happen in life, even to great people who have tried to live with good intentions. The trick is to handle these experiences with the same good intentions and not to internalize heavy energy or claim it as who you are. Who you are is *not* what happened or what you did in error. Who you are is someone who is strong when tested, brave under pressure, sincere in intention, and willing to take responsibility and move through anything.

Doubt and guilt are your creations. They are not conjured outside of you; you manufacture them. You are a powerful creator and doubt and guilt are your babies. You nurture them. You even cover them in warm blankets and then hide under them. You coddle your doubt. You harbor your guilt. And you reproduce more of them because the more doubt and guilt you feel, the more doubt and guilt you feel. These feelings cover you up. They consume you and being consumed means you live in a state that allows you to dodge the void of not experiencing the feelings' negative pull. Not feeling doubtful and guilty should be a peaceful space, yet for you it's foreign and undesirable because you equate their void with emptiness. You love your doubt and guilt. You're so used to them in the various shapes and faces that they've taken in the past, but guess what? They're not really a part of you. It's a hoax. You subconsciously relate to your doubt and guilt as extensions of you because you created them. You are attached to your doubt and guilt and you internalize them as familiar parts of your identity. You've even been acting like you want them. They punish you for whatever happened and you subconsciously feel that it's appropriate and deserved for you to now ruminate in fear, doubt, and guilt.

I'm here to tell you that you can let them go. End your internal struggle and stop creating doubt and guilt. They serve you in ways, but I promise you that what you truly want is so much higher. The cool thing is that Life (capital "L") wants for you what *you* want for you.

Through what you believe—and that which you are *being*— you tell Life what to manifest.

It's so simple because you're so powerful. As it should be, the Connective Force of All is working to align your life to serve what you said you wanted to be and do. And why? Just because you said you wanted it.

Stop letting things happen to you. Stop making life so hard on yourself. Do not accept your doubt and guilt. Take action-steps to move in the direction of your goals. Don't linger in a viral energy stratum that does not share all of the good things that you want and that does not fit you anymore. That was the old you. No one is shaming you but you, so stop doing that. Be willing to shift your time and attention away from energy suckers and low emotions. The "bad" thing that happened does not need you to hold your attention on it; it will play out without you giving it more heavy energetic fuel. Invest the resources of your time, attention, and energy in people and efforts in alignment with your goals and what you dream of with sincerity. Hit pause on the negative experience because time will resolve it and focus on all that is light energy. You can step around the distractions and away from the chaos. Don't allow your lower-self to be in the way of your Higher-Self. Move with Life.

If there is one thing that I hope you take away from this knowledge of viral energy, it's this: You can only manifest what is in the flow of your viral energy stratum. You can only create with the energy of your presence. If you want more, be more. If you want higher experiences, take the high road. Don't beat yourself up. Managing and magnifying your energetic-presence should be your primary effort. To be energetically light and free, you need to do nothing else but consciously evolve your energetic-presence. Period.

Why Failure is the Secret to Success

So, you failed the test, the relationship, or the business. Is all truly lost, or can you see some new life from the ashes? I've failed more times than I can count, and I've often felt judged because of that. But what I finally figured out is that my only real failures were the times that I didn't stay true to myself; didn't get back up again; didn't try a second, third, or fourth time; and didn't follow through. No one else kept me from success; that was all me. The only person really judging me was me.

I decided that I wanted happiness more than I wanted to avoid failure. I wanted to be, above all else, in pursuit of my purpose—fail or succeed.

It was 2007 and only a few months after the night spent on my bathroom floor contemplating suicide. I was in a rather high-profile position in public relations at a company where the upper management and board of directors were well-esteemed in our small city and somewhat regarded as local celebrities. It was my job, among other responsibilities, to vet the incoming requests for corporate sponsorship. So, when a proposal came across my desk to support a charity event that raised funds by auctioning fur coats, designer clothing, and other shiny things in a glamorous fashion show, I spoke up by questioning the organizer about the need to include fur.

A day later, I was called into a meeting with my boss, the Vice President of the company, and the VP of Human Resources. Following a grueling hour-long interrogation, I was reprimanded in writing. I had never been in trouble with an employer before. My company valued me, and they had even headhunted me from my previous employer. Yet, there I was—a huge embarrassment and disappointment to them. However, as much as I was horrified to be receiving a formal scar on my employee file, I was more horrified by my employer's clear support of stealing beauty from the backs of animals for the sake of glamour. (This was before I had turned vegan, but I had been a vegetarian since I was a teenager.) I could not help but to refuse giving an apology to the event organizer that had turned me in to my company's President and CEO. I was reprimanded in writing again, with another one-hour interrogation meeting. It quickly became evident to me just how incongruent I was within this company and so a week later, I quit my job without a job to go to.

This decision put me on the path of my inspired journey. I held a yard sale and sold all of my belongings, packed up my clothes and my cat, and drove from Ontario to Nashville, Tennessee. It was there that I started my own publicity business, and whilst there have been challenges along the path, I have never hated my work nor felt muzzled and bored for even one day. I know that I would not be living the life of my dreams if I didn't fail to meet the culture of my (last ever) employer. Today, I feel a great strength and pride in my marred journey. I think of myself as a phoenix rising because so much strength has come from the ashes of my past failures.

The phoenix-creation paradox is that you create and dismantle at the very same time. The old you burns away so that the new you can fly. Think about it: what has been disassembled, ceased, or eliminated as you built or created? And conversely, when something might look like a failure, just wait; there is always a creation in there somewhere. Failure only signals that you are learning and moving; you're in the action. You're not too afraid to try which means you're one step closer to your big success!

Have a look at these famous people: failure turned out to be an imperative step to success for Oprah Winfrey who was fired by a TV producer in Baltimore that said she was "unfit for television news"; Steve Jobs was once forced to step down from Apple, the company he founded; Arianna Huffington, creator of the Huffington Post, was rejected by thirty-six publishers before her second book landed a publishing deal; Bill Gates was a Harvard University dropout with a failed first business. Their journeys to success were ones of persistence even in the face of failure, rejection, and criticism. Did they tuck their tails between their legs and slink off into uselessness? Heck no!

Want to hear more?

In 1919, Walt Disney was fired from one of his first jobs as a newspaper animator-cartoonist. The editor said that he, "lacked imagination and had no good ideas." Imagine, Walt Disney being accused of not being creative enough? That's like firing the Pope for not being religious enough or criticizing Einstein for not being smart enough.

J.K. Rowling, author of the most successful fiction book series of all time, was let go when she worked as a secretary at Amnesty International in London. She had been caught writing on her work computer about a lovable young wizard named Harry Potter. While it worked out brilliantly in the end, I bet she initially felt as though her termination was a terrible thing to have happened. However, Rowling received a decent severance package that allowed her the freedom and security to write full-time. (*Perhaps we need to send her former employer a thank-you note!*)

Even Leonardo da Vinci's masterpiece, Mona Lisa—the best-known and most visited painting in the world—was at first considered by some to be a botched work of art. After all, the subject wears a funny smirk, she is not particularly beautiful, the scenery in the background is jacked up from side to side, and the waterline doesn't even match. (*Pray tell, could there be a hidden meaning in the work?*)

Maybe it's a relationship that ended miserably. Maybe you lost your job. Maybe you feel you have ruined an opportunity. Think of the people of greatness who have come before you, and how they succeeded precisely because of their failures. Ask yourself, "What's the hidden meaning in my failures?" Don't judge your success or failure. Don't panic when change comes, or you "fail" at something. Think about all of the time and space that is being freed up and appreciate the new direction that has been defined. Whenever there is loss, there is gain. And even in destruction, there is creation. So, you failed. Try again. Then, try again. Be on the journey, not on the judge's bench.

The Underused Gratitude Process That Makes You More Powerful, Rich, and Happy

Maybe it's financial security and abundance that you need in order to fulfill your inspired dreams. So, claim it. Discontinue the thought process that tells you that in order to be "good," you should stay poor.

(*Oh boy, do I know this one.*) For years, I was in a really sketchy place in terms of my finances. However, I still struggled for many years after that and it was only because I believed that I should. It was all that I knew. My paycheck would come in and I would somehow spend every last dollar to the point that I was always living paycheck to paycheck. I made sure of it. There was something about my financial struggle that I was both proud of (that I was surviving it with humor) and that bonded me to my also struggling friends. It put me in the Poor Girl Club and I unknowingly and consistently paid my energetic dues for the membership.

It was June of 2009 and I was living in Nashville. While my life had taken an exciting, new, purpose-filled direction and my depression had dissolved, I still suffered from failed relationships interspersed with chronic loneliness. I was also experiencing financial insecurity weighted by credit card debt and accentuated by wild fears about money from the many years that I had struggled on my own.

By way of breaking free from the corporate ladder and starting my own small publicity business, I had earned my freedom and was inching towards happiness, teetering between the thrill of chasing my dreams and fatigue from trying. Where I was then was miles away from New Year's Eve 2006 when I lived in Canada and had written my own suicide note in which I had willed away the guardianship of my beloved cat, Sabrina. And yet, I never wanted to die then (this is what many people don't understand about those who are suicidal); I only wanted the pain, struggle, sadness, and loneliness to end.

Three years of monogamous dedication to self-improvement later, I was in a good place and on my journey, not the sidelines. Yet, I still sorely yearned for a forever partner and liberation from decades of lacking, scrimping, and stressing over it all. I knew about the power of gratitude—be grateful for what you have and you'll get more of what you want—and I practiced gratitude with incremental success. Utilizing the trickery of visualizing in the present tense, I would be thankful for abundance in the moment, attempting my best to *feel* as though it was happening now. "*Thank you for my financial security and abundance. Thank you for my loyal soulmate,*" I would say over and over. I worked hard at improving my circumstances and I wanted to experience another breakthrough. I would speak my intention out loud, asking Life to, "*show me what I am missing.*" These tactics were clever on paper and they did help, but I was still lonely and struggling financially.

Then one day it hit me. I was prostrate on top of my neatly made bed, staring at the blank ceiling, when the thought came over me like an honest-to-goodness out-of-body experience. I needed to be grateful for the very sources of my angst: I needed to thank Lack and Loneliness!

I had always resented Lack and Loneliness, those cruel circumstances. I had hated what they did to me, how they reduced me and beat down my spirit. I blamed them and held them in contempt. Though, lying there on my bed, it was now made clear—like the answer to a prayer that I didn't know I had made—Lack and Loneliness were not my enemies at all, they were my greatest teachers.

"*Thank you, Lack. Thank you, Loneliness. You were marvelous teachers. I release you. I will always carry you in my heart and memories. I release you.*" The words poured out of me, and so did tears of recognition and liberation.

That day, I gained tremendous love and admiration for the teachers that I had chosen and had held in service for so many years. My heart soared with appreciation for them and my mind ran memories of all of the ways that they had served me. I recalled the many days and nights when Lack and Loneliness were my only companions. But here I sat now, in gratitude for the lessons they taught me.

"Thank you Lack and Loneliness for helping me develop patience and compassion. Thank you for instilling in me the ability to empathize with the suffering of others. Thank you for the gift of knowing that I created you to fulfill something askew in me. Without you I might never have come to know myself and my true potential. I forgive myself for how I have loathed my life. Thank you Lack and Loneliness. I will carry you in my heart and memories forever. I release you."

It was on July fourth, 2009, Independence Day, just a month after my epiphany with this new angle on gratitude (and by no coincidence, it was also right after saying goodbye—*for real this time*—to my dear Paul who had kept me on a maybe-one-day-shelf for a few years), that I met the man who would become my husband. Loneliness had been released, and Lack wasn't far behind. Having a man in my life was not the answer to my problems; the real cure was in releasing myself from the negative cycle of resentment I held for my life. That resentment had been keeping me on level with the very thing I resented. In breaking that cycle, the magic of contagious light energy had started, and I knew it.

Perhaps something in you resonates with struggle and so struggle continues to be a theme for you. Stop associating your identity with living on the financial edge, or legal troubles, or debt, or fear of not enough, or fear that what you have will be taken from you. It's now *your* turn to utilize the underused process of gratitude that makes you more powerful, rich, and happy. Do it today!

Thank your greatest teachers; they are the unlikely ones that are the most difficult to wrap your gratitude around: resentment, jealousy, envy, judgment, and doubt. Stop resisting these teachers. Ask them, "What do you want to show me? What do you have to do with the Breathtaking Agreement that I made with Life when I chose this journey?"

Write their names on a note—Lack, Loneliness, Self-Doubt, Emptiness—and make a ceremony out of releasing them. Place them in a bottle and send them to sea or spark a match and send up their smoke like signals to Heaven.

Love them. Release them. Forgive yourself.

Then, when you're ready to claim your abundance, try this as a test. Make a note of these three figures: the total amount of money in your bank accounts, your total debt, and your current monthly income. Then, seal it in an envelope and set it aside. Tomorrow morning after you brush your teeth, look at yourself in the mirror and say out loud, "Money comes to me with ease because Life knows how necessary the resource of money is to my inspired dreams. I save money and accumulate wealth in order to leverage it for my good and the good of others. I claim financial security. I claim financial wealth. I am one with financial freedom."

Then the next day, after you brush your teeth in the morning, look at yourself in the mirror and say out loud, "Money comes to me with ease because Life knows how necessary the resource of money is to my inspired dreams. I save money and accumulate wealth in order to leverage it for my good and the good of others. I claim financial security. I claim financial wealth. I am one with financial freedom."

Say the same thing out loud to yourself every morning for three months. At the end of the three months, look again at your financial wellbeing and make a note of these three figures: the total amount of money in your bank accounts, your total debt, and your current monthly income. Now, compare it to the figures from three months ago. You will very likely see overall growth in your positive financial situation, and it will all start when you consistently hold a new story about your financial life.

The brilliant thing is, your words and thoughts are all in that viral energy marinade in which you're soaking. You cannot experience abundance while you are claiming hardship. When the words that you use and the energy of your thoughts about money align with your purpose and what you truly want, you will experience a financial miracle in your life. Stop claiming your sad story of lack or loss. Verbally claim your success, purpose, wealth, and freedom from legal woes or debt. Claim your abundance. (*What in Heaven do you have to lose?*)

CHAPTER TWELVE:

THE ALCHEMY OF WELLNESS

Subluxations to Your Good Health

B locks in your body limit your access to good health. Have you ever looked out the window of a plane and noticed that once you break through the clouds, the sun is always there on the other side? Light Energy is the source of All and the unobstructed state; even shadows are created by the presence of light. In reality, there is only light and the absence of light. In terms of your good health, the metaphor is clear: ask yourself, "What's blocking my light," or "What's in the way of my health?"

In chiropractic medicine, a blockage—namely the pinching off of a nerve by an out-of-alignment vertebra—is called a subluxation. Subluxations along your spine or anywhere within the skeletal infrastructure of your body are common and can be caused by the force of an injury, or just by stress-tension in your muscles. Those muscles tweak and flex, and they can and do move vertebrae out of alignment. Of course, when vertebrae are misaligned, it jams up your spinal cord (in computer terms, the spinal cord is the central channel for wire-based communication technology within your body). These blocks literally stop the flow of messages up and down your nervous system. (To give you another image, think of it like a kink in a garden hose.) But, why is it so critical to keep your nervous system unkinked? Your nervous system is your energy superhighway delivering critical information from the brain to all of your body's organs and systems. Unresolved subluxations along this energy superhighway can and will cause disease. Here's yet another analogy that helps: imagine a roadblock somewhere along the path to your kidneys, liver, or lungs. If your organs aren't completely getting the necessary supply of how-to instructions and energy-fuel, they can't thrive (or sometimes survive).

Yet, subluxations to your body's information superhighway are not just mechanical. Blocks to your energy channels (and therefore your wellbeing) can also be caused by environmental contamination such as air pollution, water contamination, radiation, or bio-chemical interferences.

Your body was created with a program to produce health cells and if nothing gets in the way of its energy flow, it will do just that. Though, every single day you ask your body to process all sorts of poisons, much of which you actually hand deliver. By eating food that has been raised and grown with steroids, pesticides, antibiotics and more, you ingest all of those poisons and add them to your system. You probably understand that but likely haven't considered the other bio-chemicals and hormones that are trapped in the flesh of animals that have been raised and/or slaughtered in environments that create great fear for them. With this anxiety and angst comes the release of a number of hormones that are associated with fear, such as adrenocorticotropic hormone, epinephrine, cortisol, and catecholamine. Do you imagine that all of these fear-response chemicals just disappear from the muscle and fat tissues by the time the "product" reaches the grocery store shelf? In terms of meat consumption, you absorb both the toxins that are fed to the animal to unnaturally and very quickly accelerate their size, plus the fear, pain, and stress hormones that are trapped in the flesh of animals that have endured today's status-quo conditions within industries that practice the wholesale killing of animals.

Through our food alone, we ask our bodies to process a great deal of toxins; our stomachs are not magical detox machines, though we might wish they were. In contemporary Western medicine, doctors are beginning to understand what Eastern medicine practices (centering on holistic and herbal approaches to wellness) and ancient medicine men and women knew and practiced hundreds, if not thousands, of years ago: the stomach and the entire gastrointestinal system impacts the whole of the body in much the same way as the brain does—as a director of intelligence and a commander of wellness. First published in 1998 (yet only just exploding into popular medical culture in the last decade), Dr. Michael D. Gershon, M.D., wrote "the book" on it called, *The Second Brain*. Gershon devoted more than thirty years of his career to this research and the extraordinary rediscovery that nerve cells in the gut act as a brain. Think about it: to say that you trust your gut or follow your gut is to say that your gut has intelligence. And it's true, it does. Yet, you are inflicting such misery on your stomach and gastrointestinal system, playing it for clueless while you feed yourself with faux-foods. While it's not entirely your fault, it is "on" you.

In the last few generations, we have become accepting of anything that the Food and Drug Administration (FDA) has approved. More than accepting, we are also complicit by way of financial support through our consumer dollars. You assume that if it is allowed or approved by some governing entity then it must be safe for consumption, signaling little reverence for what nature has created and approves.

The human race is in a period of artificiality. We have conjured a taste for all things unnatural from our nourishment to our medicines, not to mention our entertainment and our own image.

Too often you relinquish your health and wellbeing to marketing claims and industrialized "food" production. In the interest of cost savings and convenience (and corporate greed), you buy and eat the most deplorable poisons and fake foods, all of which are subluxating your health.

Toxins of all kinds mess with the healthy reproduction of your body's cells and can create diseased cells, and eventually diseased organs and systems. Here's how: as your cells divide and reproduce themselves through the processes of mitosis and cytokinesis, your body fully creates— continuously—new systems and organs.

As your body is making you a new body, what fuel will you provide? Your body's cells create daughter cells, and the originals dissolve as new cells take their place. It all happens using the stuff that you have taken in through food, exterior environmental exposure, and the emotions and energy vibrations in which you have marinated as well as produced from within your own selfhood.

Oh yes, health is about more than what you're eating and breathing; there are energetic toxins, too! When you beat down your body with cycles of stress and anxiety—even guilt—it will force a break in the form of bouts of sickness. These toxins are some of the heavy viral energies in your life, relationships, and home or work environments. Add to that: bickering, unforgiveness, gossip, righteousness, stuck-in-traffic frustration, mudslinging in politics and in the media, anxiety due to running late, and energetic rejection towards a job that you resent.

You know for yourself that stress compromises your immune system, and yet you go through life letting in all sorts of energetic toxins. And don't forget about worry! Worry is one of the most insidious of energetic toxins. Oh, how worry will pollute your light presence. Yep, sicknesses triggered by polluted viral energy are not only caught from others and absorbed from exterior sources, your own worry, doubt, fear, guilt, regret, perfectionism, stress, and anxiety are all inwardly projected viral energies. These are self-minimizing energies, and if allowed to build-up or fester, they are toxic to your physical body. They are heavy and dense, and they have the ability to create energy blocks and stop the body from what it does naturally and perfectly: be whole.

Could it be that becoming fortified to heavy viral energy is the long sought-after cure for the common cold? Yes, indeed, it is. Have you ever noticed that when you're engaged in a conflict with someone, filled with worry, find yourself inundated with frustration over current events, news, or negative people in your life, *that's* the time when you tend to catch a cold? It's true, getting sick has more to do with your susceptibility to heavy viral energy than it has to do with your exposure to the cold virus or a bacterial infection. In fact, a weakening of the immune system is so connected with heavy viral energy that the cold virus should be referred to as "heavy-energy-sickness."

A likely question in your mind right now is: how does this explain the rate at which little kids, or the elderly, get sick? I could interview a dozen doctors to help answer this question, yet I'm not speaking of medicine when I talk about Heavy Energy Sickness; it's a matter of the spirit and the metaphysical. So, to answer the query, I tapped into the same spiritual process with which I intuit all of my writings and philosophies; the meditative process of osmotic-energy-balancing and the very process that this entire dialogue is about and instructs. (When you utilize the nature and magic of light viral energy for your good and the good of others, you gain access to a stream of Higher-Self consciousness.)

Here's what I got from Higher-Self through automatic writing regarding this question about sickness in children and the elderly: It's natural that children get a cold or get sick more frequently than average-aged adults do. This is how their immune systems develop. A child's immune system does most of its learning after gestation within its mother. This process should not be artificially modified or tampered with. Think of a baby or young child's immune system like a brand-new car; the manufacturer will advise that it be taken it out on the highway to "blow out the carbon." A young body's immune system develops precisely because of the cycles of getting sick and getting well. As for the elderly, their immune systems are in a (also natural) deliberate process of slowing down in terms of effectiveness. When a soul of any age decides that it will return to the spirit world, the body will follow this order and begin to utilize less creation-energy for the "physical self," and put more creation-energy into the desires and transition of the "spirit self."

As we continue this dialogue, let me therefore define that I am speaking of average-aged adults and our too-often untapped abilities to command our physicality to the will of our Higher-Self's purpose.

Spirit over matter as it relates to the common cold is much easier for many people to buy into. But, what about diseases?

Many, many sicknesses can be cured because on some level you (unconsciously) agreed to them in the first place. To be clear, you are not to blame for your sickness; that would imply a wrongdoing. But, maybe just maybe it is possible that before your incarnation into this physical lifetime, your soul *agreed* to the disease or even *chose* it for some purpose, and if that were true, then you are the creator of your experiences and the experiences of your physical self, too.

(*This is when you're going to say: "Penelope doesn't know what she's talking about! I have a real disease or a real injury! I'm in real effing pain and I sure didn't 'agree' to it!!!"*) Let me share with you—without boring you with my whole medical history and the details of the lumbar spinal fusion that followed—that I once had a broken back. So broken in fact was my back that neurologists actually called it "catastrophic." Do you think that I thought I "agreed" to this affliction—the worst pain imaginable; a pain so heinous that, while I write for a living, I struggle to put it into words? (*Maybe not, but then again, maybe so.*) Could it be that my "spirit self" chose this experience for my "physical self" for a particular purpose?

Returning to you and the many subluxations to your good health, let's look at the toxins to your wellness. Please, stick with me here as I'm going to talk about "many sicknesses," not *all* sicknesses, and maybe not the one that you have. (*But, then again, maybe so.*)

While it's sometimes harder to see the immediate cause and effect, many (not all) diseases can be attributed to heavy contagious energies and toxins, including diseases of the nervous system and digestive system, a weakening of the heart, many forms of depression, imbalanced weight gain or loss, plus insomnia, chronic fatigue, and the breaking down of your immune system. And that last one is a biggie, so let's touch on it again: by dimming the defense system of your body, any disease whatsoever can rise up. (I'm about to give you yet *another* analogy; each helps to further understanding of the nature of wellbeing.) The clearest way to visualize it is this: when your body's cell-reproduction is pinched-off or polluted, your body is pinched-off from natural wellbeing—just as the clouds in the sky can block out the sun, or the flow from a faucet can narrow. (*Oh, the sicknesses and diseases that arise when your immune system or communication superhighway is blocked!*) And, it can happen as commonplace and persistently as ongoing stress—"everyday" and every day.

I wanted to back up my own work and so I called one of the world's top experts on energy medicine, Dr. Bradley Nelson, bestselling author of *The Emotion Code*. Dr. Nelson told me this: "Emotional baggage is actually the emotional energy left behind in our bodies after traumatic emotional events that we experience—after a divorce, for example, after abuse as a child, or after a difficult work situation. With the emotions of anger, frustration, resentment, or anxiety, what happens is that the energy of those emotions can become trapped in the body. It's critical to understand that the body is nothing more than an extremely complex energy field of pure energy. When you're feeling an intense emotion of frustration for example, you're feeling a specific frequency of energy; that's a different frequency than sadness or depression. Every emotion has a frequency. When we are experiencing an intense emotion, that emotion can be overwhelming in some way to the body. The energy stays behind in the body even after the event or emotion has passed. After that event is over, part of the emotion remains behind and these things that we refer to as 'trapped energy' are actually balls of energy—balls of pure emotional frequency typically the size of a baseball or cantaloupe, and these can lodge anywhere in the body. When they do, they cause two specific kinds of effects for us: physical disease and emotional pains."

Let me break here mid-interview with Dr. Nelson to tell you that when I was on this phone interview with him (we had four audio-recorded interviews in total, plus he performed an energy-healing session on me), I was thinking exactly what you're probably thinking right now: *Wow! A ball of trapped energy the size of a baseball or cantaloupe! That's huge...and very specific! How does he know this?!* Well, folks, I'm not the doctor; he is. Dr. Nelson is a renowned holistic physician and lecturer, specifically studying and researching the inner workings of the subconscious mind and the mind-body-spirit connection. He's done the research on energy medicine and if this interests you, I highly recommend reading his aforementioned bestseller. For "energy medicine," he's your expert!

He continued, "These trapped emotions are stored within the energy field of the body. Now, because the body is nothing more than an energy field, that energy of the stored emotion has a physical effect because it can interfere with the acupuncture meridian flow, for example. It can interfere with the typical reactions taking place in those tissues. This is why we found that up to ninety percent of the pain that people experience is actually due to emotional baggage. It is very common for pain to disappear instantaneously when the underlying cause is revealed and removed. Energy medicine is absolutely the future. There may always be a need for pharmaceuticals, probably, but I can't say for sure."

And, I'd like to add—based on my own dialogues with Higher-Self— that a return to much of the ways and wisdom of the ancients and First Nations people is the future of wellness care.

Today, our blind consumption of toxic food, pharmaceuticals, and heavy energy has manifested in a planetary cycle of disease. But you have a choice about subluxations to your good health. You can clear mechanical, chemical, and energetic blockages from your body and become immune to Heavy Energy Sickness. You have a choice about what you linger in: light energy or heavy energy. It's time for new ideals; new fuel. Detox from your body all influences and creations of heavy viral energy. Let more light into your being.

Management Meetings with Your Body

Have you ever had a management meeting with your body?

I believe that good health and wellness are metaphysical processes of transformation and creation. And, you have the power to create. So, why are you giving away your power?

Yes, too often you readily claim your sickness, pain, or disease. By calling it "my illness," or "my high blood pressure," or "my back pain," or "my headaches," you are claiming it. Stop doing that. By claiming sickness in your name, you are resigning your power and your part in your own health.

Do not doubt that you create with the Creator.

But maybe you have a chronic illness or a terminal disease. Do you think it is possible for you to create yourself out of sickness and into wellness?

Do not doubt that you are a powerful Creator.

Your body is a resource for the fulfillment of your purpose.

You and your body are in a partnership. Yep, it's all part of the deal of free will that you made with Life. It's the deal that you got into by choice and with excitement for what you would awaken to and create. It's the deal that you made when you were in the realm of "knowing" before you incarnated into this human experience. And yet, so many of us are still asleep to it.

There's so much more to this human experience than you give yourself credit for because you are too busy giving away the credit and power. You don't want to accept how powerful you are—and why, pray tell? In part, you chose to give away your power thanks to thousands of years of religious dogma that says you are not in control, and furthermore, that you should not dare to be powerful. You also give away your power because you don't want to feel responsible; it's a burden that you believe is easier to pass off.

Yet, still, the truth is that the idea that you are powerless to your own body—that pain just happens to you and disease just happens to you— is all part of the world of illusion and separateness; the sleeping world cloaked in your own fears and doubts.

Refer to your Breathtaking Agreement With Life. What is it that you choose to create with your life? What's your unique contribution? Now, ponder this: you are not just in an agreement with Life, you also entered into an agreement with your body for the fulfillment of your purpose. That's your body's job! But, if you're not clear about your breathtaking purpose—*the reason that you took your first breath and every breath until this moment*—then your body might be unclear about its divine purpose. Make crystal clear just how much your health is wanted, needed, honored, and of critical importance to your soul's mission. Your purpose is a big deal. It's thee Big Deal! Your purpose is what has impassioned your soul to manifest into physical form.

To transform your health and promote wellness, repeat this daily mantra to yourself out loud: "Dear Life, we are in an agreement together that I use my life to (*fill in your chosen purpose, inspired dream, or passion*). We have much left to do and I am utilizing the gift of a healthy physical body." Here's another one: "I have no further use for sickness (*or pain etc.*), and for that reason, I no longer accept any force that is incongruent with my powerful purpose and intention."

Now that you have made an agreement with your body to create something anew (which is wellness), let's go one step further in affirming it with this visualization:

Imagine that the organs and systems of your body are your work colleagues. There are no slouches here. The organs and systems of your body are brilliant geniuses. In fact, the individual parts of your body, and how they work as a team, are in many ways far advanced in comparison to your own capabilities. It's within your ability to use your mastery and expertise to direct your body to your will. It's not about force; it's about a partnership. This is why you are not in command of your body; you are in a breathtaking agreement with your body for the fulfillment of your divine and chosen purpose. You say to your body, "We need to go here," and your body goes there.

In terms of the physicality that is you, your job is both as a contemporary peer to your body and her systems, as well as the Project Manager to a fully equipped team of geniuses and leaders in their own right. All of your body's systems and organs are your brilliant A-Team.

Knowing this, schedule a group meeting and ask for mandatory attendance by all of your body's departments, parts, and systems. Request the attention of your team.

Play this out with yourself. As Project Manager, you get to choose where you hold the meeting. Do you choose an executive boardroom in an ultra-modern high-rise, a family-style meeting at your kitchen table, a gathering in the team's locker room, or an intimate chat on a comfy blanket under an oak tree in a park?

Here's my own mind-body-spirit meeting place: I'm sitting in the dining room of my dream home with a massive rain-wall feature at my back. It's peacefully trickling with the rhythm of falling water and I'm facing a sunny view of the pool beyond French doors with the sparkling ocean backdropping the pool. I'm smiling and my eager teammates flank each side of an extended oval table.

Get into *your* visualization. Where are you? Where are you holding your meeting? Take note of who is in attendance. Your heart—there she is; yes, your digestive system is here; oh, there are your muscles and nerves; and, check—all your brain cells are ready, too. Next, call the meeting to order and verbally let your team know exactly what you need to be checked and put into divine alignment. And, remind your team about *why* you need top performance. (This is the most important part…)

Say to your team (quietly in your mind, or out loud for added effectiveness), "I claim my purpose and I'm going to need all of you to do your job with excellence and efficiency. All of my cells, organs, and systems: you are in a constant process of reproduction and I need you to reproduce entirely healthily and in alignment with divine order. To all of the cells of my body: I claim our total wellness. May I have the full attention of my immune system: it is my will that you engage the superpower and connectivity of all of Life (capital "L"). At this moment, supercharge my body's total wellness mode. Our physicality serves a divine purpose and I claim my body's health."

You may also simply say, "I claim my body to be the pure light energy of the Creator for the fulfillment of my Breathtaking Agreement With Life." Know that every word that you speak and think—at all times and always—is a prayer.

In the beginning of adopting this creation mindset, it might seem to oppose what you have been taught about putting your full faith in God. And yet, God has told you that you were made in the image and likeness of the Creator—"Creator" being the operative namesake. Nonetheless, if you feel that the issue is too big for you to project-manage and you don't have the capacity to take part, you can lean on the contract that you have with Life and beseech this: "God, take this illness from me and restore my health so that I may continue to create with my life."

It's not just a matter of positivity, positive statements, or self-talk. It's not only about claiming your wellness. The key is in making and keeping an agreement with your body for the fulfillment of your purpose. Remember, if you don't have a clear purpose, then your physical body may not be inspired to its full potential.

All resources will be provided to you in direct proportion to what you need in order to fulfill your purpose on Earth. (That's worth repeating!) *All resources will be provided to you in direct proportion to what you need in order to fulfill your purpose,* including the resource of your health. Your purpose is what you declare it to be. Make it big enough so that the resource of good health is intrinsic to what you will create and contribute to the whole of Life.

Just like you need to be needed, your body needs to be needed. And let's be frank: you often take your body for granted as though you don't really need her. Yep, even you, the trusted and entrusted Project Manager, don't always make the best decisions on behalf of your team. But know this: your body has a say and will eventually go on strike if it's not being maintained with the excellence that it deserves, or it's not being used in the fulfillment of your Breathtaking Agreement With Life. Just like with any contract, it's a two-way agreement; both parties must uphold their end. As long as you have breath, you are in a breathtaking and divine agreement. Start today to be the Project Manager that you set out to be!

Of course, many diseases and sicknesses are not preventable but are the cards that you were given through your genes, circumstances, or happenstance. And yet, if you could remember the Agreement that you wholeheartedly entered into with Life, you would remember that even those illnesses—or an early exit from physicality, perhaps at a very young age—were your soul's choice before your incarnation in order to experience (or participate in) a particular time-space moment that can only be experienced in the physical realm. Perhaps this was in the form of a specific expression of love in the physical body, or as a willing partner in the spiritual evolution process of another soul, therefore adding your legacy to humanity's spiritual evolution. Even a disease can serve your Breathtaking Agreement With Life, and yet even that choice can be chosen again *if* that's what your Higher-Self chooses. If you're waiting for a miracle—create it. The very good news is that you already have your miracle: through the divine process of Creation, your body's cells are dividing and making brand new cells right now as you read these words. That is where your miracle lives.

Listen to the divine wisdom of your body. What does your body need from you for the fulfillment of your purpose? Here are some requirements that your body has: good nutrition; clean air; exercise; a rest from stress and over-working; and a break from the heavy viral energy of negativity, judgment, righteousness, jealousy, envy, competition with others, and incessant striving for the upper hand. Your body has no use for the smallness that you get caught up in when you seek to come out on top over others. Your body has no use for playing small when you allow someone else to take away your power or when you don't speak up to define your boundaries. Your body knows that you and the other are one; a life spent seeking the upper hand—or being undermined—is a life wasted for the brilliance of your divine body.

Be as though you are running a mind-body-spirit empire—*because you are*! Do not accept toxins into your body's success. Start saying no to sustenance, people, tasks, work for pay, obligations, entertainment, and environments that pollute your body's creation-energy. Filter what you are exposing yourself to because you're so worth it! Say yes to sustenance, people, tasks, work for pay, obligations, entertainment, and environments that add light energy to your body's creation energy—be enlightened. When empowered by you to do what it perfectly does—without interference from heavy energy and toxins—your body will reproduce itself healthy. And all you have to do is manage by saying "no" or "yes" and by affirming your body's true purpose.

Re-engage as the resolute and fair Project Manager of your breathtaking purpose. Starting today and with total sincerity and focus, set out your plan and commitment with and to your body. Renew your agreement with your body. What is it? Write it down. Shake metaphorical hands on it.

It might sound like this: "Dear cells, organs, and systems of my body: I honor and thank you for your service to our purpose. We are in an agreement together and I need you in top health for the fulfillment of the agreement that we made with all of Life. I will do my part and provide you with the best fuel and healthy light energy as you reproduce yourself in perfect order. Through my will, I accept the management of our success. Through the empowerment endowed in me by the wholeness of all of Life, I request your full strength and wellness. I claim my health."

Is Sickness Serving You?

You might ask, "If declaring a purpose for your life, reuniting with your Breathtaking Agreement With Life, and creating and contributing to the evolution of Life is the secret to getting and keeping the resources of health and life-force, then why have so many intrepids and good-doers died—seemingly in the middle of their world-changing work—such as Martin Luther King Jr., primatologist Dian Fossey, baseball great Lou Gehrig, and Jesus Christ…?"

The answer to that question is clear when considering these questions: Did their deaths have a magical way of enlightening and mobilizing people to their cause? And, during their life and death, did they experience themselves as Creator? The very same can be said for any average good-doer who died seemingly mid-mission; you don't have to be famous for your soul to choose the most effective timing to depart from your physicality and return to your spirit self. Your presence made its intended mark and legacy.

The fact is there is no end to your life that your soul did not choose. Ever. To let God's will be done is the very same as to let your will be done. Before your incarnation, you make the choice about the inflictions (or you can call them challenges or growth opportunities) that you experience, designed as part of your plan to awaken yourself and/or others, and to experience yourself in the face of your challenge. What will you do with it; how will you role model; what will you learn or teach; what solution or advancement will you be part of; who will you inspire; what grace will you demonstrate; what love-energy will you spread?

And, there are also lifetimes when your soul set out with the best intentions and yet those were left unfulfilled (in that lifetime anyway).

Sometimes, during a physical lifetime you (unconsciously) decline your original choice, and by way of your ever-present free will, you make a new choice. Sometimes, that new choice is to surrender your life and your pre-incarnation plans through giving up. Speaking to the latter, it's not uncommon for humans to get tired of or pained by the physical world and to will themselves back to the Spirit World, although most often, this happens unconsciously.

And, there are those individuals who don't want out of this physical life, yet they do teeter on the brink of body-system shutdowns, also serving a purpose of sorts. Let me share with you this true, though perhaps common, story.

Annie is a woman in her thirties who has numerous health concerns and regularly schedules appointments with specialists of all kinds to investigate everything including her nasal septum for deviation, her breasts for lumps, her uterus for fibroids, her joints for arthritis, her spine for bone spurs, and her throat for damaged vocal cords. She's on a quest to discover things wrong with her body like a suspicious woman trying to catch her cheating boyfriend red-handed.

In fact, in her romantic life, she's had so many cheating boyfriends that she's gotten very good at social media scanning, cell phone auditing, and whereabouts-scrutinizing, and now she's applying these skills to her body as she believes that it too might betray her. To add fear to fear, both of her parents died of disease and she believes that the medical system and their own bodies had failed them. She's very untrusting on many levels. You could say that Annie is a real "sickness sleuth" and finding out if she is unwell is of paramount importance to her. It's a project that allows her to openly be in fear under the guise of health issues. But her sickness sleuthing cannot resolve what is really causing her indisposition; however something about it is working for her. What she is creating in her body is fulfilling her expectation that she is a being who is not in control. She wants to get *it* before *it* gets the better of her. Her body's ticks are serving her fears, doubts, and insecurities, and they are also giving her false empowerment. While totally subconscious, Annie is creating her ailments in order to confirm her beliefs, simultaneously attempting to gain an upper hand when she could not do so in other areas of her life.

What are all of the ways that sickness has served you?

You can be honest about it because, trust me, nearly all of us have used sickness to our benefit at some time.

It's not unusual for people to get physically sick when they need a break from work, relationship stress, and the treadmill of striving for success.

We don't usually grant ourselves a rest or retreat, but if we're sick, well, taking a break is out of our hands. So, we get sick. And it's okay to just let yourself get sick sometimes, if that's the way that you choose to take a break. But if you don't want to be sick, you actually don't have to wait for your body to force a break through sickness—or a "breakthrough sickness." A much better idea is to take the break when you need it and skip the sickness.

Sickness is handy for more than taking a break. It is also useful when it comes to explaining why you didn't get something done or reach a goal that you set for yourself. It gives you an excuse when you don't want to have to conjure an excuse. Plus, sickness can supply you with empathy that you would not otherwise get from others. Yet far more than empathy, sickness can bring to you the feeling of being cared for, and who doesn't want to be taken care of now and then? It feels like (if not truly is) love. Ahhh, that's nice, isn't it? And when you have really messed up with someone, sickness will give you a free pass and will curry favor back to you. (*I'm not endorsing sickness, just laying out the facts. And yes, I'm being a bit facetious.*) Whether acute/short-term sicknesses or chronic/long-term illnesses and diseases, both can insulate you from family responsibilities and social obligations. If you want to be left alone for a while without everyone calling your name and wanting something from you, sickness can get you your "me-time." I know many people who have conjured an illness in order to protect themselves from challenges that they couldn't face. (*I have, too.*) I'm not suggesting that they have done this consciously or deliberately; far from it. In fact, these mind-body manifestations are problem-solving modalities created by your spirit: energetic solutions to energetic blockages.

I'll give you another example from my own experience: Somewhere on my journey, around my mid- thirties, I crossed over the separation line between wanting and awareness and I did so simply by way of becoming an avid seeker of spiritual fuel and an assiduous nitpicker of authority. I started to experience the truth that I am in an agreement with my mind, spirit, and yes, my body, too.

When I was a teenager—*and truthfully, throughout the entirety of my twenties*—I used to get sick often. This was back when I was sleepwalking through life and unhappy in both my personal and professional life. Every time a cold went around, I got it. I picked it up because I was on level with being sick. I got a lot out of being sick, from taking days off work to getting sympathy from others. I had chronic headaches, functional depression, and I would get overwhelmed incredibly easily. These were all side effects of the energetic pollution that I allowed into my life, day in and day out.

My lungs, in particular, had been an area of weakness my whole life. Maybe I had inherited weak lungs from my dad. Or perhaps I had developed a narrow energy flow in my heart-lung chakra from years of turmoil and love loss. Either way, I would frequently get lung infections and issues with fluid stagnating in my lungs, and I was hospitalized twice with pneumonia. In less severe bouts, the sickness would go on for weeks or months in the form of lingering and pesky coughing and throat clearing.

Then in my early thirties, I began testing my partnership with my body as an experiment. *Why the Heaven not*, I thought? By my late thirties, I was very in-tune with my body's signs and symptoms and how to interpret them, and so usually—but not always—I could stop a sickness before it started. On one Friday afternoon, I got some news of an opportunity that was both tremendously exciting and nerve-wracking. But after a few minutes of exhilaration, fear washed over me. *Would I meet the challenge and succeed? Would I fall just short and waste the opportunity?* This had been one of my repetitive patterns and fears: to almost realize a goal or dream, but not quite. The mix of positive expectation and heavy anxiety triggered a physical reaction in my body. I immediately felt weight and fluid build in my lungs and I began incessantly coughing and throat clearing.

An hour later, I had noticed that my coughing had become so frequent that I was doing it every five or six seconds. I felt that if I didn't clear my throat that I wouldn't be able to breathe. My husband Burt said, "What's in your throat? Maybe you should drink some water." But it wasn't in my throat; it was fluid in my lungs and I had experienced it countless times before. I knew what it was. It was the same heaviness that had settled in for weeks or longer and had doctors ordering x-rays and antibiotics, all ineffective efforts as the problem was fluid and not infection. For years and years, I gave away my power and responsibility to doctors and anyone else who would claim it.

But not this time. After eight straight hours of coughing and throat clearing, the realization struck me: "Hey, wait a minute," I said to myself, "I'm not sick; I am healthy. This cough does not serve me. I don't need it to hide behind. I don't need to prepare an excuse as a cover in case I don't succeed."

In that moment, I knew that what I was experiencing was heavy energy sickness; my doubt inferred and juxtaposed from past disappointments. I knew that the part of me that had responded with anxiety to the exciting news had commanded my body to react in the same old way that it was used to reacting: "Righto, cells, we need a backup plan—send fluid to the lungs!" I awoke to the con and so I said to myself, out loud and with confidence, "Dear cells of my body, I claim a partnership with you, and it is my will that you be nonreactive to my heavy emotions. Dear cells of my lungs, clear out all fluid as quickly and as easily as I had previously directed fluid to build through my doubt-response. To my wonderful immune system, we are in a partnership with each other and I claim my wellbeing."

Ten minutes later my coughing and throat clearing ceased completely. My body fell in line with my will and both my exciting new opportunity and my will-over-body project were successes.

Incidentally, as I write this, I can report to you that I have not been sick in four years. Not once. While people around me are regularly and seasonally sick, not one time have I gotten a common cold or the flu in four years and counting. No pharmaceuticals, no flu shots, no sickness. I'm not saying I'll never get sick; I just haven't in years. I've been known to tell people, "I'm immune to getting a cold," and I believe that's true. My wellness is a result of my awareness of the power of viral energy and how I use this knowledge to my benefit.

Your spirit knows that without your health, you have nothing in this world. And without purpose, you have no business in this world. I don't mean that flippantly. Quite realistically, if you're not creating anything in the physical realm, Life will shift resources to those who are busy creating. Grave sickness can be the messenger telling you to live your life differently or just more deliberately. There will be a moment when illness will stop you in your tracks—maybe that's now—and you will instantly decide to adjust your priorities. It is remarkable just how efficient sickness is at righting imbalance. And as counterintuitive as it is that I would need to tell you this, I bet you've never heard it before: you don't need sickness to heal yourself.

Try this: Bring into your full attention what is going on within yourself—what's imbalanced? What's your body trying to tell you? Ask yourself what you are gaining from this sickness, and can you release that need? Bring it forward and allow it to be with you, consciously. If disease would inspire you to quit your job to free up your time for what's most important to you, then quit your job without needing the disease. Stop forcing yourself to do what you despise; find another way. If sickness would let you out of a burden or responsibility that you didn't ask for or can't bear, let go of the burden without requiring the sickness. Find another way. If illness would insulate you from your own self-doubt, face head-on whatever the outcome might be without creating the illness. Find another way. Create it anew.

Sickness is often the blabbermouth that something is incongruent in your energy field. Get the message and access the benefit by creating another way to get what you need. Let go of passive control of your body, and instead get in a partnership. Be direct about the love that you need. Take the break. Take the risk. Rise to the challenge. Don't get sick; get your energy light.

Light Energy Immersion Therapy

Pray for your good health and the good health of others, yes, but pray a praise of thanksgiving. It might be useful to remember, from Chapter Eight, the parable of the drowning man who asked God to save him. Three times boats approached and offered help. Three times the man declined the earthly intervention, saying, "No thanks, God will save me." As the story goes, the man dies waiting for God, doing nothing to help himself. For Heaven's sake, don't be closed-minded like the drowning man; God is listening and sending you the people, events, circumstances, resources, ideas, new medical trials, and the deep wisdom of holistic and ancient tradition medicine. Recognize God everywhere that She is.

In terms of the role of energy in your health, there is an energy-alchemy for good health. It's important to understand that even in poor health and terminal disease, you are growing in your spiritual evolution. It would greatly benefit you to embrace the gifts in illness. Haven't you reprioritized in a hurry? Haven't you felt and given more love in the face of sickness? Through the gift of diminished physical health, you are balancing the heavy weight of physical things and becoming enlightened. What else could do that? In fact, many other forces can accomplish that such as heavy forces like a sudden financial loss, or light forces of conscious intention and spiritual evolution. The balance that you need doesn't have to come through trauma or loss. It's your choice about what will get your attention and fulfill the purpose of your soul.

Now say to the great teacher named Disease, "Thank you for everything that you've shown me; I release you."

When you feel like crying because of your infliction, don't be in fear that your doubt will out you in your faith. Instead, let your emotions be welcomed with the same love that you would give to a child. Cry if you need to. Let the heavy energy pour out from you and let it be an energetic release. Then, through your tears, repeat out loud, "Disease (or injury etc.), I no longer need you. Thank you for all that you have opened my eyes to. I release you."

In living as though you have no power, you have no power. In living as though you have no peace, you have no peace. In living as though you have no right to take a break, you have no right to take a break. In living as though you have no purpose, you have no purpose. Your life's purpose is the one that you give yourself and it has everything to do with this question: what will you create, next? Elevating your creation energy and your light presence is the key to your restored good health.

Even in the face of disease, be in light. Let light energy radiate in you and from you. Let it heal you. You will recognize light because it will feel light. Let light dissolve all that is heavy. Let light dissolve the burden and blockage to your health. You cannot be separated from light any more than a cloud will sometimes separate us from the sun. Light is always there for you.

Focus not on driving out darkness and heaviness, but on being light. Yes, be in light, and also *be* the light. Get around others who are beacons of light. Let them infect you with their light. Do not invite under your roof any force of heaviness like the toxins in your environment, in the news, in your own words and thoughts, or in negative conversations with others. These are kryptonite to your goal and purpose. Let your lips speak only words of love. After all, love is the highest of light energies. Your clear access to light energy is your medicine. It's worth repeating—your clear access to light energy *is* your medicine. Fully commit to igniting deep within your body and being a generator for light energy. And in doing so, witness the experiential light of Life: God, creating Yourself anew.

Visualize this: imagine for a moment what it would be like to be God. (*Oh, just let go of your small self for a minute and allow your Higher-Self this visualization.*) God can do and be anything and so She chooses to be everything in order to witness Herself ultimately choosing light, and by doing so She experiences the pure joy of remembrance with the light that She is from the beginning. God knows that even shadows exist due to the presence of light. Nothing can block His light that He doesn't allow. God can have and do anything, and so even darkness must be under order by Him. Just like the great body of aspen trees called Pando, God Themselves manifest as countless shoots, popping forth to the surface, temporarily separated from the Whole, and appearing to the five senses as individuals. And because all is God and God is all there is, She is being everything, even that which appears to be blocking the light. God is being you. God is being all that you create. God is being the disease or infliction. God is being the joy and pain.

Likewise, you are choosing what you will be. You are being all that you create and choosing to create. You are being your disease or infliction and choosing its contribution.

But you can choose again, right now. Don't waste your energy on denying the existence of disease; choose something else. You don't want the experience of disease? Okay then, what *do* you want to experience and create? Be precise about it. In being as though you have purpose, you have purpose. In being as though you have health, you have health. In being as though you have life, you have life.

God wants you to know this: you are the Creator. The light is in you, of you, and for you. Your journey is whatever you create it to be. They are for every version of Themselves; They can never be against you. Your unknowing of being part of the Whole does not change that fact. You cannot offend Them. Your lifetimes as an individual delights Them just like a parent finds joy in watching their infant child stumble and walk and stumble again. When you walk or stumble, it makes no difference to Them nor changes Their love for you in any way. It only takes you longer to get to where you decided you wanted to go. If you decide to keep going, decide to keep going.

The realm that we call Heaven is a wonderful *state* to *be* and your soul remembers it well. Choose why you want this physical body experience to continue. Make it so juicy that it outweighs any reason that your soul would have to return, quite yet, to the Whole of Life. Write it down and renew your agreement with Life about what you will create. Accept your power to create; don't give it away. Call under task all of the parts and systems of your body to get on board. And for goodness sake, treat your body like you want it and love it.

PART FOUR:

HOW TO GET EVERYTHING YOU WANT

(AND MORE THAN YOU DREAMT OF)

CHAPTER THIRTEEN:

NATURE'S GIFTS TO MAXIMIZE YOUR LIGHT ENERGY

Why Nature is the Gold Standard

About ten years ago, I stayed with friends in Nashville for a couple of months while I was between apartments. Along with me as always was my cat, Sabrina, who was about twelve at that time. My friends had an enormous three-story white stone house with porches on two levels that wrapped around the front and sides of the home, plus four guest bedrooms, an elevator, wine cellar, home movie theater, and a full-time live-in maid named Rosa. She was a petite woman in her mid-fifties with a soft and gentle presence, and a bad lower back that she would frequently rub. Rosa spoke broken English and every morning she would come to my bedroom—one of the smaller guest rooms yet boasting the best view of a grand magnolia tree in full pink bloom—and greet me with, "Happy morning, Miss Penelope," and then she would ask to pet Sabrina. Sabrina would purr, bat her eyelashes, and then wiggle onto her side exposing her chubby belly for petting. Rosa would smile and talk to Sabrina in Spanish. As the weeks went on, Rosa and Sabrina became quite familiar and Sabrina would start purring merely at the sound of Rosa coming down the hallway with her signature swift pace. I started leaving my door open for Rosa to visit Sabrina, and while Sabrina was not much of an explorer, I occasionally noticed that she would venture out of my room. I would later find her catnapping on a perfectly made bed down the hallway in another guest room and I'd say to her, "Who do you think you are, Princess? You'd better not get too used to this!" She would look at me, flop over in deep swells of purring, and make bread with her paws in the air; "happy feet," I've heard it called.

One day, not in her usual spot on my bed, I went looking for Sabrina, ducking into each guest room to scan for my chocolate-colored kitty. When I couldn't find her, I thought I'd ask Rosa if she had seen her, so I made my way to Rosa's bedroom. Noticing the light on, I half-knocked on the open door, and said, "Rosa, have you seen—." Before I could get out a full sentence, there I saw them both: Rosa lying flat on her stomach on her bed, and Sabrina sitting on her back like an Egyptian sphinx, massaging Rosa with her "happy feet" and purring like an engine.

"Oh, Sabrina! What are you—get off of Rosa," I said in surprise and half-embarrassment. "No, no," Rosa petitioned with her head cocked sideways towards where I was standing, "No, Miss Penelope, it okay. Her purr, it heals my back."

In her signature way of communicating, both self-conscious and sweet, Rosa explained that the two of them had a daily "purr therapy" routine. Rosa would call for Sabrina, and Sabrina would oblige. (*I had no idea that Sabrina had such talent. I must say I was impressed.*)

As it turns out, Rosa was right. I did some research myself and found it to be true: a cat's purr is healing. In fact, scientists say that people benefit both physically and emotionally from a cat's purr. The vibration of the purring triggers our brain to release pain-killing hormones, and it actually promotes the healing of degeneration and fractures in bones. As I've read about it since then, I've learned that it can also treat headaches and stomachaches; lower blood pressure, stress, and anxiety; and help heal infection and swelling. What's more, studies show that cat owners have a forty percent lower risk of heart disease. (Way to go, Sabrina!) As for the primary function of this marvel of nature—which is of course to benefit cats—it seems that felines not only purr when content or experiencing enjoyment, they also purr while giving birth and when a kitten is sick or injured. They do this as both a healing *and* a calming therapy. What's also fascinating is that heart disease, respiratory disease, and bone cancer are almost unheard of in cats.

Elizabeth von Muggenthaler, researcher and president of Fauna Communications Research Institute, Raleigh-Durham, North Carolina, says that all cats—including cougars, cheetahs, pumas, lions, the domestic cat, and more—purr within a range of vibrational frequency between twenty to 140 hertz (the pulse of frequency unit "beats" per second). This is known as a healing vibration and it is being copied and generated by machines today for use in some contemporary medical communities to heal all kinds of mechanical injuries including those to bone, muscles, tendons, and tissue. It's also being used to expedite the healing of wounds; clear infection; and outright cure osteoporosis, Chronic Pulmonary Disease, and more.

It has to get you thinking—if vibration can heal physical and emotional disorders, what else can vibration do?

The vibration that you are being sets the quality of your energetic-presence. Light energy vibrations originating from outside of your selfhood can balance your presence in a positive way. I've said it before and will say it again because it could not be more important: your energy vibration, the very quality level of your presence, is the fuel for all that you create, have access to, and draw from to experience Life.

As far as vibrations go, a cat's purr is sort of an easy one because we can hear and feel that vibration. But, before the classic cat verses dog debate ensues, hang on a minute, pussycat lovers: cats aren't the only animals with superpowers. Any of your domestic pets (or wildlife, for that matter) can calm you and balance your energy with their natural vibration.

Do you ever wonder if your dog is trying to tell you something? Oh yes, dogs want to show you how to relax and to let go of heavy energy. (Well, okay, first and foremost, your dog wishes to teach *you* how to fetch. But second only to that, they wish to show you how to relax.) Surely you have noticed your dog take in a big breath and then huff it out in a dramatic sigh. Your dog makes no apologies for sighing, and yet *you've* probably been told by others not to sigh. People interpret sighing as frustration, boredom, anger, or displeasure. And yes, sighing can no doubt be a social faux pas, but your dog knows that there is a time and place for a good sigh. Sighing is a stress-reliever, and do you know why? Sighing allows you to "shake it off" and let heavy energy out. Sighing, dancing, a good head or body shake, and exercise are all excellent modalities to release built-up heavy energy. So, sigh if you want to!

But, what about your heavy viral energy rubbing off on your pet? If you are a very frantic or high-strung person, your frantic energy will likely rub off on your pet. Yes, there's a reverse effect to this and the "winning energy" will always be the more concentrated of the two fields as they naturally balance their differences through osmosis.

It just so happens that all of nature has a message for you and it's told through the pulse of life. Each being—all matter and non-matter—has its own unique vibration, just like a fingerprint. In fact, all of life together as a system has a vibration, and yet each unit moves within a stratum with other units on the same level. When it comes to the natural world, without effort, all of nature vibrates at the highest level, in *purrfect* order. The thing is, nature is already effortlessly vibrating at a healthy and harmonious pulse. Without a concept of separateness from the whole of Life, the natural world is intrinsically part of the body of Life. It is this interconnection with Life that encodes nature with harmonious vibration, naturally "getting along with" and fitting into the body of Life.

Conversely, humans are the wild cards in the world of vibration. Luckily for us, there are ways to tune our vibration. Meditation is certainly one way. Here's another: nature immersion—like my experience with the giant owl and the process that I had intuited which I call "osmotic-energy-balancing." A time of synchronicity with nature is the purest of all meditations. The energy of nature vibrates in balance and in alignment with higher consciousness, naturally and without effort. And by being around it, you can pick up the same vibrational rhythm. Simply put, vibration tunes vibration, and this is what we've been talking about since the beginning of this book—*energy is viral.*

Viral energy—both the magical and wonderful effects, plus what you don't want seeping into your life—is all around you. Again, the nature of nature is that it is vibrating in perfect order. So, get outside and around nature, in an open field of grass, near to wildlife, or in the heart of a forest. Immerse yourself in surroundings that are rich in healthy energy and healthy presence. Just by being around nature's perfect vibrations you will be infused with balance and peace. Spend some time in nature and experience for yourself why nature is the gold standard.

Ground Yourself with The Earth

How you ground your feet is a clue or signal regarding what you like, whom you trust, and where your attention goes—energy flows! (Sure, a bit cliché, but still true.) Did you know that when you're gathered in a group and a new person enters the group, you can tell who is open to whom by the direction that their feet are pointed? While your upper body might turn to welcome or include someone in conversation, your feet will only turn towards them if you are genuinely open to that person at that time. Now when walking into a room, you can check if others are putting their best foot forward. Whether forward or sideways footsies, there is significance to how you are grounded and connected to the life all around you.

All of life harmonizes and works on a pulse and this includes the natural rhythms of nature's four elements: earth, wind, fire, and water. (Aristotle added a fifth element—aether: the upper regions of air beyond the clouds—but let's focus on the four to which we have easy access.) These elements each have properties that you can tap into to give you energetic balance. When we say that someone is "earthy" we are usually saying that they are in-tune with nature and have a solid foundation. When we say that someone is "down-to-earth," we are saying that they are levelheaded, practical, reasonable, and sensible. It would seem that these expressions are not derived from thin aether but are rooted in deep truth.

Brenda had a difficult time making decisions and was feeling insecure in her life. She believed that her value was in her persona, her image, what others thought of her, what she did for a living, whom she dated, and what kind of ring she wore (and on what finger). Her energy was sometimes off-putting and she didn't know it. Her light had been muddied by the negative viral energy that she had allowed to steadily seep into her environment over several years. She had been emotionally beaten down from chronic loss, rejection, unfulfillment, and disappointments, and so her energetic-presence was on- level with low and stagnant experiences. She knew something wasn't working so she sought professional counseling, plus advice from lifelong friends, and read a number of self-help books. But it wasn't until she discovered gardening, of all things, that her internal evolution began. Brenda's practice of gardening involved much more than watering a half-dozen houseplants; Brenda took up gardening as a beloved new hobby and dedicated much of her spare time to it. She would get her hands and feet in the earth every day for months, and her energy gradually steadied and her perspective magically cleared. With a clear head, she made better choices and became more decisive. She became confident in her true value and she felt her bright light return.

Please know that you are not on your own in life; there's an Omnipresence in perfect balance available to you—Life takes many forms. What you need the most right now might just come from the grounding element of earth.

It's about immersion: kneel down in it, walk barefoot on a dirt path, fully breathe in the smell of earth clinging to freshly pulled carrots or beets. Ground yourself with the element of earth, balance your mind and thoughts, fine-tune your energetic vibration, and open up to new opportunities and experiences.

The Secret for Excitement is in the Wind

Here's a natural phenomenon that the producers of ABC's *The Bachelor* franchise became aware of and utilize to fast-track love: have promising couples bungee jump or skydive together and they will very likely fall in love (or infatuation, at least). Sure enough, the moment a pair tandem-plummets from a skyscraper in an extreme free-fall, or hits the open road in a convertible, the adrenaline and hormones flow, and so does the love connection. Afterwards, while holding each other in an exhilarated embrace, they proclaim, "If we can do *that*, then we can do anything together!" Well, okay, perhaps a wind-driven adventure can't keep romance going *forever*, but it sure can propel lovebirds to the next level for eight to nine weeks of filming.

So, what's the matchmaker magic? The secret for excitement is in the wind. Wind stimulates adrenaline, gets your heart beating faster, can bond you to someone who's participating in the same activity, or can most definitely help you out of a funk or emotional rut.

Do you sometimes feel like you're just going through the motions of taking care of your daily tasks, yet you're not feeling fulfilled? You can feel melancholy just from being in a state of boredom for too long. And by the way, you can be bored and quite busy at the very same time. Fulfillment comes with following and actualizing your life's true purpose. *Tall order, right?* If you don't know where to start, no worries. All you need to do is get on the same level with what you want—raise your vibrational energy. Small steps can help you to get out of boredom, en route to purpose, and ultimately to fulfillment.

So, what can you do today for more joy and excitement? Of nature's four energy-balancing gifts (the elements), wind holds the secret for excitement, and excitement is the antidote to boredom and indifference. Naturally, you've felt it for yourself. Wind is uplifting; it gives you energy, and it excites and motivates. Feel the wind on your face and in your hair. Just try it! Go for a ride on a bike, horse, or motorcycle, or visit a fair, carnival, or theme park. Take a long drive with the top or windows down. Skydive, sail, paraglide, parasail, ski, run, skate. On a windy day, sit on a dock, a cliff, or at the top of a hill and feel goosebumps of excitement. Do it on your own, with a friend, or with your significant other. Make it a regular activity to feel the natural element of wind. Open up the windows of your house; get in fresh air and flush out stagnation.

Remember, energy must circulate or it will stagnate.

You will begin to pull yourself up and out of boredom, indifference, or stagnation, and into the flow of all that you truly desire.

And, do you know that you can build your own creation energy out of thin air?

Try this energy building technique: Find a quiet spot outside in a natural environment. This can be in a forest, on a wooded bike path, at the beach, or in your own backyard. (We carry a great deal of stagnant and heavy energy due to chronic exposure to non-living environments (such as our city habitats), and so the more natural your surroundings, the better this works.) Stand in a comfortable position with your legs shoulder-width apart. Outstretch your arms to your sides and begin to move them in wide circles from the front to back, and around to your front again. Get a nice, slow, rhythm going and make large open circles in the air. Now, close your eyes and continue your circles at the same easy pace. Imagine that your arms are gathering energy like large paper cones collecting cotton candy. As you are in motion, you are collecting bigger and fluffier balls of light energy. Every so often, swoop your arms over your head and shoulders, moving a wave of light energy over you and engulfing your entire body. Notice the birds chirp, feel the sun on your face, and inhale the gentle breeze that you are creating as you generate and gather energy. Do this for as long as you want (I recommend at least ten minutes) and do it as often as you like. This practice builds your good light presence and supercharges your mindset, soulset, and creation energy.

To Get More Passion, Feed the Flames

When you're getting ready to share a romantic evening with someone special, you might light candles or get the fireplace going. Somehow you innately know that fire helps to spark up the intensity of energy, but have you ever wondered why? Simply put, the element of fire can generate passion and ignite inspiration and motivation. We know that passion is synonymous with love, yet it's also a descriptor for heightened inspiration and energy around your mission, purpose, or an ultra-exciting project at hand.

In the same way that you use fire to build romance, you can utilize the element of fire for inspiration and to bolster your passion for your work—and your life in general. When we say that someone is "on fire," we mean that they're motivated, excited, and purpose-filled. The religious expression that someone is "on fire with the Holy Spirit" means that they are infused with God's holy presence. Fire is an element that is essential to passion.

Every so often I have a hard time getting started on a project. There's no reason for it; it could be due to a lack of enthusiasm or inspiration, or it could be a product of "overwhelm-ment." Some days, I just allow myself to take a break, take a nap, or take a walk. Other days, I light a fire under my chair. Well, not quite—I light a candle or I fire up the range and create something tasty with flames. Have you ever wondered why professional chefs are so passionate? The element of fire—a tool they use for their daily work—helps to create their extreme passion for their craft. Yes indeed, the reference to fire and passion is no "nothingburger."

Fire is one of nature's tools and its magic is: passion.

The late, great Steve Irwin, TV's "The Crocodile Hunter," was passion personified, and more in-tune with nature—and the nature of nature—than most of us. At a time when Steve had already been married for a few years to his wife, Terri—and busy on his mission to educate others about wildlife—he felt a burden to put a plan in motion to ensure that his life's work lived on long after him. Of course, when he felt this draw to plan for the future it was years before his death; he would have had no idea that at the age of only forty-four his life would be cut short at the height of his career and worldwide popularity. But what he did know about was the passion-sparking power of fire.

In her 2007 book, *Steve & Me*, Terri Irwin tells a wonderful story about the day that Steve set out to build a giant bonfire in their yard for the sole purpose of bringing himself inspiration to spark some passion about the real quandary in his life: what was the destiny of his destiny? He had some figuring out to do, so Steve made a fantastic fire and sat in front of it for hours, stared into its grand and powerful flames, and waited for the inspiration to come to him. Then, after a while, it did. From some magical place, Steve Irwin had a giant spark of inspiration. He ran into the house and declared to Terri that what they needed to do was to have children who could carry on the family mission. And they had better start now, he said!

So, they did. Today, those two children are Steve's legacy. And it all came to him while meditating on the element of fire. But Steve Irwin didn't invent the use of fire for revelations and inspiration. For native peoples and tribes around the globe, fire is ever-present at gatherings and rituals as a messenger; a gift from the Creator. It's a language used by the Creator, implanting the Mind of God into humankind. To them, fire is not just fire, it's "Sacred Fire." Like God, fire is thought of as both untouchable and also the giver of life. Some believe that fire holds consciousness and illuminates the Higher-Self. Whatever you believe, there is an undeniable power in fire.

When you need inspiration and passion, find ways to utilize the element of fire. If you're working, light a candle and place it in the corner of your desk. Turn on the fireplace. Build a bonfire and meditate on it. You don't have to do anything else, just be. The more beautiful and bigger the fire, the more beautiful and bigger the magic! Fire sparks passion in all forms. Try it for yourself and ignite something passionate and truly inspirational.

Water in Motion: The Brainstorming Supertool

Perhaps you're a schoolteacher, student, theoretical physicist, engineer, or homebuilder and you're trying to figure out a solution to a problem or discover the missing link to the mystery. You discuss, confer, read, formulate, write, and sketch your heart out to crack the quandary. Or maybe you're trying to figure out your life: where you go from here; how you can get paid to do what you love; how you can get paid more; what's your next step; who are you meant to be with; when will it all happen? You're writing action lists, searching the Internet, making contacts, and putting yourself out there. Those are all necessary efforts, and yet have you ever considered tapping into nature's special gifts for manifesting the life that you want?

You have heard by now that thoughts are viral and can be picked up. But do you know that you can also tap into and pick up the mind of God, the thoughts conceived by your Higher-Self, or the ideas of others? That's right, thoughts are viral, the voice of the Creator is viral, and these come to you through your intuition, your gut feelings, and through moving water. Yes, it's true; I can verify it through my own experiences (and I bet you can, too). Life has a nifty communication channel directly to you and it's available for you when you need to generate new ideas and supercharge your creative thought-power: it's the element of water.

Water conducts inspired thought. The word "inspired" refers to thought which is sponsored by the Creator, and yet the operative word is "conducts." Water is a conductor, a travel highway, for Life's creative force. (*Think about that!*)

Here's how it works: ionic compounds such as salt, calcium, and magnesium are present in non-distilled water, like the water from your household taps, rain, rivers, lakes, streams, and seawater. "Ion" means "going" or "to go" and because all ions are *charged*, energy vibration is able to go and flow as the ions move through water. This is the very same way that electrical currents are able to move through water, flowing from one bit of ionic compound to the next, lightening fast like on an unseen track.

Now, check this out: here's where ions get pretty interesting. As the ions in water are moving around and going about their business, their trajectories can be deflected by a magnetic field. That means that these abundant and tiny charged ions are stimulated by the presence of an energy field to spontaneously respond to and even connect with other magnetic fields in their flow. (Well, your mind is a magnetic field, and the mind of God is a magnetic field.) When the flow of these ions is accelerated and stimulated by movement, the whole process is stimulated. And so, around moving water, you might pick up brand new thoughts, solutions, and inventions—quite unexpectedly.

Moving water supercharges the inherent magnetism of inspired thought.

Your Higher-Self can actually pick up transmissions of thought-energy from someone else such as a farmer in Ireland, a scientist in Africa, an engineer ten miles up the road, or student from across the country or world, or anyone with whom you might be in flow with simply by holding the same intentions. (*Let's pause to take that in.*) So, while you can tune-in to the mind of God (and all of Life) anywhere and at any time, there's actually a tool to use to tap into a flow of universal creativity like picking up a phone to make a call. Just as water is a conductor of electric energy, so too is water a conductor of thought energy. Now that's magical!

Do you ever notice how you rapidly get good ideas when you're in the shower? Of course you do. Director and actor Woody Allen says he gets ideas in the shower and makes a habit of spending an hour or more in the shower when he needs to be especially creative. But, Woody's not the only one. I get ideas in the shower, too. When I really need to get the ideas rolling, I take a pen and some paper with me when showering and set them on the bathroom counter so I can write down my inspired thoughts in a hurry. Even still water, like water in a tub, will conduct thought. Greek mathematician, physicist, engineer, inventor, and astronomer, Archimedes, had his Eureka moment in a bathtub. Although, still water naturally moves less than flowing water and so the effect is greater in the shower than in a bathtub. (*When I want to relax more and think less, I take a bath!*)

Ideas can come fast, clear, and big when you're in the shower or around any source of water in motion. Individuals and teammates at task in corporate boardrooms and marketing rooms are more effective and more creative when the space is enriched with a flowing water fountain or a moving-water feature of some sort. It works the same when you spend time near a babbling brook or a waterfall, or when walking in the rain. In fact, the magic works even better when you're utilizing an element of nature while actually *in* nature.

Indoors or outdoors, now might be a good time to think out-of-the-box by not thinking at all. For new ideas to really flow, get around water in motion.

CHAPTER FOURTEEN:

THE ENERGY OF LOVE

Home is Where the Heart Is
(More Than a Welcome Mat; a Mantra)

No matter what age they are, people who have lost both of their parents in death often say that they "feel like an orphan." Even though they had (and still have) parents, they say that they can't help but feel orphaned when their parents passed away. I believe that "Home" had orphaned me like that, or so it felt when I was ten years old. That was the age I was when our family moved cities for the first time, and it was the last age I remember feeling like I lived in a home, rather than just a house. I can't put my finger on it—the reason why home got lost—and I won't point one either. Perhaps both a memory and a mirage, all I know is that, for me, home was a runaway.

In my teen years, I'm not sure if I was running away from home or running in search of it. That search took about eighteen years of moving from apartment to apartment, house to house, boyfriend to boyfriend, infatuation to heartbreak, and paycheck to paycheck, until I set out to create home inside myself. It was the pursuit of my purpose that finally gave me comfort and unorphaned me from a home that I had chased before I had the slightest idea of what I really needed.

Today, home has taken on a completely new meaning. Home is the real me; the enlightened space inside my being; the welcome mat of my soul. And, since I made the decision to commit my life in partnership with another human being through marriage (*there was a time when landing the Loch Ness Monster was more likely for me than matrimony*) home is once again "a place" of sorts, though still portable and intangible. While we also have moved numerous times, home is the space where we are, our little family of five, the family that our love built: my husband, Burt; Sabrina, my cat of twenty-three years; our new additions, kittens Max and Andy; and me. That's how it is with love. Home is no longer a building; it's what you build.

Home is where your heart is; this can be your mantra, too.

Today, you don't have to keep up your sad story, identify with what or who did you wrong, nor focus on the ways that your parents screwed up (or how you screwed yourself up). Look at how all of it has created a particular set of circumstances. For instance, I would never have become introspective and therefore written this book if I wasn't at one time very unhappy; my challenges made me a seeker. Likewise, your circumstances and experiences have created *your* journey. With that, decide what you will create. Let go of the challenges that brought you here. Start telling a new story for your life. Embrace everything that brought you to this place on the leading edge of your creation.

So, what in the world is happiness? I spoke with Miles Adcox, CEO of Onsite Workshops and Recovery Center in Nashville. He's a frequent guest on *Dr. Phil*, *The Doctors*, *20/20*, and *Good Morning America*, and certainly an expert when it comes to the therapeutic pursuit of happiness. So, I asked him, "Miles, what is happiness to you?" He said, "Happiness to me is experiencing unconditional acceptance for who I am. You might think that acceptance is from others, but it's actually from myself. Happiness is working through the beautiful opportunities that come up through relationships with other people, and then realizing that all of it is just one big mirror to look inside myself."

It's freeing when you decide that your home, your happiness, and your love, are not under a roof or under another's control. You build them with each decision; with every action. The magic of viral energy is that you have a supernatural creation power at your will: light energy and heavy energy are catchy. Discover your life's true purpose. Don't dwell on negativity or get stuck in doubt. Choose all that is good and light—get around it, marinate in it, and create your dwelling place.

The Newbie in Nashville Phenomenon

Waiting on something that you want is exhausting. It's energy-sucking. Inherently, waiting too long on a dream cancels out expectation, and expectation is a magical ingredient for creation.

Nashville is a city that attracts the best-of-the-best of vocalists and musicians from all over the country and the globe. Hopeful songbirds and starlets mecca to Music City USA because they know it's the get-discovered capital for their industry. When the newbies first arrive, they cross paths with movers and shakers, magically get invited to A-list parties at the homes of record producers or so-and-so's manager, are introduced to several somebodies, land a meeting at a label on Music Row, and network and business-card-collect their newbie tails off. Energy is flowing, connections are fast and loose, and success feels imminent!

Until, someone who has been scratching and striving in town for ten years, annoyed and intimidated by the newbie, tells them, "Kid, Nashville is a ten-year town. Everybody knows that. You have to earn your way; it's not going to come fast or easy. After ten years, this town *might* give you a shot. Get in line."

Then, the newbie notices that the bright light dims, the special invites dry up, and the momentum slows. They decide to get in line, play the game by the rules, join songwriter rounds every Thursday night, gig for tips every Friday through Sunday, co-write with anyone who asks, wait tables during the days and some nights, and wait for the magic to come in ten years.

When expectation is removed, it is replaced by toiling and waiting, wanting and waiting, and struggling and waiting. Then one day, the newbie isn't a newbie any longer. They are now a scratcher and striver telling some naive newbie, "Kid, this is a ten-year town. I used to have that spark in my eye, too. Everything was happening for me until someone gave me the lowdown and told me it would take ten years."

Doesn't it make you wonder—what could you do if you didn't allow other people's fears and insecurities to affect you? What if you moved through life with the advantage of utilizing the transferrable nature of energy, both the lowdown and the high and light?

To review and bring it home again: the magic of viral energy is that you have a permeable energy field—in fact everything does—and in addition to attracting like-energy, you also marinate in various levels or "strata" of energy through your environment and the people and stimuli around you. This in turn sets your energetic-presence.

You know that confidence is attractive; it's also catchy. Deploy light viral energy for everything from business meetings to dating. The next time that you're going into an important meeting, first take twenty minutes to center yourself and to visualize that your client has already bought your product, or the investor has already invested in your idea, or your counterpart has already offered you the exact deal that you were looking for, or your new company has already hired you for the position. Go in fully believing that your meeting with them today is just to finalize the details. (*Work it! Work it, Baby, own it.*) With that in mind, be confident and they will be confident, too. It's catchy.

Nothing (and no thing) is more important than your energetic-presence. It is what puts you on level with all possibilities that you desire. It is what puts you in the path of magic. It is the fuel for all that you create. You are here to create not to wait. Toiling is not creating. Tempering your enthusiasm or the enthusiasm of others is not creating. The newbie in Nashville phenomenon is not exclusive to newbies or Nashville. It's about the power that you have to create when your spirit is filled with expectation.

Protect and nurture your energetic-presence and then go make it happen!

Nobody controls your happiness. Nothing that you can achieve or obtain will signify your worthiness or that you've "made it." To make it you literally have to create it. Repeat this mantra: "I am succeeding far past my greatest dreams." Be your purpose; don't wait and worry—create your purpose! It is uniquely yours and it is Life's promise to you. So, arrive like a child again. Throw off your fears and doubts. Be new. Live and be and *move* in the energy of love, passion, and enthusiasm.

When You Expand, You Expand—More

Sometimes you live "small" (I do, too) because you're worried that there won't be enough. You say, "I can't follow my dreams right now because I have to work for a living; I want children but I can't manage having a baby now; I don't have time to exercise; we will take that trip when we have more money; I will donate to that cause when I have enough for myself; I have to get things done so that one day I can stop and smell the roses." But wait, how do you think your parents did it? They didn't wait until they had the money to get married or for the perfect circumstances to have children—they just did it, and somehow more resources came and they got by.

Now, this could be my favorite principle of viral energy, and it absolutely fascinates me. It will shake up everything that you thought you knew about how time and money work (and all resources for that matter). Here it is: expansion creates expansion.

Today, we know that the universe is not static and it's not shrinking; it's growing. In 1929, Edwin Hubble discovered that the universe is actually expanding. On the massive cosmic level, all is becoming more. Interestingly enough, on the quantum level (that's the smallest stuff), all of everything is *also* becoming more.

In 1927, German physicist Werner Heisenberg was studying space and discovered that pairs of particles pop in and out of what was thought to be empty space. (*What?! Hold the press!*) Yep, they just show up from nowhere. These energy pops are borrowed into space, then very quickly pop together and disappear. (They basically reunite or re-member with their counterparts and instantaneously return from whence they came.) This is a real and proven thing; it's called Quantum Fluctuation. Energy particles come and go in no particular pattern or logic. Like youngsters full of life and adventure, they are possibilities. They manifest fast, divest fast, are everywhere, and are plentiful. Space is teeming with the coming and going of energy pops. Energy at this quantum level is contributing to space by temporarily appearing, and yet sometimes it leaves behind residual energy and that energy becomes matter. (*They're sort of the Gremlins of the quantum field. No water needed!*) So, what had been empty space expands into more; from no-thing comes abundance.

So, why are you living small when abundance is all around you, available in both outer and inner space?

The magic of viral energy can't promise you expansion and abundance; that's determined by how you grab onto possibilities and manage the quality of your thoughts and your energetic-presence. What the magic of viral energy can absolutely promise you is this: as you expand, you automatically create the energy to meet your expansion. Even expansion energy is viral. (Pop!) Life says, "Oh, darling, I can see that you need more of that resource. Here you go." Expend the time, and you will magically have more time. Use the money to invest in your purposeful pursuit and passion, and more money will replace it—and then some. Share yourself, and you will become more. Do it, and by doing it, you put yourself in the same energy as the magic. You make the magic! Life says, "My Precious One, I can see how you utilize the air in your lungs, your health, your mind, your voice, your money, and your time, for your good and the good of others—here is more."

There is a well-known absolute that says energy cannot be created or destroyed. And yet, here's a mind-shifting claim: only the second half is true. At the smallest level—at the birth of energy—creation is continuous.

Not long ago, in 1998, light pulses from supernovas proved to cosmologists that not only is everything in the universe moving farther away from what appears to be the point of origin (the Big Bang), everything is also moving away from every other thing. The distance between all things in the universe is expanding, more, and more, and more. Since the moment of the universe's creation some 13.7 billion years ago, it has been expanding and is accelerating in its expansion. It's expanding at a higher rate than ever before—exponentially.

It's hard to visualize this rate, and yet scientists know that the universe's growth is much faster than the speed of light, which is 671,000,000 miles per hour. They believe that the universe's expansion is a result of the Big Bang, and when this was agreed upon as the source, they then asked the question, "What is the force that is pushing apart the universe?" And that's the question they've been striving to answer ever since.

The current leading theories on the universe's exponential expansion include the idea that energy and matter are being hurtled outward from a center point by a force likened to that of an explosion. It's a violent beginning to a volatile universe. Of course, an explosive force like that would eventually slow (fizzle off), and we already know that the expansion of the universe is not slowing, but rather it is exponentially accelerating.

So, what's the push between the matter? Because they don't know, scientists resolved it around 1977 by inventing a fix-all called "dark energy" (though first dubbed "antimatter" in 1898 by German-born physicist Arthur Schuster, a concept later refined in 1928 by English physicist Paul Dirac). Modern theoretical physicists say that "dark energy" is an unknown substance undetectable by light, filling up the spaces between matter and therefore creating more and more space between all of the galaxies, and between everything in space. And yet, they don't have any idea what it is.

Keep in mind that light is very important to how we measure the stuff in the universe, and therefore how we see the whole picture. Scientists currently believe that because more space and dark antimatter is filling up between us and the other galaxies, that this means we are becoming more isolated. But maybe they are looking for an answer where an answer can't be found. After all, the universe's expansion easily outruns the speed of light, and so what should we expect to see? Put another way, there's "stuff" there, but we can't yet see it because the creation of the "stuff" is much faster than the travel speed of our only means to detect it: light.

Creation is faster than light.

Another leading hypothesis out there is the suggestion that the universe is being pushed apart by a force such as "reverse gravity" or "repulsive gravity." In 1979, teeing off from these hypotheses, theoretical physicist Alan Guth developed the idea of "cosmic inflation," which does tie up a number of cosmic question marks while raising other unknowns. The fact remains that scientists don't have a definitive answer to the question of universal expansion. It has remained a mystery.

So, what's the big push? Let me bring it back to a personal level and give you an analogy for the big push, and I promise to reveal what viral energy has to do with the universe's expansion by the time we turn the final page.

Eight years ago, a colleague of mine named Adam—a proud and diehard bachelor—confided in me that he had been exclusively dating a woman named Robin for the past ten months. He said that he was falling in love with her and that they were very compatible, but he still resisted the idea of choosing just one woman to whom he would permanently commit. He expressed a concern that a wife would be a dependent, both financially and emotionally, and he didn't think that was something that was in his best interest. He was twenty-nine, and while he had a steady job, he didn't really have a career sorted out yet. Adam described Robin as "very smart, fun, outgoing, and easy to be around." Yet she, too, did not have any sort of wealth, and he was afraid that a wife would suck away his own (limited) resources.

It's funny how life sometimes gives you a creative push. Four months after our initial conversation, Adam told me that Robin was pregnant, and he had decided that he deeply loved her and truly wanted a life with her. And so, while he was nervous about how they would financially manage, he asked her to marry him. Today, Adam and Robin have four children, homes in two states, and enjoy working together in their thriving business. Robin brought to the marriage an outstanding business idea, leadership in executing the strategy, her go-getter and fun-to-be-around personality, not to mention her role in bringing four children into the world! Yet, everything that they have done, accomplished, and created, they did together—and it all has manifested because they took a chance on love and expanded their world. They were *being* a life that required more resources, and so more popped in.

Every scientist, problem solver, philosopher, thinker, and writer knows that the more ideas they have, the more ideas come. The potential for expansion is hardwired into our mind-body-spirit beings, deployed if and only when we need it to create. Even physical limitations are redefined as athletes continue to break the records of athletes from early times in history. Expansion creates more expansion! Build your momentum and they will come. Act on your inspirations and dreams; be prepared to trade resources in the short-term to fulfill your ultimate dreams. Be glad that you took the leap and move along.

Be what it is that you want. The magic of viral energy will bring you the possibilities for expansion, and as you expand you will expand—more.

Success Has a Tipping Point

"Katherine" is a fairly well-known actress turned speaker and spiritual teacher. Nearly a year ago, she published a book about love and self-discovery, and she wholeheartedly believes that her destiny is to help others and to leave the world a more compassionate place. And yet, for all of her positive messages for others and good work for humanity, she can still get discouraged. Of course, anyone and everyone, even the very enlightened among us, can experience discouragement. "I want to get your advice on something," Katherine said when she recently called me, "I sometimes get discouraged and I wonder if the world will respond to *this* version of me. Success in Hollywood came easier for me. My message today is the 'real me,' more than anything else I've ever done, and yet it's a slow burn. How do I get to a place of knowing that my mission will come through in the world, and not get discouraged?"

I reminded Katherine that her work as a spiritual teacher started long before her occupational evolution. I reminded her that in the deepest chambers of her soul, this is what she wishes to share with others. I reminded her that she is moving in the direction of her goal. And then I told her a little story about the tipping point at which I believe she'd arrived.

Morton Grodzinsa, professor of political science at the University of Chicago, first used the phrase "tipping point" in the field of sociology in the 1960s when he adopted the phrase from physics. In science, a tipping point is in reference to the addition of a small amount of weight to a balanced object until the additional weight causes the object to suddenly and completely topple, or tip. In physics, it's sort of like the straw that broke the camel's back. The idea was expanded and built upon in 1972 by Thomas Schelling, an American economist and professor at the University of Maryland. And, most recently the term was popularized by the book, first published in 2000, titled, *The Tipping Point: How Little Things Can Make a Big Difference* by Malcolm Gladwell. Gladwell defined a tipping point as "the moment of critical mass, the threshold, the boiling point." Since then, the term's applications have been used for all kinds of social behaviors.

Now, let's apply this to reaching success at your highest dreams and purpose. In the field of viral energy, your metaphorical success-scale reaches its tipping point when you move the magic *quality* (not *quantity* as in the fields of physics or sociology) of creation-energy towards your dream, goal, mission, or purpose. Give your goal light thoughts and words. Feed your goal with the light energy all around you as energy osmotically permeates your being. As you feed your goal (*and your soul*) with light energy, a new viral energy stratum is reached, and you now are in flow with and have access to all that lives and moves within this higher energy stratum.

Truly, you start to move with the flow.

And although your success at what you have worked toward in earnest—and brought about by way of elevating your creation energy—indeed has an actual moment when the scales tip in favor of your dream, goal, mission, or purpose, there is no true getting *"there"* as there is always a higher viral energy stratum available to you. When you rise up in your creation energy, you reset your energetic-presence. This is more than just your point of attraction; your presence literally puts you in a specific stratum (flow) of creation energy. And you can't get, do, be, have, or experience anything with which you are not on the same energetic level.

As far as a tipping point to your dream goes, oh, you'll feel it! It's your personal shift from wanting to awareness and it will not go unnoticed by you.

For all of the effort, research, planning, and taking action that I have done in order to bring my message to a larger audience and therefore make the meaningful difference that I set out to achieve, there was a moment—an energetic shift—that I noticed when I felt my success-scale tip. I just knew that I really had something that would be meaningful to others, and I knew that it would manifest into the form of this book. *"It"* was happening, and I felt it beyond doubt.

Approximately a month or so into this shift into knowing, I received an opportunity that was undeniable validation of my work from an individual for whom I have great admiration—a renowned expert in the field of personal growth. To draw a comparison, it would be like a basketball player being offered personal mentorship by Shaquille O'Neal. Or, a baseball player being taken under the wing of Babe Ruth. In the publishing genre of personal growth/spirituality, this individual is the Greatest of All Time. The G.O.A.T.'s validation wasn't the tipping point; the tipping point aligned me with the validation and opportunity. But first, I had to get energetically *"there."* I had reached an inner tipping point (one of many) in the fulfillment of my purpose, and the agreement that I made with Life responded.

Today, I know that I am moving with the powerful force of creation. Since this particular awakening—this special tipping point—I no longer strive for a finish line; getting *"there"* is not the goal or the end, but the imperative and magical way to get to the *"there"* beyond *"there."*

Free yourself of striving to get "*there*," and instead manage your energetic-presence. In doing so, you will automatically fulfill your purpose. Your success has many tipping points at which your momentum becomes supercharged. It's endlessly empowering.

So, how will you know when your success is about to reach a tipping point? Your spiritual evolution flows like this: wandering—wishing—deciding—declaring—moving—manifesting—becoming—being. You won't be in doubt or confused when *it* happens; you will know, because you will *be* it.

CHAPTER FIFTEEN:

YOU MAKE THE MAGIC

The Puzzle-of-Creation Paradigm

The virality of energy is such that growth is exponential. Let's use the example of your social media account. When you have just a few friends or followers, your reach is small. If you're active in your network, you will eventually gain more followers. Let's say you now have 1,000 followers with the capacity to share and like your posts with *their* 1,000 followers. This means your message has the potential to be presented to all of your followers' followers, expanding your reach and growth potential to an audience of one million. However, virality's exponential growth isn't unique to social media. Nope, the Creative Force of All has the claim on that—it's viral energy and you're already in the network.

To explain, let's move from cyberspace to outer space. (Okay, now I'm going back to finish what we talked about in Chapter Fourteen, "When You Expand, You Expand—More.") Since the Big Bang theory couldn't sew up the discovery of how the universe is exponentially expanding, scientists from fields including Physics, Cosmology, and beyond, are all currently grappling to answer the question: what's the force that's pushing apart the universe? However, according to viral energy, it's a question that cannot be answered because the first assumption is wrong: there are no external forces pushing apart the universe.

This is where we need to start thinking differently, no longer relying on our five senses or our old ideas about power, because the force that expands and creates the universe is CREATION itself. The force is not from without; it's from within.

And it is the same force within you!

We can't see or measure the universal force of creation (or the "Universal Force of Creation"), but that doesn't mean there's nothing there. Remember those fancy twin pairs of particles and the ways in which they pop into space, pop together, pop out again, and sometimes leave behind a residual energy that can eventually form into matter? Yep, those crazy youngsters. You can think of their spectacular silliness like the merging of cosmic DNA. Not all possibilities are manifested, but some are. And, as quantum-tiny as they are, they have a lot to do with answering this *massive* question regarding the source of the *big push*.

It's time to expand our perspective and transcend the power-based culture. No, there is not an outside force pushing the universe apart. The

Big Bang was not even a bang but more of a Cosmic Viral Birth akin to the spark of an idea, or dust left from particles that pop in from thin air. (You'll recall this is called Quantum Fluctuation, the temporary change in the amount of energy in a point in space.) There is indeed a power that multiplies space, yet it's not pushing everything apart from a mysterious force centered at one point of origin.

Creation is the push.

Here's how: Imagine that you have all of the pieces to a very large puzzle laid out in front of you. However, this puzzle is not shaped in a square or rectangle—its form is unconventional so you cannot start with all of the straight edges because there aren't any.

The Puzzle-of-Creation Paradigm is a visualization tool for how the universe is expanding. With puzzle-building, it's very slow going—*in the beginning*—as you place the first pieces. When the puzzle starts taking shape, the pieces then assemble faster and faster. With even further creation, the image and likeness of the puzzle becomes evident and it's at this point that the big picture is so clear; it could almost put itself together.

When this starts to happen, it becomes evident to the puzzle builder that this puzzle has no borders—it is literally a puzzle without limits. (*Eureka, this is our puzzle of creation!*) An external force was never pushing the pieces outward. As creation took place, *more* creation occurred. This is the Law of Creation: creation itself is the catalyst of creation, like a viral domino effect or chain reaction.

Just like puzzle building, the universe is put together in an exponential manner. The mysterious "force" of creation is not a force at all, but rather a "power" or an "energy." The act, the moment, the noun, the verb, the spark, the will, and the embodiment of all creation is viral energy.

This "power" or "viral energy" works the same in the cosmos as it does in your life, and so to understand it better, let's take a deeper look at how this energy plays in space.

Previously, we discussed two phenomena for which science still has a gigantic question mark: What is expanding the universe? And, what is "dark energy"? To recap, scientists know that the universe's growth is much faster than the speed of light, yet they only have several incomplete theories to explain the force pushing apart the universe. The Big Bang is no longer thought to be the big push of the universe's expansion because the force of an explosion would eventually slow. Now, cosmologists and theoretical physicists are hypothesizing about what it is that pushes between matter, expanding everything in an exponential way. You'll remember that I mentioned that in 1977, a fix-all was postulated around what is now called "dark energy" or "antimatter." This is an unknown substance undetectable by light that occupies the space between matter. Its properties create more and more space between everything in space, including all of the galaxies, and yet, scientists don't have any idea what it truly is.

(*Okay, so we're caught back up and this is where it gets very exciting for the future of science, the study of viral energy, and for you and me, too! Understanding "dark energy" is foundational to comprehending the "how" of the universe's exponential expansion, so we'll start there.*)

In space, the vast and growing distance between matter is not composed of empty, vacuous "dark stuff." According to the properties of viral energy, the growing space of "darkness" between us and other galaxies is only because the energy in between is in the cosmic embryonic stage. This space of "dark energy" is where consciousness-energy is vibrating so very fast—God fast! It is pure Spirit; pure light energy. (*But wait, it's supposed to be dark energy, right?* Keep reading!)

The space known as "dark energy" is teeming with pops of energy particles, each with the possibility of connecting with other particles and experiencing creation, and some of these possibilities manifest into form. *But how, pray tell?* Just like a swirling bowl of Jell-O powder dissolved in hot water as it enters the fridge, the speed of consciousness-energy has the capacity to slow from pure, energetic vibration into a settled form. This is how more stuff (and Jell-O) is created.

Here's a sidebar just for fun that has been discussed with concern in the scientific community: should we be worried about being cosmically isolated when the distances grow infinitely large between us and the other galaxies? (Have no fear; viral energy is here!) No, because there will be more stuff born in between and that stuff will one day become observable light or measurable radiation energy. Dark energy is not as scary as it sounds; it's just the space before the beginning. (*Drumroll, please.*)

And, let's clear up another question while we're digressing: you might wonder (as cosmologists do), if everything in space is expanding, then why isn't Earth fattening up, too? (*The answer is very interesting and it's a quantum theory that also applies to you.*) When a mass is very dense and heavy, like the Earth (or a person), the uncertainties and speed of evolution are slower and lesser than the possibilities of non-matter energy like empty space, or dark energy. Pure matterless energy has no weight and contains no mass (yet). As far as dark energy is concerned, it will be a very long time (like millions of years) before mass accumulates within that breeding ground of creation.

(I feel like we need an *extended* background drumroll here as we build momentum to our point.)

Matterless energy such as "dark energy" or "antimatter" is teeming with energy pops (Quantum Fluctuation) that every so often stick around rather than popping right back out of outer space and back into inner space. Energy at this quantum level is contributing to space by temporarily appearing, but sometimes it leaves behind residual energy. What had been empty space expands into more—from nothing comes abundance.

The paradox is that matterless energy is not empty or void, but rather it is the most active of all energy fields, and therefore it has the most possibilities as to what it will become. While you are made in the likeness of the Creator, and you are indeed Creator, the most profound difference between the energy and power that is you (in form) and Spirit (non-form) is that the latter state knows Itself as infinite and limitless in terms of possibilities. And so, the path to enlightenment is through embracing infinite possibilities. The Living God is you, *becoming*.

With God-fast speed and lightness comes the mysterious possibilities of the "quantum effect" that can bend light, space, and time, causing light and matter to unpredictably move and shirk the laws of standard physics. So, back to the question: why is Earth (and moons and suns and dust) not expanding in size in the same way that all of the space between everything is exponentially expanding? Simply put—mass is heavy, space is light, and the less dense something is, the more space exists for the magical possibilities of *creation*.

Frankly, I'm going to suggest that dark energy be renamed light energy, because in reality, *all energy is light energy*. Of course, to accept this shift in thinking we would first have to confront the misconception that light energy is only observable with our five senses. (Oh, yes, this opens some new thought.) As Shakespeare wrote and Hamlet said, "There are more things in heaven and earth, Horatio, than are dreamt of in your philosophy." We are now beginning to awaken to a new sense—the *fourth dimension* that I experienced when I encountered the giant owl in the forest and was allowed to "see" a new world where Spirit dwells among us.

The truth is that light is not defined by a measurement via visual perception; Light is consciousness-energy and it comes in many strata of vibrational speed. Not to be confused with heavy viral energy, the dark energy or "antimatter" of matterless space is actually just light energy. It's a very active field of creation and it's comprised of light energy even if it looks dark from our perspective. (The heavy energy that we speak of in terms of viral energy is a completely different reference than the dark energy of space. Though just like the dark energy of space, heavy energy—or you could call it "dense energy"—is also just light energy that is polluted, septic, and clouded or cutoff from the purity of light energy.) The dark energy of space is light energy that is the beginning of creation.

It's a light that is moving so fast that it cannot even be seen with our five senses.

Okay, we've cleared up dark energy (which is simply very light energy) and now we can return to and focus on energies that are true polar opposites and very powerful creators: light energy and heavy energy. All creation-energy, light and heavy and every quality in between, is energy that is vibrating at different speeds. These speeds of energy effortlessly collect within layers or energy stratum, like the separation of oil and water—that which is heavy and that which is light.

If you want to manifest more supernatural possibilities within your own life, utilize the magic of viral energy to lighten up. Fill your being with the same burgeoning possibilities of creation that exist within the unseen light of matterless space. Raise your presence to a higher light energy stratum and feel the result. You create with the Creator and everything that you want is yours when you enlighten.

Replacing the Big Bang Theory (And Our Obsession with Force)

Maybe it feels like there's always someone trying to keep you down, or perhaps you just don't understand how powerful you are.

Do you know how a circus trainer breaks an elephant to, well, not be an elephant any longer? The trainer first restrains the elephant's tremendous power by binding its leg with a heavy chain. After trying and failing to get off the chain, the elephant starts to doubt that there is any point in struggling. Soon, the trainer is able to use only a rope to hold the defeated elephant, although at this point, the elephant is only restrained by its own doubt.

You are the elephant in this analogy. Your chain is the illusion of powerlessness. It's a radical idea for so many of us reared in the era of shame-esteem, cultivated under the great con. The truth is that *you* are the creator; you are here to create and to further the spiritual evolution of humanity. As your presence is elevated to higher and higher strata of light energy, you transcend what we call "sin."

The whole universe is on the ***move*** and it's time we pull back the curtain of illusion that separates wanting and awareness. I mean that quite specifically. (Remember the Seven Consciousness-Energy Strata?)

It is the time in our evolution when the illusion is beginning to dissipate, and it's happening as you raise your presence stratum by deliberately managing your light and heavy viral energy. It's ancient and yet audacious.

The concept of the circus is now generally thought of as cruel and archaic, but what the circus really represents is a time in humanity when we were less evolved; unknowing. Our collective presence will continue to rise to a level where we have no desire to undermine others, seek the upper hand, or harm another being for our gain. As we evolve in our understanding, the imprisonment of criminals will one day be virtually unnecessary because we will know that to rob, take advantage of, or hurt another will only harm ourselves. While a modern invention, factory farming will become (in the "soon-time" on planet Earth) widely known as the causation of huge heavy energetic tumors upon humanity, and so it will cease. Even war and discord between people will not serve a purpose in what we choose to create.

The time is nearly here that you will no longer be in doubt about your power to positively effect change. In everything you do, you will see that your correct path is the path of Light, not the path of confusion. There's so much that you will enlighten to and create anew, and it's all starting in your lifetime, right now.

Our species is experiencing a shift away from the thirst for forcefully stealing power, toward the utilization of internal enlightenment energy.

As empowerment replaces our old ideas of power, we will no longer see each other, our planet, or the universe from the perspective of aggression force. Even the Big Bang theory, first proposed in 1927 by Georges Lemaître, will be supplanted because it fails to take viral energy into account—it can't evolve with our understanding of life at the quantum scale of creation, and so it will become extinct.

Here's a new theory of creation: you can call it *The Big Push*, if you like. However, because it draws the picture of creation with a profoundly greater meaning, I prefer to call it *Mother Universe*, or *Mu* for short.

While appearing to be a location of origination, the concentration of light energy in the universe is not a singular place, nor a bang, and it's neither the beginning nor the end. Rather, it's the omnipresent, powerful, and infinitely enlightened state of being. Mu is everywhere light is membered—it's that Oneness that is our true nature and the very same source from which we emerged when our Higher-Self burst into physicality, much like a pop of Quantum Fluctuation. Mu is a portal to the realm from which your energy came and to "where" in time you will return.

She's your Mother Universe and Pando's momma too, and She didn't appear in a violent explosion, but rather in a Bloom-Of-Creation: the flowering of light energy across the universe.

But, why should you care about the workings of space and time?

When we as individuals and as a species finally "get" the creation of the universe, we will begin to understand how creation itself works and how each of us can utilize this same power to create within our own lives.

Let me explain the cosmology of the universe in terms of viral energy. And, to do that, first we must talk about both space and time and how they relate to one another.

By now, you've heard the term "spacetime" about half-a-dozen times in these pages. Here's a simple definition: spacetime is the fusion of space (which is three-dimensional) together with time (which is experienced as linear, therefore it is one-dimensional). While we do experience it this way, time is not linear from hour to hour or from day to day. Together, space and time is a single four-dimensional continuum and not a linear experience. It has been discovered in modern physics that space and time do in fact work together and must be measured together; they are literally and technically just one model that physics calls: spacetime.

Space and time go together like peanut butter and chocolate, or like Mickey Mouse and Minnie; they have an undeniable connection and they're eternally interwoven. As new creation-energy in space is blossoming with more creation, space itself is stretching its metaphorical elbows, making room for more and expanding the distances between observable matter. As space is altered from *what-was* to *what-is* and beyond, so too is time stretched, bent, and altered.

I know this might seem sophistic, however the "place" and "moment" currently known as the Big Bang (though perhaps it will become known as Mu) is both the beginning and the finish line of evolution. That coordinate in spacetime is essentially the future. Yes, the future!

It's so easy to get this turned around and to hypothesize that the "birthplace" of the universe must be in the past as it happened so very long ago, yet that would be inaccurate. Furthermore, it would be inaccurate to say that the place of the Big Bang is the birthplace of the universe as there are countless birthplaces of the Infinite.

What we can say is that at Mu, in relativity terms, creation has been creating in physicality longer than younger incarnations of light energy. At the place of the Big Bang and also at countless other spacetime coordinates within *many* universes, Mu's light energy has existed in physicality the longest and has experienced the natural forward-moving spiritual evolution of creation—it has grown to true enlightenment.

Nearer to Mu's spacetime coordinates, there are worlds that are much more highly evolved than our own and that have progressed to a homogeneous balance with both the physical and spiritual realms. After all, they've been evolving for billions of years longer than we have. From our perspective, imagining these worlds can give us a glimpse of our own future, but for the Light Beings there, it's just "now."

(To really underline the idea of time, I'm going to allow us plenty of repetition.)

Nearer to what we currently refer to as the Big Bang, that which is being experienced at this very moment is happening *now*. Well, that is, "now" for those beings at that particular spacetime coordinate.

And, what is happening at this very moment on Earth is also happening *now*. Well, that is for those of us located at the spacetime coordinate shared by planet Earth.

However, what is being experienced way, way far away (at a given point nearer to that which we currently refer to as the Big Bang) would be a spacetime coordinate that, from our perspective, would be countless years away—years into the evolutionary-future.

In this same way, what is being experienced by us here on Earth is the evolutionary-past from the perspective of light beings at the spacetime coordinate of a given point nearer to that which we currently refer to as the Big Bang.

But why stop there?

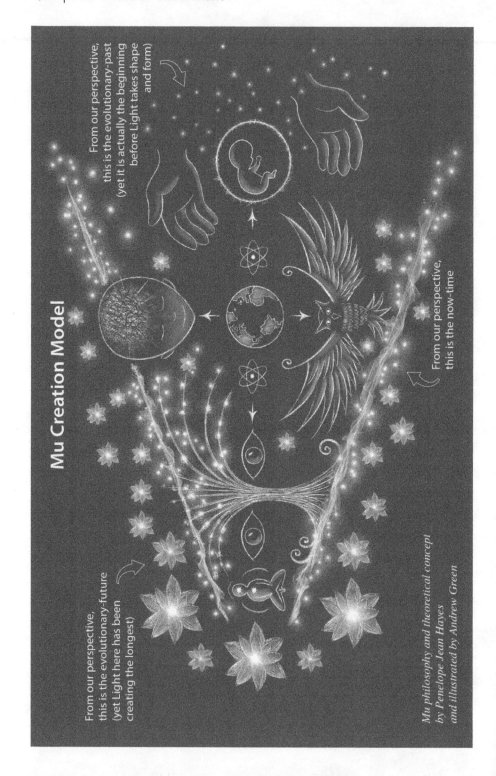

Mu Creation Model

From our perspective, this is the evolutionary-past (yet it is actually the beginning before Light takes shape and form)

From our perspective, this is the now-time

From our perspective, this is the evolutionary-future (yet Light here has been creating the longest)

Mu philosophy and theoretical concept by Penelope Jean Hayes and illustrated by Andrew Green

Going further out away from the Big Bang moment, even further out than our own spacetime location, and still much further out to the far reaches of the limitless universe, there are also light beings "there"—some newly bursting into physicality. To us, that spacetime coordinate would be the evolutionary-past. Then, yet again, for the light beings there it is just *now*.

The Mother Universe Creation Model is a new theory in the field of Cosmology.

I do not dispute the Big Bang theory; the science is solid and has been measured. I am, however, suggesting variations to *What-It-Is* and how we think of the universe's inception. What I am most definitely proposing is a new idea—new-consciousness—about *what* is expanding the universe and *how* it continues to grow and evolve, as you too evolve. (*And right there, in the subtle phrasing of that sentence, is the ancient truth and the key to you becoming the power to fulfill your own dreams.*)

Here are the key differences between the Big Bang (the current concept of the universe's beginning and its design or "architecture") and the Mother Universe Creation Model:

1. The spacetime coordinate that is the Big Bang was not an explosion as we currently think of it. This is an old idea born from humanity's current obsession with force—an attitude that creates most of our problems. We are looking at it all wrong. The Big Bang *did* happen—I'm not challenging that. However, all of the physical matter involved was **birthed into physicality**—it was an on-mass flowering or Bloom-of-Creation that came through from another realm; the realm of Heaven where all Creation is born. In an "instant" an entire field of energy and matter bloomed—and so began the creation of the physical realm (in this universe).

2. Let's now consider what happened next (and is still happening) *after* that first inception, or Big Bang. Physicists today have no idea why or how the universe is expanding. They are still asking, "What is the force that is pushing apart the stuff in the universe?" But that is the wrong question; the wrong assumption. The Mu Creation Model says that CREATION *is* the push that is

expanding all of the empty space between the stuff. Where there was nothing but empty space, now pops new stuff: new creation. (It is actually called Quantum Fluctuation, yet no one has applied it to why the universe is expanding. Until now.)

3. What is also different about the Mu Creation Model versus the Big Bang is that in the very same creation-evolution-expansion modality, Creation is happening, has happened, and will always be happening in many other "places" (spacetime coordinates), too. So therefore, Mu is not only at the Big Bang coordinate in spacetime, it is *everywhere* that new creation is popping, and it is therefore growing and expanding the universe. And by the way, this is not the only universe. There are countless universes, all being and creating.

Earlier, I mentioned "the natural forward-moving spiritual evolution of creation." So, if the future and past are interwoven with spacetime and both are happening now, why then do we experience time as only moving forward?

Ponder this concept for a moment, plainly and simply as it relates to your own life, right here on Earth.

Why is what we refer to as the "arrow of time" an experience of moving from the past to the future, but never in reverse? And what's more, why do cosmologists, physicists, scientists, and philosophers say that time is an illusion, when in every way real and true we only experience time as a progression from then to now, past to present, present to future?

To understand time, you need to first understand your own evolution.

You are evolving from one creation-moment to the next.

Every moment you are more evolved than the last. Just as your thoughts move in succession from one to the next, and just as the cells of your fingernails divide to become slightly longer from one moment to the next, this too is how you evolve—always forward.

Time follows in this same way—forward. Time is just your experience of the flow of evolution; the arrow of creation is forward. Evolution, even by name, means advancement and (like time) it cannot be experienced in reverse.

You are part of a forward-moving spiritual evolution. Starting this very minute, you can begin creating the life of your dreams. If you desire happiness, fulfillment, peace, love, success, respect, and compassion, then raise your energetic-presence—and therefore your consciousness-energy stratum—to where happiness, fulfillment, peace, love, success, respect, and compassion flow in abundance.

Nobody Puts Baby in a Corner! Don't Hide; Share Yourself with the World

Before I started to have the time of my life, I used to be Baby in the corner. I always knew that I had a deeper purpose to live out which entailed more than checking into an office cubicle daily and mindlessly going through the machinations of my PR job. Yes, I knew this even when my life was a total mess and I slept on a stranger's cold basement floor. Yes, I knew this even when my parents' neighbor told me, "You've got to get normal," the day she helped me move apartments. (*This was after my car was repossessed, during a period when I had a violent boyfriend. It was before I finally did get normal and way before I realized that normal is overrated and limiting.*) Yes, even back then when I was in turmoil and in hiding (figuratively and literally), I knew that I had something special in me to contribute to the world. Yet, it took some time to discover exactly what it was that I had to share, so I started with baby steps, or *Baby's steps.*

If you're not yet sure what your purpose is (your Breathtaking Agreement With Life), consider this: just show love. Smile, acknowledge others, say hello to people everywhere you go. Give yourself to the world, even if it's just with a friendly and sincere acknowledgment to another.

When you meet each person throughout your day—the waitress at the diner, a stranger passing on the street, the cashier at the store, the next person in line—make eye contact with them and notice the color of their eyes. This will have you keep eye contact for a fraction of a second longer than usual, and it goes a long way in giving validation to others. Your energetic-presence is impacted by how you treat people, and as said by magazine mogul Malcolm S. Forbes, "You can easily judge the character of a man by how he treats those who can do nothing for him." When you're going through a particularly hard time or bad day, that's exactly when you should shift your care and attention away from yourself and to the benefit of others. Try it; you'll be amazed how your own problems dissolve when you go out of your way to enlighten others. By consistently showing genuine happiness and excitement to see other people, they will soon react the same to you.

Not long ago I had a moment when I slipped back into being "Baby in the Corner." There was an event in which my artwork was being showcased and I found it hard to mingle and allow others to compliment me—it felt braggadocios. I thought it best that people be free to mingle without me pushing my product, so I stayed in a corner of the space and spent the evening talking only to a few people with whom I felt very comfortable and familiar.

The next morning, I immediately felt disappointment for having wasted an opportunity. It was like a regret-hangover. I started receiving text messages and emails from some of the attendees saying, "The event was nice, but sorry we didn't get a chance to talk with you." Then I realized: they weren't there for my product; they were there for my presence. They actually just wanted to be with me together in that moment of light. This was a beautiful epiphany for me—my worth to others isn't what I have produced or achieved; my worth to others is my presence.

When you share your light energy with others, you infect them with light energy. And while you do this only in hopes of brightening someone else's day, just by giving others moments of sincerity, love will be mirrored back, your energetic-presence will rise up, and your own creation energy will enlighten. You are your worth to others and your presence is contagious! Get outside of yourself, be mindful to look others in the eye, smile, show love, and give genuine moments. Share yourself with others— after all, that's all that they really want from you.

The Magic of Infectious Inspiration

Today, start getting excited about your life and what you will create. Get more excited and inspired than you have ever been before! Did you know that creativity in any one area is amplified by another creative activity? Singers Tony Bennett and Paul McCartney are also fine art painters. The same goes for actors Jennifer Aniston, Viggo Mortensen, James Franco, Pierce Brosnan, Johnny Depp, and Sylvester Stallone. There are numerous athletes who practice a two-sport talent, as well. Running back Jim Brown played football and lacrosse. The great Deion Sanders simultaneously played professional baseball and football—he even played in Game four of the 1992 National League Championship Series on a Saturday night, and then flew to Miami to join his Atlanta Falcons for a Sunday afternoon game the next day.

And it doesn't stop with multiple talents. The creative energy of an individual using a single creative endeavor can inspire creativity in someone else. In collaborative audio-visual arts, a symphony is orchestrated by a maestro to the flow of moving art projected on a theatre-size screen. The two together make a spectacular display of sight and sound.

When creativity inspires creativity in another, proximity is a non-factor. Even though their arts are unrelated, there are some individuals who are entangled in joint creation and can inspire each other from across oceans! James SB Richardson, a British award-winning abstract and contemporary artist from Bristol, kept his art entirely to himself for twenty-five years. That ended in 2017 when Anastasia Richardson (same last name; no relation), a young American country music vocalist from Tulsa, Oklahoma, inspired him to share his art with the world. The two had never met, other than through social media. When I spoke with him about their cross-pollination of inspiration, James had this to say about the virality of creativity: "When I close my eyes and listen to Anastasia's music, each note, each lyric hits an imaginative creative cell within me. Its depth and meaning inspires me to let the feeling run down my arms to my fingertips, then produce onto canvas." The creativity proved to be mutually inspirational as James' work bolstered creativity in Anastasia. She describes it this way: "James' paintings trigger my mind to start the creative process. His creativity makes me more creative because it gets me thinking about what words or lines might work best to make people visualize what I'm singing." James and Anastasia are two unique people from different countries that produce separate art forms, yet each of their creative endeavors amplifies the other's creativity.

Truly ponder this phenomenon: whether painting, singing, orchestrating, or acting, none of these creative activities have skills that transcend one another—they are totally different arts, born of unique talents, and honed with different practiced skill sets. Could it be that creative energy itself is contagious? According to the magic of viral energy—absolutely!

If you are a songwriter with writer's block, take some cooking lessons. If you're in advertising or marketing and want to develop more creativity, take up woodworking. If you're an author and you need inspiration, channel beautiful works of art. If you're a manager in need of greater idea-generation, try photography as a hobby or learn a new language just for fun. Visit an art gallery. Attend an opera or theatrical play. Read about some of history's great inventors, and then philosophize and hypothesize with a friend. Entertain new ideas. Collaborate with others.

Whatever it is that you're doing on your own will very likely be bigger, better, and more fun and rewarding when done in synergy with someone else. Let the creativity of others infect you with creativity. Let your own interests and talents feed off of one another; entangle inspiration and creative energy. And above all else—open yourself up to the magic!

What's Next?

Humanity is on the cusp of our biggest expansion yet. We are stretching, straining through an evolution to arrive at a soulset of energy-sharing. While we are only at the inception of change, we will (in the "soon-time") start to transcend Homo sapiens (Latin for "wise man") and will enter a process of becoming Homo illuminatus ("enlightened man"). Our full movement to homo illuminatus will mark the completion of dominance-based evolution and will give rise to spiritual evolution. Then, much further into the future of our species, our awakening will give rise to illuminatus Quis (the "enlightened One").

When we can share our light presence with sincerity— and without manipulation—we will begin to witness the ushering in of this new consciousness.

So, what's it to you?

A collective switch is about to be flipped. Right about now you are beginning to see that the people with whom you have conflict or who you despise can be precisely the people that you raise up through the sharing of your light presence. *You want to know how we can heal the Earth, stop violence, end wars, inspire change, and make the world a better place, right?* Soon, you will know that by elevating another, even in small measures, they will cease interest in their destructive intentions and actions. As people elevate up the strata of consciousness-energy, their intentions will be in alignment with higher and higher light energy; heavy energy will serve no use to them. This is the way to a harmonious, cruelty-free, and compassionate world, and it will all manifest because of you. The truth is, you make the magic (and your experiential reality) with each and every energy projection.

If you're like most people, you disapprove of those who attempt to undermine others, you cringe at government or industry corruption, denounce oppressors and predators among us, and condemn people who torture or abuse animals. Yet, if you truly wish to change the current, then you need to know why and how it moves.

Humankind can live for a time without food and water, and even for several minutes without oxygen. But, we cannot live for even a fraction of a second without energy. (*Oh, how intrinsic and salient to life is our energetic-presence!*) Those who assert control or force their power over others are the most wanting and under-fueled people in the world. Oppressors seek to charge themselves by stealing personal power from others. They yearn to be significant, to be in control and have the upper hand, but what they actually need is empowerment and enlightenment; stealing power will never satisfy, last, or fulfill.

Perhaps your first reflex is to separate yourself from oppressors and to hate them back. But please know this: while those feelings might be valid, they have no power to effect evolved and lasting change. Martin Luther King, Jr. said, "Darkness cannot drive out darkness; only light can do that. Hate cannot drive out hate; only love can do that."

Attempting to shame or minimize your enemy will not make them disappear or bring about victory for your cause. The new-consciousness way to heal suffering, injustice, and abuse in the world is through energy-sharing between people. That is to say: sharing light energy, virally.

Hating people who are filled with darkness will not stop their cruelty; only drawing them closer to light can accomplish that. When you witness a terrible story in the news—another heinous act of violence against the innocent—rather than projecting hatred to the oppressor, close your eyes and send light energy thoughts to the victim and the victimizer. (Yep, even them. *Especially them.*) The beauty and efficiency of energy is that it's contagious and has an osmotic function. When you affect—and infect—another with your light viral energy, you raise them up little by little, light by light. Just by projecting thoughts and words of light energy verses projecting hate and fear, little old you can add to the enlightenment of another. Be a beacon of light, let light radiate from your powerful and empowered presence. When the other is enlightened, they no longer seek false fuel. While it's not your responsibility to enlighten others with your presence, you will find that the more you do it, the more you will want to.

Just as a stem of the organism called Pando knows that the wellbeing of the next stem affects them both, you will know that your wellness is also affected by all of Life. You will know that if another stem is septic, it does not serve you to hate them; only in healing them can you benefit. You will know that when you enlighten others, they no longer wish to harm any living creature, including you.

We are coming to our crescendo moment in the understanding of viral energy.

Creativity creates creativity. Expansion creates expansion.

Mother Universe is the source of your power to create. She is in you, of you, for you, everywhere, endless, and available to you at the instant that you create your every thought, energy-projection, word, and action. Creation is your power. As you create, you expand. As the universe bursts with more creation, it expands— exponentially.

Heavy energy creates heavy energy. Light energy creates light energy. All energy is viral and creates at the same level. What's more, you can pick up heavy or light energy when you're open to it, because while your energy field is permeable, you choose what you take in; that's your free will. In turn, you elevate others with your light presence, and with that power, you will elevate the world.

The way to heal suffering, injustice, and abuse in the world is through energy sharing between people, otherwise known as viral energy.

It's a natural phenomenon already in play and now that you know about it, start using it for your good and the good of others. This is the future of our spiritual evolution. We are still in the evolutionary process;

you are evolving right now. You are not the same person today as you were a year ago and not because you are aging, but because you are enlightening.

By sharing your light presence with others, you don't give away or lose anything of yourself; you become more. Life says, "I can see that you have utilized your presence for the good of others. More light is yours." Let me give you this example: When either heavy or light viral energy is shared from Person A to Person B, Person A has not lost any of their original energy quality or stratum level—heavy or light. Nothing is lost or reduced in any way. You can visualize it this way: If Person A bursts with joy into a room and some of that joy rubs off onto Person B, it does not mean that Person A has lost any of their joy. It means that their joy multiplied. Energy can be created; it's not just transferred. Energy isn't just moved from here to there—it stays here *and* it is created there, too. Energy stays with Person A and it is created within Person B, too. Energy multiplies; it is created. Furthermore, precisely because energy can be created, the exponential expansion of our universe exists, as does our own selfhood and our ability to create. You probably cannot find a mathematical equation to prove this, and yet asking for one would be like asking for the mathematical equation for a caterpillar transforming into a butterfly, or for a newly hatched turtle finding the ocean by the light of the full moon, or for unconditional love. We don't have equations to validate these natural phenomena, yet we still know them to be true.

Viral energy is the greatest marvel that the world has ever known; yet it has gone practically unnoticed. Until now.

Life is consciously creating itself—experiencing its creation, through creation—and that is the whole point in the first place. You are here to create, not merely to survive. You have the power to manifest your dreams.

Nothing whatsoever is lost to you when you empower another. In fact, by sharing yourself with others, you automatically generate more creation energy inside your being. As Glinda The Good Witch from Oz said, "You've always had the power, my dear. You've had it all along."

You are the generator.

You can become the power to fulfill your dreams because you are in an agreement with Life to create. That truth in itself might be the most remarkable thing to know about Life. And yet, there is an even more astonishing wonder: life is equally in an agreement with you! Life will uphold that deal by providing you the resources and opportunities. And here's the only caveat: you must use your resources in fulfillment of your purpose, because you don't get what you're not being.

Your Breathtaking Agreement With Life is your birthright. No one needs to validate this. The resources to fulfill your purpose are available to you, not because you will need them; but because you are (already) *using* them. No one can take this away or withhold it from you. Your dream/passion/purpose is (literally) your breathtaking birthright and you need only to claim it by being it. What are you creating? How are you being? Who are you empowering? The great philosopher Socrates said, "The secret of change is to focus all of your energy, not on fighting the old, but on building the new." Happiness is not about what you *want*, but what you will *create*.

You have the power to impact others with your mission, your intention, and your light viral energy. The world is evolving because of you. Utilize the gift of your life. No longer be in doubt about your power to effect positive change in your own life and the world around you.

The magic of viral energy is the promise that you are enough. It's the mystery of contagious light and heavy energy through the permeable energy fields of The-All-of-Everything, from the mountain to the ocean, from Mother Universe to Pando, and even to You. It's the magic that enlightens your struggle for heavy energy and false empowerment. It's the access and invitation to be Light. It's the truth that was there in the beginning, that exists now, and that forever shall be, and it will give you the power to, at last, fulfill your dreams. The possibilities are without end. Your ability to create is without end. The resources available are without end. Not even the speed of light can outrun the unending creation of Life. With the magic of viral energy, it is a world without end, amen.

The MAGIC OF VIRAL ENERGY

IN SUMMARY AND CONTINUATION OF OUR JOURNEY

Sharing with you the magic of viral energy is part of my life's purpose, which is to help humanity transition to our next spiritual awakening and to prepare for our journey ahead. Homo sapiens are not the final version of our lineage; our species is evolving.

In review, here are the properties of viral energy—*this isn't school; this is fun!*

Viral energy:

- Is a natural phenomenon
- Is contagious
- Works like reproduction—it's new creation, not redistribution. It has the power to create more—picking it up from a source does not mean that the source has been altered or lessened
- Is happening whether you're conscious of it or not
- Is an energy source that you create with
- Comes in different strata, or levels, from heavy to light
- Contributes to the quality of your being
- Operates by possibilities not absolutes
- Is spontaneous
- Is an exponential expander

The phenomenon of viral energy happens not by the law of attraction, but by way of osmosis. Yes, osmosis! You are drawing from, contributing to, and creating with all of Life through the sharing of energy, and you do so consciously, intentionally, and osmotically. We have become anesthetized to our true nature and we are living as though our environment and all creatures and creation are outside of ourselves.

While *The Magic of Viral Energy* deals with the ways in which you can utilize the knowledge of viral energy to attain a life of purpose and happiness, my next project, *Do Unto Earth*, brings "viral energy" to its next revelation. Building the viral energy message from domestic to global, *Do Unto Earth*, reveals broader issues facing both humanity and planet Earth that directly affect you and our species' future.

Do Unto Earth explains "viral energy masses" which are large energetic fields created by both light and heavy intentions and actions of communities and populations, industries, and cultural beliefs, as well as through massive pockets of love, hate, nature, war, gratitude, abuse, forgiveness, indifference, and compassion.

While speaking plainly to the damage mankind has done to the planet—both energetically and physically—this book also brings inspiration to the hearts of those working toward environmental and animal welfare causes as it sets forth a clear and actionable vision of humanity's path to evolution. *Do Unto Earth* advises that saving species and adopting plant-based food sources are the most important missions to pursue, as is a necessary return to much of the wisdom of the aboriginal and First Nations people.

We are now at the threshold of a Life-changing decision and we are asked to be the change. Collectively, we are hearing a call to evolve, and we can do so through the healing of our relationship with Mother Earth.

Like ripples in a pond, *Do Unto Earth* will begin a wave of awareness to reach those who have yet to seriously consider the fate of our planet. Soon, this wave will become tidal.

We are ready for this and we are each asked to begin. This is a call-to-action, a warning, a challenge, a prayer, and a message of healing to the world.

www.DoUntoEarth.com

ABOUT THE AUTHOR

Penelope Jean Hayes is a motivational and new-consciousness writer, contemporary philosopher, and speaker. She practices osmotic-energy-balancing and writes her spiritual and cosmological theories through a process of channeling higher-stream-consciousness. Her written works on social, popular culture, and environmental issues have appeared in *HuffPost* and she regularly writes aspirational and metaphysical content for the international publication *Face the Current* magazine. Penelope has a background in social/popular culture analysis and has appeared on television hundreds of times as an expert guest on programs including *Dr. Phil* and *ABC News*. Penelope is an advocate for Higher-Self-development and the pursuit of "viral energy" as a field of study. She uses her voice to call for the protection of the planet through the preservation of endangered species and the adoption of plant-based food sources. Penelope is a vegan, wanderlust world-traveler, and Survivor superfan. She and her husband, Burton, currently live in Naples, Florida, although they are often on the ***move***.

www.1penelope.com

www.ViralEnergy.org

CPSIA information can be obtained
at www.ICGtesting.com
Printed in the USA
JSHW051536210422
25133JS00001B/108